Challenges for China's Development

There is now no doubt that China is a major economic force, and the country's phenomenal recent rate of growth means that it is primed to become an even bigger player on the world stage. The pace of reform for China's enterprises of all kinds has quickened as the Chinese have sought to cope with the challenges of self-determination – strategic, financial and governmental – in a rapidly evolving social and political context.

This timely collection explores China's current challenges from the perspective of the enterprise. It includes discussion of current and likely future overall trends, reports on new research findings on the true extent of governance and accounting reforms within enterprises, and considers the impact of increasing global competition on strategy, business relationships and management culture across a range of different kinds of enterprises. Starting with the macro view, contributors then focus on aspects such as Chinese-European co-operation, Chinese shareholders, corporate governance, the insurance industry, value creation and business style.

As China confronts large-scale economic, environmental, political and welfare problems, this book will be an invaluable resource for academics and business people examining the underpinnings of the Chinese economic system and its probable course.

David H. Brown is Senior Lecturer and was previously Head of the Department of Systems and Information Management at Lancaster University. His research interests are in the field of systems and strategy. In recent years, he has taken a special interest in the Far East and particularly in China, where he has worked since 1986.

Alasdair MacBean is a Professor Emeritus and Director of the Lancaster Centre for Management in China at Lancaster University. He has previously been head of the Economics Department, a College Principal and a Pro-Vice-Chancellor. His research is mainly in international trade and economic development, the economy of China and transitional economies, and he has authored or edited eight books.

Routledge Contemporary China Series

Challenges for China's Development

An enterprise perspective

Edited by
**David H. Brown and
Alasdair MacBean**

Routledge
Taylor & Francis Group

LONDON AND NEW YORK

First published 2005
by Routledge
2 Park Square, Milton Park, Abingdon, Oxon OX14 4RN

Simultaneously published in the USA and Canada
by Routledge
270 Madison Ave, New York, NY 10016

Routledge is an imprint of the Taylor & Francis Group

Typeset in Garamond by
Newgen Imaging Systems (P) Ltd, Chennai, India
Printed and bound in Great Britain by
Antony Rowe Ltd, Chippenham, Wiltshire

Transferred to Digital Printing 2006

British Library Cataloguing in Publication Data
A catalogue record for this book is available from the British Library

Library of Congress Cataloging in Publication Data
    Challenges for China's development: an enterprise perspective / edited
by David H. Brown and Alasdair MacBean.
      p. cm. – (Routledgecurzon contemporary China series; 4)
    Includes bibliographical references and index.
      1. Business enterprises–China. 2. Privatization–China.
3. Government business enterprises–China. 4. Government
ownership–China. 5. China–Economic policy. 6. China–Economic
conditions. I. Brown, David H., 1946– II. MacBean, Alasdair I.
III. Series.

    HD4318.C418 2005
    338.951'05–dc22   2004065147

ISBN 0–415–34133–7

Contents

Figures

Tables

Contributors

David H. Brown is a Senior Lecturer in Management Science and Deputy Director of the Lancaster University's Centre for Management in China. His research interests are in the field of systems and strategy including their international context, especially China. He has published widely in journals and edited three books, including *Management Issues in China: Domestic Enterprises*, with R. Porter (Routledge, 1996). He has held China research grants from the British Council, ESRC and the EU. In 1998, he was awarded a Fellow Professorship in Management Science by Renmin University of China.

Jean Jinghan Chen is a Senior Lecturer in Financial Management and the Deputy Director of Centre for Research in Corporate Governance in Emerging Markets in the School of Management, University of Surrey. She obtained her PhD in Economics from Lancaster University. Her main research interests include corporate governance, capital structure, foreign direct investment, and the Chinese economy and business studies.

Tony Fang is Assistant Professor of International Business at Stockholm University School of Business and the Founding Director of SABEC (Sweden Asia Business Education Centre). A graduate of Shanghai Jiao Tong University, he completed his PhD in Industrial Marketing from Linkoping University, Sweden, in 1999. His research has focused on China and Asia-related cross-cultural management and strategy areas and is the author of *Chinese Business Negotiating Style* (Sage, 1999).

Fan Gang is a Professor at Peking University and at the Graduate School of Chinese Academy of Social Sciences where he received his PhD in 1988. He was Harvard Research Fellow before becoming Secretary-General of the China Reform Foundation and Director of the Institute of National Economy Research. His writings focus on macroeconomics and in 2000, he edited *Finance Market and State-owned Enterprises Reform* and co-wrote *Chinese Macroeconomic Policy Facing the New Era* with Zhang Xiaojing.

Nick Hawkins teaches International Marketing and Industrial Marketing at Liverpool Business School. He is a Chartered Marketer and specialises in the teaching of the Chartered Institute of Marketing case studies. An experienced marketing practitioner, he has worked as a consultant to many international companies. Currently, he is a Director of Community Integrated Care, a large UK-based charity and is also a visiting lecturer in International Marketing at the School of Management and Commerce in Poitiers.

Xiaoling Hu is a Research Fellow at the University of Gloucestershire. She graduated with a PhD in Economics from Nottingham Trent University in 1998 and joined Portsmouth University as a Research Associate, where she worked for two years. Her research areas relate to the problems of transitional economies, and particularly, the reform of China's financial sectors. Her current interest is the growth and transformation of China's insurance sector.

Philip Lawton has taught corporate law, corporate governance as well as general business and commercial law for 25 years in leading international institutions. In 1987–8, he was a foreign expert based at the Chinese Ministry of Commerce's College in Beijing and from 1989 to 1999 he was associate professor at City University of Hong Kong. He is currently teaching at Lancaster University where he is researching the experience of minority shareholder actions in Hong Kong and their relationship with sociological models of the Chinese family firm.

Yunyan Li received her MA degree in Marketing from Liverpool John Moores University in 2002. Her dissertation was awarded the best Dissertation prize by the Chartered Institute of Marketing. She has worked in Ningbo Jide Electrical Appliances Co. Ltd (in China), as an Assistant Manager in the Sales and Marketing Department. Her interests are in Industrial Marketing, Relationship Marketing and Strategic Marketing, particularly in the context China's small and medium-sized enterprises.

Guy S. Liu obtained his PhD in Economics at the University of Oxford, and he is a Lecturer at Brunel University and Adjoint Professor of Sichuan University (China). He was a Guest Editor for *Economics of Planning*, *China Economic Review*, *Corporate Governance – An International Review*, and an Editor of the *Journal of Chinese Economic and Business Studies*. His main research interests cover comparative corporate governance, enterprise reform and industry in China, industrial economics and firm performance.

Alasdair MacBean was appointed Professor of Economics at Lancaster University in 1967 and later became a Pro-Vice-Chancellor. His research is mainly in international trade and economic development, the economy of China and transitional economies. He has written 6 books, edited 2 and published many articles and contributions to books including *Trade and Transition: Trade Policy in Transitional Economies* (Frank Cass, 2000). Currently he is Professor Emeritus and Director of the Lancaster Centre for Management in China.

Martin F. Parnell was an EU Fulbright Scholar at the Georgia Institute of Technology, Atlanta, USA. He teaches International Business at the Liverpool Business School, specialising in the socio-cultural dimensions of business, particularly of marketing. He has published extensively on the German political economy and business, including DTI-initiated research on German small businesses. His recent work on Sino-German business relations has been published by the Society for Chinese Economic Studies, Giessen University, Germany.

Lord Powell of Bayswater, KCMG is President of the China Britain Business Council and Director at Jardine Matheson. He has also been a prominent diplomat, active in the diplomatic service in Europe and the US, and served as Private Secretary to two successive Prime Ministers – Baroness Thatcher and John Major.

Hantang Qi graduated in Management Science from Fudan University, Shanghai, in 1984. Following completion of his Masters he joined the faculty at Fudan. In 1995, he took the PhD programme in the Department of Management Science at Lancaster University Management School. His research focused on township and village enterprises and their strategic development. He obtained his PhD in 2000 and joined Greenwich University where he is a Principal Lecturer in Strategy.

Pei Sun is a PhD candidate in Business and Management Economics at Judge Institute of Management, University of Cambridge. He obtained the degree of MPhil in Economics at the Faculty of Economics, University of Cambridge, and BA in Economics at Peking University. His research interests include comparative corporate governace, enterprise reform in transition and developing economies, and the impact of industrial policy upon firm competitiveness in newly industrialising economies.

Cheng Wei-qi received her LLM degree from Warwick University, England and PhD degree from City University of Hong Kong. In 1999, the Ministry of Justice in Vietnam invited her to help amend the Vietnam State-owned Enterprise Law under a project sponsored by the United Nations Development Programme (UNDP). She is now teaching at Law School, City University of Hong Kong. She has published *Investing in China, Legal Perspective* (LexisNexis Butterworths, 2003). Her research is mainly in corporate governance and foreign investment in China.

Ian Wilkinson is Professor of Marketing at the University of New South Wales. Previously he was Foundation Chair in Marketing at the University of Western Sydney, Nepean. He has published 3 books and over 100 research papers. His research is collaborative and internationally based and has been supported by grants from the Australian Research Council and the Australian Trade Commission. He has been a consultant to many firms and organisations, and from 1992 to 1994 he served as a member of the Australian Federal Government's Trade Policy Advisory Council.

Dermot Williamson is a Lecturer of Accounting and a member of the Lancaster Centre for Management in China. He received his PhD in Management Control from the University of Glasgow. His research interests are in management control, effects of national culture on perceptions of control and operational risk management. He is a co-author of *Perceptions of Trade Credit Control in Mainland China and the UK* (CIMA, 2001). Prior to becoming an academic, he was a Manager with the Royal Dutch/Shell Group in Europe and the Far East.

Kevin Yeoh recently completed an Arts degree in History and Chinese and an Honours Research degree in International Marketing at the University of New South Wales. He is presently working in banking and finance with Macquarie Bank, an Australian investment bank. His main research interests lie in Chinese business and foreign affairs. Kevin is also an editor of *The Backbench*, an online current affairs magazine.

Yong Zhang graduated from Henan University in 1993 and worked in the state textile sector where he co-ordinated purchasing at the local, provincial and national levels. In 1999 he went to the University of Strathclyde for his MBA and obtained a distinction in his dissertation. Currently, he is completing his PhD at Lancaster University Management School where he is researching strategy formulation in large corporatised SOEs with special reference to organisational processes and personal networks.

Preface

This book has its origins in the Inaugural Conference of the Lancaster University Management School's Centre for Management in China in April 2003. Two speeches helped to set the scene. Professor Fan Gang, Director of the National Economic Research Institute of the China Reform Association, outlined three main problems threatening China's prospects for continued high economic growth – the reform intentions of Premier Wen Jiabao and the other new leaders, the issues of financial reform and the social problems arising from increased unemployment. The response from Lord Powell, President of the China–Business Council, focused on China's role in the world economy, and in particular the trade with Europe and the United Kingdom. Both speakers were optimistic for China's prospects. Such optimism, however, depends on China's enterprises and their ability to cope with the challenges of self-determination. These challenges have exercised both the government and the management since the early beginnings of the corporatisation policy in 1992, and in 2004 it remains central to China's prospects.

The research reported here explores these challenges from the enterprise perspective. The conference brought together Chinese and Western scholars, specialising in the economic resurgence of China. Between them they explore the influences of culture, institutions and recent history on business enterprises. They cover all types of enterprise from State owned through Joint Stock, Township and Village, Foreign Invested and Private companies. Both the regional variety of 'Chineseness' and the continuing pervasive influence of SOEs over many Joint Stock Companies are brought out.

The initial chapters highlight the problems of achieving adequate methods of corporate governance. The reasons range across failures in the attempts to commercialise SOEs through conversion to Joint Stock Companies to 'agency' problems that result from weak incentives for managers to maximise share values. Social, legal, cultural and historical experiences are drawn on to explain the difficulties in using foreign regulatory models in the Chinese context. Later chapters deal with the managerial agenda and approaches to strategic development and marketing, including the 'new' service industries' insurance. Case studies feature in Chapters 6, 8 and 9. They illustrate the successes and weaknesses in ensuring effective research and development in one setting, and of managing strategic change in others. Finally, the common assumption of a homogeneous Chinese style of business is confronted by recent research in Beijing, Shanghai and Guangzhou.

The perspectives offered in these chapters are the result of recent work in China. Although access for academics has improved, research at the enterprise level is always difficult, and the problems of interpretation and generalisation are formidable in a quickly changing economy and society. The potential advantage of a compendium, over the single author, is the scope of the research that is possible and the value of different discipline viewpoints. As editors, we hope that this volume will contribute to knowledge base on China and prove of value to management students, researchers and practitioners alike on some of the issues facing China's varied enterprises and insights into the ways in which they are coping.

1 Introduction

China's macro environment and enterprise challenges

David H. Brown and Alasdair MacBean

Following the Sixteenth National Congress of the Central Communist Party (CPC) in November 2002, the pace of reform for China's enterprises of all kinds has quickened as they seek to cope with the challenges of self-determination – strategic, financial and governance – and to do this in the context of difficult social and welfare changes and the realities of increasing international competition. This book explores these challenges from the perspective of the enterprise. The enterprises operate in a macro environment, conditioned by the state of the economy, external relations, politics, laws, institutions, resource constraints, demography, income distribution and the potential for social unrest and this is where our book begins.

No economy can achieve phenomenal growth for over twenty years without meeting serious challenges. For a country as big as China, sheer size not only exacerbates some of the problems but also creates problems for the rest of the world. Whether China can overcome the challenges and maintain high and sustained growth will profoundly influence the prospects for enterprises, in China, East Asia and elsewhere. This chapter and the one that follows, seek to survey how these factors will influence the prospects for the successful development of China's enterprises. They set the scene for Chapters 3–10 in which Chinese and Western scholars, specialising in the economic resurgence of China, offer an insight into some of the institutional, cultural and management issues of enterprise development.

China's macro environment

China's recent history shows an economy of unprecedented dynamism: annual GDP growth averaging over 8 per cent for the last twenty years, and foreign trade growing at an annual rate of 15 per cent since 1980. China's exports are now larger than Italy's. In terms of world trade share in both exports and imports, China ranks sixth. Based on purchasing-power parity estimates (a better measure for cross-country comparisons than using official dollar exchange rates), China's GDP is already second only to the United States. Over the last ten years China has attracted more foreign direct investment (FDI) than any other developing country, and in 2004 FDI into China reached $60.6 billion, exceeding FDI in the United States, though there are questions about 'round-tripping' (investment in China of moneys sent to China's overseas companies reinvested in China to evade regulations and gain tax advantages). But China also has one of the highest savings rates in the world, averaging over 40 per cent of national income (data from IMF, 2003). These high rates of saving combined with the inflow of foreign investment have supported massive annual investment while maintaining a trade surplus. Combined with a plentiful supply of labour and rapidly improving transport and communications, this investment has driven China's consistently high growth.

It has been achieved with little improvement in efficiency (total factor productivity). Most of China's growth can be explained by investment, increases in labour inputs, and the shift of labour from the agricultural to the industrial and service sectors (IMF, 2004: 24–6). This low level of efficiency is a concern for China's planners, but it is quite similar to the experience of the other 'miracle' economies of South-East Asia and is scarcely surprising when investment rates have been so high and China has such an elastic supply of cheap labour into manufacturing from the rural areas. Given China's enormous reserves of relatively cheap labour, at 59 cents per hour China's manufacturing labour costs are among the lowest in the world. With relatively high levels of primary and secondary education, China's vast labour endowment gives it a substantial comparative advantage in labour intensive products and components. This relative advantage seems likely to persist as the flow of basic labour from rural to urban areas is so plentiful that wages for unskilled labour are unlikely to rise much. Average labour productivity is likely to continue to rise as rural labour continues to flow from low-productivity agriculture to higher productivity jobs in industry and services. This trend will be reinforced by improved education and training, and increased competition at home and abroad as the continued opening up of the economy under WTO rules forces the adoption of more efficient methods on both private and public sectors. China should retain for many years to come its relative advantage in production and assembly of products where the main costs are labour costs.

Main threats

The main threats to long-run sustainable growth in China, probably, are resource constraints (including the ability to absorb wastes), the risk of social instability, partly due to increasing unemployment and inequalities in incomes, demographic change, inefficiency and insolvency in State Owned Enterprises (SOEs) and in the banking system and the resulting lack of adequate credit for the non-state sector enterprises. China's economy will go through cyclical swings, like that of any other country's, but there is no reason why China should not succeed in maintaining an average growth rate of 7–8 per cent, if these more fundamental constraints are overcome. This assumes that there are no major shocks from the external environment such as a surge in Organisation for Economic Co-operation and Development (OECD) protectionism or widespread financial crises.

The pattern of high growth sustained for many years until income levels reach about half OECD levels seems common. Japan, South Korea, Taiwan, Singapore, Hong Kong and the later industrialising economies have all managed to sustain high rates of growth for 20 years or more before slowing significantly at income levels far above China's current $1,000 per head. China, as these countries have so successfully done, can play 'catch up' for many more years. China's huge reserves of labour, 150 million or more surplus workers in agriculture (IMF, 2004: 26) and others in overmanned SOEs, will enable it to avoid any bottleneck from general labour scarcity and rapidly rising wages.

A huge, rapidly growing economy such as China, places demands on the natural resources of the whole world, let alone of China's own territory. China's consumption of energy from coal, oil and natural gas together has risen by 260 per cent over the last 20 years. In 2003 the prices for crude oil and products rose by 11.8 per cent and for coal by 2.6 per cent, and for basic industrial materials such as steel, pig iron, copper and natural rubber by 20, 44, 14 and 42 per cent, respectively (Li, 2004: 2). By 2020, China will be faced 'with difficulties in the shortage of energy reserves, production capacity and transport capacity as well as environmental capacity for the discharge of waste gas' (Ibid.: 2). China can meet many of these shortages by imports financed by continuing buoyant exports albeit at rising energy and resource costs to her economy and to the rest of the world. Already, China's terms of trade have worsened as a result of falling prices for her exports and steeply rising prices for imports of materials. But, a more serious problem is the high and rising environmental costs of air and water pollution. A World Bank study estimated that the cost to China of pollution-related damage to health, productivity and agriculture amounted to $54 billion or 8 per cent of GDP in 1996 (World Bank, 1997: 104). Several major cities such as Beijing, Shanghai and Guangdong have significantly reduced levels of pollution, but this is not true of most less important cities. Despite extensive regulations to control environmental damage, China's pollution levels have continued to rise and are among the highest in the world. Between 2000 and 2002 wastewater discharges rose by 12.8 per cent and waste industrial gasses by 28 per cent (Li, 2004: 5). Aside from contaminated water from agricultural run off, industrial and domestic wastes, China has serious water problems, floods have grown worse in the south whereas water tables are falling in the north resulting in, irrigation wells running dry. Desert areas are expanding by 3,000 square miles per year – grain harvests are falling, partly as a direct result, but also indirectly and farmers are being encouraged to plant trees to prevent desertification (World Bank, 1997: Ch. 7; *The Economist*, 2004b: 14). In addition there is commercially sensible switching to higher value crops in the areas near cities. Agricultural land is also being lost at a high rate as a result of massive construction operations of houses, factories and roads.

China can, of course replace domestic food production with imports. Indeed, this may make economic sense, but the damage done to agriculture exacerbates China's social problems. It will create even greater unemployment in the rural areas and increase the pressure to create more jobs in manufacturing and services to avoid social unrest. It will increase the income disparities between rural and urban areas, and between the northern and the coastal regions. Although, by most definitions, the numbers of Chinese living in absolute poverty have fallen, incomes have become less equal between urban and rural areas and regional per capita income differences have increased. The per capita income difference between urban and rural residents increased from 1.8 : 1 in the mid 1980s to 3.2 : 1 in 2003 (Li, 2004: 3).

Sustainable growth with equity has become the objective of China's new government, but efforts to reduce environmental damage and inequality will prove difficult. Extensive corruption among party officials makes enforcement problematic and adds to the strains on social equilibrium. The Central Communist Party Disciplinary Committee revealed that it had reviewed 134, 692 cases of large-scale corruption before the end of 2003 (*The Economist*, 2004b: 14–15). The new leadership appears to be taking seriously the issues of rural–urban income disparities and of official corruption and is operating a more open economic and political system than did its predecessors. The best guess is that China will be able to avoid serious unrest. This is certainly the view of Professor Fan Gang expressed in Chapter 2. But unless China adopts much more energetic environmental policies and succeeds in their rigorous implementation, continuing environmental degradation will seriously damage welfare and generate costs that will eventually slow growth. Chinese enterprises will have to adhere to strict standards on waste disposal and significantly improve the efficiency with which they use energy and other resources if China is to meet its target for sustainable growth.

China's demographic change will present serious problems for its social security system. The number of people over 65 by 2020 will have risen to 16 per cent of the population; a higher figure than for any other Asian developing country and coming close to the average for the industrially developed countries of 18.6 per cent in 1990 (Li, 2004: 2). If China's development follows a similar path to most countries, family support for aged parents will decline and the State will have to take much more responsibility for the retired. The one child policy that has been followed since the 1980s and increased labour mobility will increase these problems. The rising burden of social security costs will worsen China's already difficult fiscal situation. Enterprises will have to share in these increased burdens through higher taxes and pension contributions for employees.

Despite many years of structural reform, burdened by over-manning, continued social costs and poor management, most of China's SOEs continue to have low efficiency. According to a recent World Bank study by William Mako and Chulin Zhang, 51 per cent of all SOEs that were losing money are saddled with a lot of uncollectible debt and unsaleable stocks (*The Economist*, 2004a: 13). China's biggest and most modern shipyard in Dalian, despite cheap labour, the latest shipbuilding equipment and subsidised loans, has productivity of labour that is one-seventh to one-tenth of its Japanese and Korean rivals. The average return on industrial SOEs' net assets is slightly under 5 per cent (*The Economist*, 2004a: 12–13). Many are highly in debt, but aided by pressure from regional and local governments they have been able to continue in business and even invest heavily with soft loans extracted from China's weak banking system. SOEs form practically all of China's heavy industry, still account for 35 per cent of urban employment, and in the past have taken 80 per cent of all bank loans according to Nicholas Lardy of Brookings Institution (Zhang, 2003). China's industrial policy has included the aim of developing a few global giants after the Japanese and Korean models. But according to a leading commentator this has been a total failure so far (Nolan, 2001). Without further structural reform and greatly improved management the SOEs will continue to be a drag upon China's economy. Their persistent demands for finance deprive private enterprises of access to bank loans to fund the expansion of their highly successful activities. In terms of financial constraints on private companies China was ranked as the fourth worst out of 81 in a World Bank survey in 2000 (Huang, 2004).

Despite financial constraints, the private sector has been the great success story of the Chinese economy. Measuring its size is difficult because of confusion over which enterprises should be defined as private. Narrowly defined, the category classifies only officially registered firms as private. That excludes collectively owned and foreign-invested firms, but many collectively owned really are private, choosing this form for various advantages conferred on collectives. But also some private firms are owned directly or through investment trusts by SOEs. The broadest category is one that treats as private all that are not fully controlled by the state. As a result there is a range of estimates from 30 to 60 per cent for their share of GDP. The China Statistics Bureau shows the share of total industrial output of non-state industries as rising from about 20 per cent in 1980 to just over 70 per cent in 1999 while the SOE share fell from about 80 to 30 per cent.

Whatever the precise share, there is no doubting the rapidity of the growth of the private sector. Its distribution, however, contributes to the widening gaps in regional income, as over 70 per cent are concentrated in the east of China, with over half of all private companies in the six leading provinces (Zhang, 2003). In Zhejiang province average incomes are more than twice those in the north-east and the province is home to 62 of the 400 richest Chinese. Its success is due to the dynamism of the private sector: 91 per cent of Zhejiang's enterprises were privately owned in 2002 (*The Economist*, 2004b: 14–15). But, even more rapid expansion of private enterprise in China is handicapped by the difficulty of obtaining finance for startups and expansion. This is due to weaknesses in China's stock markets, tiny corporate-bond market and, more importantly, the state of the commercial banks. Over 90 per cent of business funding comes from the banks. But their lending has been almost exclusively to SOEs, and for development or purchase of property. For many years China's banks have been saddled with a great burden of loans to SOEs that were unlikely to be repaid. Until recently, the managers had little or no discretion over who to lend to, and none over the terms of the loans. Political, rather than commercial factors, determined the pattern of lending. Instructions came from the centre. In the past, some 80 per cent of bank loans went, under government direction, to failing SOEs (Zhang, 2003). But, even when the central government wanted to curb loans to insolvent SOEs, often local and regional governments, for political or social reasons, put pressure on the managers to circumvent such instructions. As neither SOE managers nor bank managers paid much attention to profits, this has meant the continued accumulation of an enormous quantity of non-performing loans (NPLs), amounting at a recent estimate to 4 trillion yuan, about $483 billion (*The Economist*, 2004b: 17).

Without fundamental reform, the banking sector will fail to supply the finance needed for rapid expansion of China's private firms. Fortunately, China's leaders are aware of the problem and are taking action. Two earlier attempts in 1998 and 1999 were made to relieve the state banks of some of their NPLs. Four State Asset

Management Corporations were set up to purchase NPLs from the banks and repackage them as equities and sell them to the public. They had little success and only a small proportion has been sold. An unfortunate effect is that, relieved of some of their burdens, but un-restructured, the state banks continued to lend to SOEs, thus building up yet more NPLs. Yet another attempt has been made by using some of China's foreign exchange reserves to increase individual bank's capital so that they can resume lending. But as most of the managers remain the same, there is little cause to suppose that their abilities or attitudes will change. They have excessive numbers of branches and employees and few have the ability to assess the creditworthiness of applicants for loans. It is claimed that 'branch managers have closer ties to local officials and businessmen than to their own bosses' and that their recent behaviour gives evidence that in making loans the banks still follow political orders rather than commercial criteria (*The Economist*, 2004a: 17). Current risks of inflation have led to measures to restrict lending, but they have invariably been of an administrative rather than a market-directed type. It was only in January 2004 that the central bank took a small step towards liberalised interest rates by permitting banks to allow for risk by charging up to 70 per cent more than the low fixed benchmark rate. Potentially, the opening up of the banking sector to foreign banks under WTO concessions will improve the situation. But given worries about the quality of information, the weakness of corporate governance in China and the difficulty of understanding the accounts of firms, it is unlikely that there will be many foreign banks willing to rush in to set up joint ventures with Chinese banks.

These are the main problems facing China's aim to maintain sustainable growth of about 8 per cent and together they provide a context for enterprise development. In the next section of this chapter we summarise some of the key insights from the authors and draw the reader's attention to the common themes.

Some issues for enterprise development

It is now 26 years since Deng Xiaoping set the programme of economic reform in motion. That decision taken in 1978 forever changed the direction of Chinese society and the role of managers within China's industrial enterprises. But the programme in essence was more an acceptance of the necessity that domestic and international exchange was needed for national development rather than a thought-through strategy or blueprint (Garnaut, 1999). The reforms themselves have been well documented and commented upon (e.g. Byrd and Lin, 1990; Child, 1996). From the enterprise perspective – the focus of this book – there have been three main developments. The first, from 1978 to the early-1980s, saw increased autonomy to enterprises and the re-emergence of some private production and free markets in agriculture. The second main development from 1984 sought to further encourage the autonomy of enterprise managers through the implementation of the contract responsibility system and later the director-responsibility system. By 1988, the policy of decentralisation had firmly placed the director in the role of the formal legal representative of the enterprise. Both these stages were experimental, controversial and subject to reversals but they prevailed. At the same time the non-state sector grew rapidly to the point where by the early 1990s at 58 per cent of GDP it exceeded the contribution from SOEs (*China Statistical Yearbook*, 1992). Recognising this reality, the third stage of development from 1993 until today has focused on the corporatisation and governance of the state enterprises and the legitimisation of other forms of ownership as a means of increasing competitiveness and productivity. This is the so-called modern enterprise system.

Set against a history of central plans, allocated resources and price controls these changes towards full enterprise autonomy, within an increasingly marketised economy, presented enormous challenges to enterprises and their managers.

As a result (of these changes) a completely different mindset and range of competencies is being demanded of China's managers. In short, their traditional focus on how to meet targets has been replaced with 'What are the targets, both now and in the future?' And then 'How can we meet them and be profitable?' (Brown and Porter, 1996: 2).

From the first part of this chapter we know that the sustained success of China's economy is, in part, evidence of the ability of enterprises and managers to meet the challenges referred to earlier. But the situation is dynamic – with solutions come new problems and changed circumstances. The research presented in this book is recent. Based on empirical work largely from 2000 onwards the authors offer their insights into the issues facing enterprises both now and in the near future. The chapters reflect two main themes. The first derives directly from the Government's reforms of the early 1990s referred to earlier and is the key theme of corporate governance. The second theme is that of enterprise development and the approaches that managers are adopting for dealing with some of the emerging issues. A final chapter outside of these two themes is a reminder of the pitfalls of treating China as a homogeneous entity and that awareness of the regional differences is important in understanding enterprise behaviours.

The rationale for China's shareholding system and corporatisation is both political and economic. The SOE reforms of the 1980s were characterised as improving firm performance by giving management greater autonomy and incentives to operate on a commercial basis free from political intervention. These measures, however, failed to address the fundamental problem of SOEs' economic inefficiencies and losses (Lin, 2001). In particular, these changes did not deal with the core relationship between 'ownership and management'. The challenge posed to the owners has been summarised:

> How the owners (the principal) can achieve efficiency, profitability and accountability while also permitting the managers (the agents) the necessary degree of autonomy to operate the corporation in a competitive market environment. Corporate governance is about solving this principal–agent problem, which arises due to the separation of ownership and management, and for ensuring returns on the shareholders' investment.
>
> (Kagawa, 2002: 5)

China's approach to this has been to been to adopt a governance structure, which comprises the board of directors including outside specialists, and a supervisory board. The board of directors represents the shareholders' interests. In practice there are many issues arising from this governance structure and its implementation including insiders' control, over representation of the state and the failure to improve performance (e.g. Qian, 1996; Xu and Wang, 1999; Lin and Zhu, 2001).

In Chapters 3, 4 and 5 the authors address this theme from very different perspectives and contribute to fresh insights. Cheng and Lawton in their chapter revisit the historical and legal background to the development of the uniquely Chinese system of corporate governance. They explore the regulatory and governance issues of converting SOEs into joint stock mode. This is done from a number of perspectives including the lingering difficulties in the pre-reform SOE system, the importation and or adaptation of foreign regulatory and governance norms and the lessons of the earlier pre-revolutionary period in failing to attract Chinese entrepreneurs. In exploring these issues socio-legal and cultural perspectives are used to question the validity and applicability of the corporate governance system in China and in particular the issues of independent directors and minority shareholders are explored and suggestions are offered in terms of likely improvements. The chapter concludes by making observations on the likely areas of convergence and divergence in corporate form and governance between China and the Anglo-US system in the light of the earlier analysis.

Liu and Sun in Chapter 4 are concerned with the critical links between ownership, shareholding classes and performance. The relationship of ownership and control to corporate performance has intrigued economists since the work of Berle and Means in 1932. Recent discussion has focused on the effects of concentrated shareholdings, managers, institutional investors and banks. But little work has been done on the effects of concentrated shareholding in developing countries. Previous work on China has relied on official statistics that report only shares owned by the state and those owned by 'legal persons'. But this latter category can conceal the ultimate owner that may be a state, provincial or local government owned enterprise. The work presented here traces ultimate ownership through a survey that covered over 95 per cent of listed companies in 2001. It serves two purposes. It reveals ultimate owners and enables a more useful analysis of the relation between class of owner and performance. As a result Liu and Sun make the important observation that the earlier work that tried to relate class of shareholding with performance is misleading.

The final chapter in the corporatisation theme is Chen's on corporate governance (Chapter 5). The author argues that the corporate governance structure per se causes much of the inefficiency in the joint stock companies. This arises from the failure of the current corporate governance arrangements, which embody elements of Western practice, to adequately incentivise directors to create value for the owners. Managerial stock option plans are one such example of a Western mechanism that has failed in China because of the excessively speculative and poorly regulated nature of the market. Chen argues that in the specific context of China's economic and social environment that China needs to rethink its own governance approach and not be overly concerned with 'other' country models. One approach that may have advantages is a neo-corporatist two-tier board model in which the shareholders have an explicit and direct involvement, and there is less reliance on the ability of the market to regulate the firm's actions.

Despite a ten-year focus on corporatisation – both the practice and the regulation – problems remain. Many joint stock SOEs continue to under perform or have stopped trading. The governance system of itself does not lead to profitable enterprises. This relies on managers making the strategic and tactical decisions on products and markets in order to develop their enterprise. This is our second theme. Four chapters deal with three kinds of enterprise – SOEs, collectives and private. The authors report on different issues faced by management from formulating strategy to management control. A sub theme to emerge is the significance of relationships in the four very different research narratives.

The enterprise development theme starts with Brown and colleagues in Chapter 6 on Township and Village Enterprises (TVEs). Originally TVEs were the unsung heroes of the economic miracle and recognition was slow. Not until the late 1980s, did government policy actively support TVEs, before this they were subordinate to SOEs. By 2000, however, they accounted for 47 per cent of total industrial output and their annual average growth rate over the ten-year period 1988–99 was as high as 19 per cent (Fu and Balasubramanyam, 2003).

In their research the authors try to understand the sustained success of two such enterprises from a process perspective. A framework to explore the process of strategy formulation at the organisational level is presented consisting of three perspectives: an environmental or outside-in perspective, a resource based or inside-out perspective and an inter-organisational or network perspective. The research shows the importance of the environmental-fit approach to both companies but that the commitment to a resource-based approach is less evident. The importance of networks as a mechanism for strategic development is confirmed and in particular the significance of inter-personal networks.

Yeoh and Wilkinson in their chapter develop the sub-theme of relationships further by some interesting comparative work between European and Chinese enterprises in terms of the nature of their business to business relationships. The work was survey-based and sought to bring a dimension of quantitative analysis to the research area. Different models emerged for the Chinese and European and the results confirm the importance of trust and social bonding in facilitating relationship functions and value creation in both Chinese and European contexts. The authors' findings suggest that trust is more important in China and that trust is significant in the fulfilment of indirect or network functions. The greater the trust, the more likely is a customer to engage in actions of potential value to a supplier, such as divulging market sensitive information, introducing new customers, or even collaborating in innovation or product development.

The third insight into enterprise development is a focused, in-depth investigation into a private manufacturing company in the electrical sector. Li and colleagues in their chapter explore how the practice of developing and using *guanxi*, which is a common feature of business relationships in China, relates to the Western concept of relationship marketing. The authors develop a conceptual framework to clarify the relationship between the two and go on to suggest these concepts can reinforce each other. The nature of the analysis is such that the insights, even though developed in a particular private enterprise, have a wider validity.

Williamson, in Chapter 9, completes this second theme of enterprise, but also provides a link back to governance. Markets and business organisations operate within their social context, and these contexts are very different between mainland

China and the United Kingdom. Based on empirical studies of Chinese and British managers, Williamson investigates how social context affects managers' assurances about the state of control. Control here means the provision of some level of assurance of achieving one or more objectives for an organisation, including avoiding undesirable outcomes. Totally seven areas of control are investigated and compared including contracts, laws and regulations, accountability, empowerment and hierarchy and attitude to risk and uncertainty. The work confirms that differences in contextual factors are associated with what gives managers assurance that their business is under control. Williamson extends the analysis to suggest that the assurance of stakeholders also depends upon their social context, as does the value that they place on control assurance given to them by managers. Evaluation of control assurance is thus an example of the social embeddedness of markets, and in particular of the transformation of data about performance into values. Since cultures develop slowly, the consequences are that Chinese institutions and markets are likely to develop with Chinese characteristics. Despite China's accession to the WTO Chinese institutions, cultures and philosophical traditions are likely to continue to shape how international regulation is acted out within China. This view of the importance of social embeddedness echoes Chen's observations in Chapter 5 on the need for a Chinese approach to governance.

The book concludes with two chapters about enterprise development – both very different. In the first of these, Hu reports on the insurance industry – one of the fastest growing service sectors in China. The work is ongoing and the chapter is a reflection on the industry at the end of 2003. Starting with a review of the major stages in the development of the industry and in particular the process of liberalisation. This has led to joint stock companies, with their historic incumbent advantages, coping with the challenges of competition from foreign firms, with their technological and financial advantages. Hu sets out the major challenges for the industry many of which derive from China's accession to the WTO. The chapter argues that despite the increasing foreign competition the position of China's domestic insurers will remain strong in the future.

Our final chapter is from Fang (Chapter 11) and is fundamental to enterprise development. In it Fang challenges the notion of a single 'Chineseness' and the homogeneity of China. For enterprises doing business in China, whether inter or intra, the importance of geography and ethnicity is significant but underresearched. The existing knowledge of Chinese style of business is based largely on the perception of China as one single homogeneous entity and the Chinese as doing business in one and the same 'Chinese style'. But with a vast land area, 1.3 billion inhabitants and deep ethnic, linguistic and regional cultural variations, such a view is clearly simplistic. In his chapter Fang sets out to capture the diversity of the Chinese way of doing business from a regional or sub-cultural perspective. Findings are presented from a survey of Swedish companies' perceptions of Chinese business behaviour in three major regions of China: Beijing, Shanghai and Guangzhou. The study reveals considerable differences between regions in their styles of starting business process, decision-making, communicating, and negotiating and leads to a profiling of businesspeople from Beijing, Shanghai and Guangzhou. These differences highlight a further dimension of relationship complexity that managers in enterprises, both domestic and foreign, will need to take into account.

In conclusion, the aim of this book and the international conference on which it is based, is to disseminate quickly and effectively our many different research findings and insights about China. The twin themes of corporatisation and enterprise management in this book underline some of the major challenges facing China's enterprises from their increasing autonomy, trade liberalisation and deregulation. Since 2000, the pace of change has quickened even further and the collective view of our authors is largely positive; that China's pragmatic experimentation will continue to deliver workable 'solutions' for enterprise development regardless of their ownership characteristics.

References

Brown, D. and Porter, R. (1996) 'Introduction', in D. H. Brown and R. Porter (eds), *Management Issues in China: Domestic Enterprises*, Vol. 1, Routledge, London.

Byrd, William and Lin, Qingsong (eds) (1990) *China's Rural Industry: Structure, Development, and Reform*, Oxford University Press, New York.

China Statistical Yearbook (1992) China Statistics Press, Beijing.

Fu, X. and Balasubramanyam, V. N. (2003) 'Township and village enterprises in China', *The Journal of Development Studies*, 39(4): 27–46.

Garnaut, R. (1999) 'Twenty years of economic reform and structural change in the Chinese economy', in R. Garnaut and L. Song (eds), *China: Twenty Years of Reform*, Asia Pacific Press, Canberra, pp. 1–26.

Huang, Y. (2004) 'China's growth masks weakness', *Financial Times*, 22 April.

International Monetary Fund (2003) *China: Competing in the Global Economy*, IMF publications, Washington DC.

International Monetary Fund (2004) *World Economic Outlook*, IMF publications, Washington DC, Chapter 11, p. 26.

Kagawa, N. (2002) 'The modern enterprise system and corporate governance in China's state-owned enterprise reform', Online. Available at http://www.gwu.edu/econ270/Noriko.htm

Li, Jiange (2004) 'China's economy towards 2020', Mimeo paper presented at the Conference, 'China's 2020 Vision', Royal Institute of International Affairs, London, 29 March.

Lin, C. (2001) 'Corporatisation and corporate governance in China's economic transition', *Economics of Planning*, 34(1-2).

Lin, Y. and Zhu, T. (2001) 'Ownership restructuring in Chinese state industry: an analysis of initial organisational changes', *China Quarterly*, 16(6): 305–41.

Mako, W. and Chulin, Z. (2003). 'Management of China's state-owned enterprises portfolio: lessons from international experience', *World Bank Report*, World Bank Office, Beijing, 3 September.

Nolan, P. (2001) *China and the Global Economy: National Champions, Industrial Policy and the Big Business Revolution*, Palgrave, Houndsmill.

Qian, Y. (1996) 'Enterprise reform in China: agency problems and political control', *Economics of Transition*, 4(2): 442–7.

The Economist (2004a) 'Behind the mask: a survey of business in China', 20 March.

The Economist (2004b) 'Letters from John Burton and Erping Zhang', London, 17 April.

World Bank (1997) *Clear Water, Blue Skies*, Washington DC.

Xu, X. and Wang, Y. (1999) 'Ownership structure and corporate governance in Chinese stock companies', *China Economic Review*, 10(1): 75–98.

Zhang, A. (2003) 'The development of China's private sector and its implications', talk presented to Lancaster Centre for Management in China, Lancaster University, Lancaster, December.

2 China's economy and cooperation with Europe*

China can maintain high growth in its economy despite serious problems. The new leaders are better educated than their predecessors and placed in a post-cultural revolution environment. They are conscious of the need to maintain growth and that this means continued efforts in reform. They will not be radical, but gradual progress in reform should be maintained. China is becoming more open. Freer debate is being encouraged. The main problems are in the banking sector, unemployment and income disparities. The large volume of non-performing loans (NPLs) is undoubtedly a threat to the banking system, but China's huge financial reserves represent a cushion against any international credit crunch. Unemployment due to reforms in the State-Owned Enterprises is another threat. Pressure to adhere to WTO rules would further add to this. But the huge excess supply of labour in agriculture seems a greater threat in the longer term. Admittedly, the expansion of industry and services needed to absorb the labour flow from the rural areas, is hard to envisage. But China's economy should prove remarkably resilient in the face of external shocks. China would benefit from expanded demand for its exports, should the world economy recover and grow quickly, but its exports could also benefit if a sluggish world economy pushed consumers towards a search for cheaper versions of the products they wanted. Despite these threats, China's fast growth can continue for the next twenty years at least as shown by the examples of Japan, South Korea and Taiwan. Lord Powell endorsed most of the points made by Professor Fan Gang and went on to stress the importance for Europe and especially the UK, of greatly expanding their share of China's imports. China's size, rapid growth and modernisation make it a key target for exporters and investors. The current share of both Europe and the UK in China's imports is far below that of the Asia-Pacific region. There is great scope for further expansion of a variety of products from Europe, in particular, – agricultural products as China's own ability to produce many of these lags behind the growth of its demand for them.

COMING COLLAPSE OR CONTINUED HIGH GROWTH?

Fan Gang

It really is a great honour for me to speak to this distinguished group and gives me great pleasure to attend this inaugural conference of the new centre. As a Chinese economist I am really delighted to find one more new centre for economic and business studies on China set up in Europe. In recent years, I have seen this growth of interest in China. I have been told, that some classes in this management school already have over 50 per cent of their students from China – this constitutes my only worry. Perhaps you should re-name your school 'The Chinese School of Business Studies' in Lancaster University, with both Mandarin and English as official languages.

As I am a macroeconomist, I propose to give you a brief review of what is going on in China and on the macro background of your business studies.

When I prepared this speech, I thought that it would be interesting to make an assessment of what is the actual economic and social situation in China today. In recent years, the assessment of China's situation, the perceptions of market sentiment, about the Chinese economy have fluctuated wildly. I remember two years ago, in the world outside, most people talked about when China should devalue its currency. However, since last year, everybody is talking about when China would revalue the yuan upwards against the dollar. Two years ago a magazine cover story was that the Chinese 'cook' the statistics and the growth rate was seriously overestimated. But last year some American wrote a paper (I haven't seen the original paper) claiming that much of the contribution to China's income is unrecorded and the actual growth rate is not 8 per cent, but closer to 28 per cent.

Last year, about the same time as now, the Singapore Government College organised a conference, actually, more a one-to-one debate before an audience, between me and Mr Gordon Chang, author of *The Upcoming Collapse of China*. At that time he had quit his job as a lawyer and was travelling around the world, devoting himself to telling people that China is going to collapse. Now I don't think I need to explain to you why the Chinese economy is not about to collapse. But what may still concern you is how China will be able to continue it's high growth and what are the problems that China must solve to permit this. Is it not likely that these problems will cause major setbacks or crises that will halt China's growth?

To answer this question, I should like to discuss some of the major problems that China faces which may be the focus of your concerns. I should like to review three key questions:

- Is the new leadership going to carry on with the reform agenda and are they up to doing the job?
- What about the financial risk? What about the non-performing loans (NPLs) and China's whole set of financial problems? Are they going to cause some kind of crisis?
- Finally, what about the social problems that may arise because of high and rising unemployment?

I believe that these are issues every one is concerned about.

Calibre and intentions of the leadership

Well, first of all, what about this new leadership and the reforms? When this change of leadership took place, I think most Chinese people were really happy. It is not about who transferred the power to whom. It is just the fact of transfer. For the first time, power was transferred according to pre-set rules, which is one major example of progress. But then people worried about whether this younger generation of leaders were capable of doing the job. Perhaps it is true that there is no individual among the new leaders as outstanding as Zhu Rong-ji, our previous prime minister. But, as a generation, I think the new group is better than the older ones. They are better educated and they have direct experience, or some experience at least, of the market economy or market-oriented reforms. In this they are unlike the previous generations, whose basic background, was the planning system. This generation is more pragmatic, carries less ideological burdens, and have been more exposed to international issues.

Some people say that at least the older generation had experience abroad, particularly in the Soviet Bloc, whereas this new generation is just home grown. But most of their working experience has been after the Cultural Revolution. In daily life they have met all kinds of foreign investors and they have encountered every issue in international affairs. I believe that they are capable as individuals and as a collective body, particularly at the ministerial level. Most belong to the generation who were educated after the Cultural Revolution. Now they are concentrating on several things: further reform of the state enterprises with further reform of the state assets management system. A new body has already been set up, the so-called 'The State Commission for Assets Management'. It combines the power of relevant ministries of the past with the management of the state enterprises. The most important feature of this commission is that it has the authority to sell off assets. But, also important is that this authority has been de-centralised to the local level. Now the local government has ownership rights over the local state companies. A friend of mine, who is a senior official, attended a meeting of high-ranking officials and provincial governors that was addressed by Mr Wen Jiabao, the new Prime Minister, before the party congress. My friend said that a particular provincial governor was listening without much attention, half asleep. But when Mr Wen Jiabao mentioned the local rights of ownership he suddenly opened his eyes, realising that this was really something important and relevant to his situation. Now you can see provincial and city governments rushing into the further sales of those state assets. One city says, 'I have 50 billion yuan in assets', another province says, 'I have 100 billion to put on the table'. Recently, I spoke with a governor who said that the question now is not about whether we shall sell, but who and where are the potential buyers. I think this process will definitely continue. It is not necessarily the initiative of this generation of the government, but a kind of consensus is emerging that this sort of process must go further.

A greater concern for this government is reform in labour issues and the social security systems. They will continue the experiment with social security reforms in Liaoning Province and will speed up the process and put these reforms into nation-wide operation.

Another pointer is that Mr Wen Jiabao, the new Premier, is himself very concerned about the rural situation. He has committed himself to the reform of local government, and the local taxation system, and to reduce the burdens on the rural people. He has vowed that China will not repeat its history of rural rebellion.

Further, you may notice that the document of the Party Congress contains a word about the political situation. I am not saying this leadership is ready to go very far in political reform, but it seems that they have committed themselves to some progress in this area. In a way, we have already seen something new take place. On the evening, previous to my arrival here, I did two interviews with the central TV station, – two live half-hour interviews. Of course, the topic was the impact of the war in Iraq on the world and Chinese economies. But the novelty is that this was a live broadcast. This is really something historic. It was the first time we had had a live half-hour interview on the national TV. Whereas things are progressing, I do not expect dramatic changes, but I think that things are moving forward. The base line is that the leadership does not have many policy options. They can't go back – that would be political suicide. They cannot move forward very much either. They cannot jump, but move forward, they must. They have to follow the trends, to continue the programmes, and to show some creativity on the reform and development agenda. So, basically, I am not too worried about political reform. I think that the course of reform will continue and that perhaps we shall be in a better shape than we were earlier.

Financial reform

My account may so far seem a little too rosy. The next question, about the financial issues, is much more difficult. China is infamous for NPLs. At the moment, the official figure for NPLs is still, I think, about 40 per cent as a ratio to the GDP. Bank NPLs are about 26 per cent. Additionally NPLs, which have already been transferred to the balance sheet of the so-called State Assets Management Company (SAMC), and which are still unsold on the balance sheet are about 12 per cent. So, it is still a very large number.

Whereas these large numbers have not really caused any major financial problems with China's growth which continued to grow at over 8 per cent, it did cause a kind of financial crisis in the past. The deflation over the years 1997–9 was not caused by the Asian crisis, but by a domestic credit crunch. The credit crunch came because at that time, NPLs reached such a high level that the monetary authority had to act. It had to take that problem as its first priority. It had to impose many rules on the banks and as a result the banks just stopped lending. It was a kind of financial crisis. But it has already taken place, was not on a large scale and did not involve any financial crisis with the international balance of payments. It was simply a crisis in the domestic banking sector.

In general, the financial situation is still manageable in the macro-economic sense. But I think that the basic reason that it is less worrisome is that the overall financial situation is not as bad as that of the bank situation appears to be. The key point here is that although having a high NPL ratio, China still enjoys a very low government debt ratio. After four or five years of stimulus to macro policy, China, still has a government fiscal debt balance equivalent to only 18 per cent of GDP at the end of the previous year. In the EU, the Maastricht Treaty standard for this ratio is 60 per cent and in Japan, the current government debt to GDP ratio is 150 per cent. Also China's foreign debt is quite low. If we leave out the long-term governmental debt, and take only the short-term financial debt owed to foreigners, that debt is only equivalent to one per cent of GDP. So if you add together the NPLs of the banks, the net debt held by the Asset Management Companies, the government debt and the short-term debt owed to foreigners $(38 + 18 + 1) = 57$ per cent, which is still lower than the Maastricht Treaty standard. Such a level of debt is well below the warning line and totally controllable. That is why the overall position is not as bad as the NPLs figure implies.

The reason China enjoys this lower government debt ratio is that, since the mid-1980s, the Chinese government stopped subsidising the state-owned enterprises (SOEs) from the fiscal budget. From then on all the funding for the SOEs came from the banks. From the beginning, both the fixed investment funding and the circulating funds, to the SOEs, came from bank loans. This, plus the fact that the government did not, until recently, use fiscal policy to stimulate the economy, is the reason why the government was able to keep its debt low and that's why the bank loans/debt should be regarded as quasi-public debt. When you see the low government debt, you should also take the bank debt, the bank NPLs, into the calculation of the overall financial situation. It is all ultimately a liability of the government. So, in recent years, the government continues to take the reduction of the NPLs as the first priority of monetary policy, particularly since the last year. With WTO entry, China faces more international competition and the bank managements have to become more serious. It is reported that the major state banks reduced NPLs last year by 3 per cent. I tend to believe this, although the relationship between the state banks and the state companies is still in many cases the same as before. But now the state banks lend more to the local state companies and to the local government for investments in real estate or for infrastructural projects. The banks are more cautious than before. Market forces and competition have forced them to be more careful about their financial performance.

If the growth of NPLs can be effectively controlled then I am not too worried about the total outstanding amount. With continued growth of GDP of 8 per cent and with the enlargement of the monetary basis, the ratio of NPLs to GDP will probably decline. As long as the ratio is not increasing, I think the situation will be manageable.

I do not like the programme of so called debt-equity swap, which took place four years ago under the leadership of Zhu Rong-ji. It just doubled the bad loans in the next period. It created a kind of a moral hazard problem as, when the banks were relieved of the bad debts, they did not believe that the exercise would never be repeated and simply lent more.

The best way to deal with the NPLs is to keep them on the balance sheets of both the state enterprises and the state banks. That way, they create pressure for reforms, for the necessary changes in performance, and these institutions should not be relieved of such pressure. In that manner, the Government can keep control of the stock of debt, and the main effort can be put into trying to control the growth of NPLs. The bad loan is already bad, and it cannot really be taken back into the operation. It is better to just leave them to serve as the incentive, or pressure, for new reforms. I do not know if a debt-equity swap will take place again, but some people in the leadership once talked about another round of the swap, but so far it is not on the agenda, and hopefully it will not be.

There is still a lot of work to do in the financial sector. Banking reform and financial reform have been too slow. The current bottleneck for reform in the whole economy, which slows financial growth reforms, does remain a serious issue, but will still be manageable. I do not think that we will see a financial crisis in the near future.

There is an even less likelihood of an international or external crisis because China has a good external balance. If you reduce the possibility of a further crisis over the next couple of years, and continue to move on, extending, postponing the crisis for the future, then during this time you can start to solve the problem. I do not expect the problem can be solved overnight or even in five years. But if you have five years without the risk of a crisis and you do carry on with increasing the GDP over these five years, you gradually outgrow the problem.

Unemployment

What about unemployment? Well, this is still the major concern, the major political issue in China. Everyone is talking about it. Behind it lie the issues of income and regional disparities. Basically the problem is about the employment of 3–4 hundred million people, particularly people from the rural areas. There are two aspects to the unemployment problem. One is the layoff of workers of the state sector and the other, – the issue of the rural people. Concerning the layoff, it remains the biggest political issue and the focus of the government's concern. But I think the peak of the layoff is already over and the most difficult time has passed. Over the last five years China laid off 26 million people from the state sector. This is probably the largest layoff in history. Then another, approximately, 20 million jobs have been lost in the township and village enterprise sector and the so-called collective industry sector in the past five years. The previous five years were not good. The years 1997–9 saw a downturn in growth. That slow growth in GDP meant that the creation of new jobs was very slow. The last five years saw the most difficult time for redundancies in the industrial sector. In the future, perhaps another 15 million people from the state sector may be laid off. Last year, that slow down produced a layoff of 7 million people. Now, or in the near future, another 3 or 4 million may be made redundant. In the late 1990s annual creation of new non-farming jobs was only about 6–8 million. But with higher growth since 2001, the creation of new jobs annually was 12–13 million. So with fewer layoffs, the higher growth rate and the better social security system, I think this issue of industrial layoffs is going to be manageable.

The real long-term challenge is to create enough jobs for the rural people. Recently, I did some calculations with reference to agriculture and agricultural employment, in Japan, the US and Australia. Using their experience as guidance, China eventually may only need, approximately 40–60 million farmers to farm the relatively small area of cultivable land in China – which means that in the long run, over the next 40–50 years, a total of 300–400 million people should be relocated from agriculture to the non-farming sector. But the present situation is that in each year, at the current level of technological progress, we shall only create 10–12 million new jobs. This means that over the long term, even with rapid GDP growth, there will still be a huge under-employment situation in rural areas and even more people will flock to the cities looking for jobs.

That is a real challenge, and because it is a long-term issue it cannot be solved overnight. In the future you will see increased social disparities: unemployment, income disparities and maybe some urban poverty. Is this likely to lead to a social crisis? If the growth stops, we can no longer create the jobs. But if we assume that growth can continue, not necessarily at 8 per cent, but at least at approximately 6–7 per cent, then we shall have increasing numbers of people moving out from the countryside. This is important because at present you have, in some places, particularly in the interior regions, a very tense relationship between the local government and the rural people because of the poverty and taxation burden issues. But now the rural people at least can go out and look for new opportunities. They do not have to stay in the same place and continue dealing with the same issues. Such an ability to move is different from our recent history when there were tough legal restrictions on labour migration within China. Second, as long as the opportunity to move exists, people can move around and earn additional income from new, non-farming jobs, and some will send some money back to families on their farms or rural towns. Life in rural areas may be tolerable even though agriculture is no longer the source of the growth in income. Incomes in rural areas can still increase through increasing work in non-farming jobs.

So, as long as growth continues, a situation can emerge in which few, if any, major groups in the society become worse off in absolute terms. They may still be worse off in relative terms. Indeed, many, especially rural, people will be worse off in relative terms because in the cities, earnings will be so much more. But, as long as no major groups are absolutely worse off, the basic social stability will be preserved and social unrest prevented. Further, China may have the opportunity, even though it is a large developing country, to avoid the typical problem of huge urban poverty. This is because China is the only country where people in the rural areas have the title to rent a small piece of land, which cannot legally be sold. The tenant leases it and can transfer the lease contract if he or she finds a job in the city. If such a person loses his/her, job he/she can still come back to his/her home and reclaim his/her lease contract. This means that although the small piece of land is not the source of income growth, it can serve as a form of basic social security in rural areas.

That is the reason why after 20 years of migration and labour mobility you do not see much urban poverty in the city. You do see a type of floating population. When the spring festival comes people travel all the way to their home town. Why? Because there still is a home there, and they still have that small piece of land there. That small piece of land under a leasing contract, is not owned, if it were, it could be sold. Then it would no longer serve as a form of social security and for all the usual reasons you could have urban poverty as experienced in other developing countries.

Income disparities are a significant and growing problem both intra- and inter-regionally. China's politicians and officials in the Government like to come to Europe to learn how European countries use fiscal transfers to narrow the gap between the rich and the poor. You can narrow the gap by fiscal transfers when there is a 20 per cent difference in income shares, but not when the gap involves a 20-fold difference between the highest and lowest incomes. That means that income inequalities will remain with us as a social issue. The only hope is that, as long as the majority of the people can share some of the prosperity, then in absolute terms, no one is really worse off. China can still hope to continue to avoid a major setback.

All this may still sound rather rosy, but basically today I am quite hopeful about what is going on. People worry about the effects of the war in Iraq and the possibility of world economic recession. My view is that China is now in the position to sell its goods in either scenario. If the world economy is getting better, China will sell, China's exports will grow along with world growth. If the world economy goes into recession, China may still sell because during a recession, people become more cost-sensitive and may switch to cheaper goods. The Chinese are now producing those cheaper goods – in accessory not luxury goods. China's exports to Japan actually started to increase after the bubble burst in Japan, which is one of the reasons why, last year, when the world economy was not doing well, China's exports continued to grow by 30 per cent. So, China really now is in a position where the increase in the export growth of its products is almost guaranteed.

Export growth is also guaranteed because so many foreign companies are now manufacturing in China. They have to sell on international markets, which is the reason why two years ago, we, as an institute, kept saying to the government:

> Don't worry too much about the growth. Now you have a good opportunity in that growth is guaranteed and in some sense automatic. Now your job is to concentrate more on the reforms, on institutional changes, so that you can prepare for the next round of growth. Then you can deal with the long-term issues.

I think this will be the situation for some time and will provide a good test for the new leadership. Will they use this good opportunity? But the problems will always be there. When we talk about the 'good situation' it does not mean that the problems will disappear. This is the fate of a developing country, you have to grow with your problems. You cannot just solve a problem and make it vanish. China's problems remain but China is still in a comparatively good situation, so one can see that it is possible to make real progress.

Sometimes when you have better growth, ministers do not worry or feel a sense of urgency to reform, to do the hard job required by reform. But progress in reform is the real test of the government. If the government can really do the job satisfactorily, I think China can have at least another ten years of high growth. If reforms progress well, China will hopefully have another 20 years of high growth.

Actually, this is not so very difficult to believe when we make a simple comparison with Taiwan and Korea. If they can maintain, as they have, high growth for over 40 years, China, with a much larger labour force and with a bigger domestic market is likely to have another 20 years of relatively high growth. But I still worry that even with such a 20-year period of high growth, it is still not enough to ensure adequate employment. This is because we still have that 400 million rural people to be re-employed in other sectors. If we are to have a total solution to the current problems we need at least 40 years of very high growth. That's the real challenge. It's not the challenge for the near future, but the challenge for the long-term.

COOPERATION BETWEEN CHINA AND EUROPE

Lord Powell of Bayswater

I am most grateful to Lancaster University for the invitation to speak and congratulate the University on its imaginative initiative in setting up its centre for management in China. Just to explain why I am here: I am President of the China–Britain Business Council (CBBC), the UK's leading agency helping British organisations to do business in China. We are delighted and honoured to be involved with the Centre: and we greatly value Lancaster University's support of our work as a member of the CBBC. Despite my role as President of the CBBC, I do not classify myself a China expert. I first visited China with Margaret Thatcher in the 1980s to meet Mr Deng Xiaoping – an unforgettable experience. Over the ensuing decade we had visits to London from many leading Chinese figures including Mr Jiang Zemin, Mr Zhao Ziyang, Mr Hu Yaobang and Mr Li Peng. In the 1990s I paid frequent visits to China, as a director of Jardine Matheson, the oldest of all China's trading partners. Therefore, I have experience, not expertise.

We are meeting at a time of high tension in world affairs with a major conflict with Iraq under way. We shall not be debating the rights and wrongs of the conflict in this forum. But it has caused a significant rift within Europe, across the Atlantic and within the UN Security Council. We need to heal that as soon as possible and ensure that the UN plays a very full part in the reconstruction of Iraq once Saddam and his murderous gang have gone. If we fail, the UN itself and the hopes for finding multilateral solutions to world problems will suffer a severe blow. China and the UK have a common interest in avoiding that and I applaud the even-handed approach which China has taken.

We must also hope that the war's impact on the world's economy and markets, which are already limping badly, can be contained by ensuring that the conflict is reasonably brief and completely successful. If that is the case, a cloud will be lifted from the world markets, oil prices should settle quite quickly to more sustainable levels and we should be able to look forward to an economic recovery. That again is in all our interests and particularly in China's case in achieving its ambitious economic development plans.

On a more cheerful note we would all wish to congratulate the new government of China on taking office. Many of you at this meeting will know individual members of the government, in particular the new Premier Wen Jiabao, and will wish them well. They are a talented group, strongly committed to continued reform and to the development of China's economy. None of us – least of all, they themselves – underestimate the economic, financial and social challenges which lie ahead for China. But the achievements of their predecessors under Premier Zhu Rong-ji – who is very widely admired in this country, have created a firm platform for tackling those challenges and propelling China forward. That is what all of us here want to see and we shall work to help achieve it.

Under the circumstances that the new Chinese Government is starting its first five-year term and given the fact that Europe's relationship with China will become increasingly important over that period – not least, as we seek to repair differences and strengthen ties following the war in Iraq – I propose to give you some views on how political and economic cooperation between China and Europe should develop over that period.

The core of my remarks is: there isn't enough political and economic cooperation between China and Europe – there needs to be much more. Europe lags behind the US and some Asian countries in the scale and scope of its involvement with China. That applies to the volume of trade and investment and equally to the level and frequency of political contacts, particularly of course in Asia-Pacific regional organisations, from which Europe is generally absent. Europe has a lot of catching up to do, in order to develop a relationship with China which matches the traditions and ambitions of both parties.

To form a view on what we can realistically expect to achieve between China and Europe over the next five years, let me speculate at how first China and then Europe are likely to develop over that timescale.

My basic forecast for China is a very positive one. An important leadership and generational change is taking place which will accelerate the overall pace of change in China. Membership of WTO will further hasten economic reform and multiply China's engagement with the rest of the world. China's manufacturing base and exports will expand rapidly as China becomes a global manufacturing centre. Foreign direct investment will continue to flood in. The role of the private sector in the economy will grow. And the legal system will rapidly develop.

Less positive will be the continuing problems of China's vast rural population, in particular the downward pressure on rural incomes and consequent social dislocations; unresolved difficulties in restructuring SOEs; the weak balance sheets of state-owned banks; and a conflict between the social discipline needed to safeguard growth and raise living standards and a desire for greater freedom of political expression. I would summarise this as the typical problems of rising expectations. I also suspect that the opening up and development of China's West will take longer than is hoped. There will also be difficult natural problems such as the shortage of water in parts of China.

But on balance, I believe the positive outweighs the negative, and that China will resolve or at least manage the problems which I have described and that five years from now China will be a significantly stronger and more influential player in the world economy, as well as a more open and self-confident one in world affairs, with less of the sense of insecurity which has in the past been a characteristic of China's foreign policy.

What about Europe in five years? Hopefully Europe's economies will have recovered from their present trough. Enlargement of the EU will be a reality despite French threats to block it. Europe will be, by a long run the world's largest market. But I suspect the pace of integration in Europe will have slowed somewhat. Absorption of new member countries will be a major preoccupation distracting from the more ambitious plans to create a federal Europe. Europe may, by the end of the five-year forecast, have a full-time president to symbolise and represent its unity. But in other respects, I doubt it will act much more as a unit than it does now. For a great power like China, that will mean continuing to balance bilateral dealings with individual European countries some of the time and engaging with the EU as an institution at other times. Looked at, from the European perspective, European countries will be both competitive and cooperative in their relations with China.

I would not expect to see the EU – as compared to some of its individual members to be a significantly weightier player on the political stage of Asia than it is now. I do not sense there is – yet anyway – great impetus behind ASEM: certainly nothing to compare with APEC. And I detect no enthusiasm at all for European military or security engagement in Asia – that will be left to the US.

You could say that my forecast is rather sedate and makes no allowance for surprise. I remember Margaret Thatcher's first law of politics: the unexpected always happens. But I think it represents a probable outcome. What conclusions do I draw?

First, China will play a significantly larger part in Europe's calculations than it does now. That is a function both of China's remarkable growth and increasingly attractive market, and also resulting from the relative political and economic eclipse of other power centres notably Russia and Japan. Europe will focus more on China and pay more attention to China's views. China will seem less mysterious, less distant, and approachable, more relevant to Europe and that will be a good basis for more active cooperation.

I would expect to see that growing attraction mirrored on the Chinese side. China will not want to be too dependent on the US market for its exports and will find Europe a useful counter balance, not just in trade but also politically. Although remaining primarily focussed on the Asia-Pacific region, China is likely to become a more active member of the UN Security Council and therefore more drawn into active discussion of world problems with its European Permanent members. And as it grows economically stronger and still more politically engaged internationally, China will have a legitimate interest in other world decision-making bodies: not just the formal institutions of the UN and the WTO but the real wielders of influence like the G8. Overall, I would expect to see China identify its interests increasingly with the developed world rather than with the developing countries.

So the incentives for deeper and more substantive engagement between China and Europe are there. How can they be translated into practice? Let me suggest a number of ways:

- A higher level of European involvement in China's economy, so that we come closer to matching that of the US and Japan. At the moment, our trade, especially Europe's exports to China, is not keeping pace with the expansion of China's imports, though we are now doing rather better on the investment front, coming after only the US and Japan. Some European companies and countries are already quite heavily involved: one thinks of Volkswagen or BMW or BP or Shell. But the business opportunities will grow rapidly with China's WTO membership and if Europe fails to grasp them, others will not. Our national trade promotion bodies need to do an even better and more active job of leading European companies into the China market.

- This extends also to agriculture. As China's farmers switch to cash crops and as more agricultural land disappears under concrete, China will have to import more commodities, in particular, grain, which will offer trade opportunities for individual European producer countries. But in order to compete with the US and Australia, they will have to combine under a European banner.

- In the same context, it would be good to see an expansion of Chinese investment in Europe, as well as the listing of more Chinese companies on European stock exchanges particularly London.

- I would additionally like to see a further major expansion of educational and training exchanges between Europe and China. Actually, we now have some

50,000 Chinese students in the UK on courses lasting one year or more, which represents a ten-fold increase in six years, pretty dramatic by anyone's standards and Lancaster is playing a leading part. This, more than anything will establish the links and determine the style which will characterise our future relations. In Europe we need to train more Chinese speakers who will be the front line of Europe's future presence in China.

- There is a likelihood of a huge increase in Chinese tourists visiting Europe at some point in the next five years. That will in itself extend knowledge about Europe within China. But I am not sure that St. Peter's in Rome, the Louvre in Paris or the Tower of London have yet thought out how to cope with this.

- Although it sounds a hackneyed diplomatic cure-all, I see scope for extending the range, and deepening the substance, of exchanges on international issues between European countries and China. Our global interests touch each other at a large and growing number of points – from arms control to the environment, from terrorism to trade and many points in-between. We also need to get many more institutions involved in these contacts, including parliaments, cultural organisations and learned societies. Political dialogue should not be restricted to government ministers in China or to European Foreign Ministers and Commissioners.

- We should also look at the structure and institutions of the Euro-Chinese relationship. I sense there is scope for a more substantial and durable framework without becoming overwhelmed by bureaucracy. In particular the Euro-Chinese political dialogue is not very strong. Last year's Euro-Chinese Summit in Copenhagen in September lasted only two hours. We should consider matching some of the issue-specific working groups set up between China and the United States.

- And surely by the end of this five-year period if not before, we ought to be considering China's association with the G8 Summit, where Europe is already strongly represented and where China's absence as a strategic partner will seem increasingly strange that will of course, stimulate claims by other countries such as India and Brazil to be included. But I believe China will have an unanswerably strong case – always assuming of course, that it wants to be a member.

- Last, on a matter of style I would like to see us get away from the rather ritualistic nature of political exchanges between China and Europe. This is a generational and cultural phenomenon. There is scope to ease up on formal declarations, develop franker and easier relationships and communicate in a more modern way. This conference and dinner is an excellent example of easier communication. I hope it will prove to be the beginning of a series, which will develop and blossom as an important contribution to strengthening Euro-Chinese ties.

Note

* Opening speeches given at the LCMC Conference Dinner 3 April 2003 by distinguished guests Professor Fan Gang and Lord Powell of Bayswater.

3 SOEs reform from a governance perspective and its relationship with the privately owned publicly listed corporation in China

Cheng Wei-qi and Philip Lawton

There are a variety of reasons explaining the lack of development of the privately owned, publicly traded corporation (PPC) in China. This chapter examines the development of the private corporate sector against the background reform of state owned enterprise (SOE). The latter reflects a number of problems, including typical agency issues involving exploitation of state assets by managers and officials against a background of ambiguous regulation and an overall lack of transparency. This corporatisation, rather than privatisation, of the SOE sector typified by an ostensibly communitarian approach in a 'socialist market' with 'Chinese characteristics' retains an underlying ideology hostile to the private sector. Whereas this has allowed considerable expropriation of SOE assets and at the same time, helped fuel the rapid development of China's economy, it has meant that the private sector has taken a back seat despite its important contribution to economic success. Finance, whether by way of bank loan or listing has been relatively difficult to obtain for the private sector. We argue that only with a change in both law and official attitudes to private property and business (including the privatisation as opposed to corporatisation of many SOEs) will the PPC be able to develop and contribute to China's development in ways similar to other parts of Asia.

Corporations and business in China: a brief historical overview

China has long had associations similar to partnerships, companies and trusts. That they should have had, then and have presently, a concept of 'kinship' embedded in a long cultural tradition is unsurprising (Jamieson, 1921; Ruskola, 2000: 1599). Probably some element of kinship was often a cementing factor in European business relationships and in some parts of Europe, is still vital (Wilson, 1995: 24; Colli and Rose, 1999: 47). But in the West, at least in the Anglo-American corporate world, the dominant norm is that of a 'nexus of contracts' as perceived by economists (rather than lawyers). Such differences may mean inevitable limits to the convergence of law and corporate governance in systems with disparate basic norms (Ruskola, 2000; MacNeil, 2002: 2).

The assumptions of Chinese reformers in the early twentieth century that the anonymous private corporation on the Western model would 'facilitate commerce and help industries' proved over-optimistic. The record shows that organisational structures and values rooted in networks of family and regional ties, 'Capitalism with Chinese characteristics', resisted the corporate structure even in its heyday in the first half of the twentieth century. China's capitalists appeared even more leery of public participation than they did of government. That the public would be invited to share in one's business's control and profits, was found hateful. In essence, this view of W. C. Kirby (1995) laments the absence of privately owned, publicly traded corporations (PPC) in China. A simple explanation relies on the concept and role of residual claimancy in ownership and its interaction with the Chinese Government's tradition of relying mainly on discretionary fees (*Kejuan Zashui*) as a source of revenue rather than explicit taxes.

Discretionary fees invite government opportunism through fee adjustments to profit levels and this, according to some economists, attenuates an important aspect of owner's property rights – to be the residual claimant[1] to the firm's income. This may be sufficient to make the corporate governance structure unattractive, relative to a simpler family firm. Private economic activity will tend to be driven into family firms. It may be further argued that the emergence of state corporatism in China with SOEs and state-sponsored stock markets will actually impede the emergence of true PPCs (Bowen II and Rose, 1998: 442).

Traditionally the centralised government wielded by a generalist Confucian bureaucracy was always suspicious of specialist knowledge and of the accumulation of wealth as the basis for a potential threat to central authority. Officials were dominant. Merchants ranked below artisans. They paid dearly for the privilege of pursuing their chosen social roles both in the abstract sense of moral condemnation and also in cash as officials squeezed them for their 'tea money' or bribes. Frequent official interventions in mercantile activities and periodic squeezing of profits combined with a regular debasing of the currency and issue of paper money which was often non-convertible led to a widespread distrust of public officials and currencies by merchants (Whitley, 1992).

The introduction of the Western type of corporation in China during the first half of the twentieth century appears unsuccessful. State corporatism of the late twentieth and early twenty-first century may also have impeded the development of the PPC. Nearly thirty years of state ownership of enterprises and central planning have added to these earlier cultural and institutional inhibitions. The history of central planning in China and its industrial policies is a familiar story and will only be briefly rehearsed in the following section.

Characteristics of state-owned enterprises (SOEs) under the socialist system

Most limited or joint stock companies in China today are transformed from SOEs. Their current problems in structure and governance may be retraced to the problems that SOEs had under the pre-reform socialist system.

Industrial plans were formed by an iterative process. Drafted first by the ministries in accordance with the national plan, they were then adjusted by industrial departments at local level in the light of local conditions and SOE views. Plans were then returned to central government for the final approval after which, change was nigh impossible.

Under this system the state claimed absolute ownership of all assets as well as managerial rights in SOEs. The only job of the SOEs was to fulfill, and where possible, to exceed the plan. The government arranged all else. All the elements of business, normally carried about by company managers and independent agencies such as materials, finance and personnel were dealt with by different departments of government in charge of these subjects: oil, steel, coal, chemicals, finance, personnel and so on.

Various privileges associated with the size of the SOE, such as administrative rank and influence brought more personal gain to the directors than efficient production or profits. Responsibilities were mutual in law. The SOE directors, appointed by the department of personnel had to manage the SOE according to plan, but under the guidance of local communist party committees (CPCs). But the state owed duties to the SOE. Plans had to be provided in a timely fashion; staff should be adequate to meet the real need; similarly, materials, energy and tools; and finally, overall coordination of SOEs rested with the government. These complex arrangements meant it was difficult to pin down responsibility for failures. Later reforms tried to take care of this by transferring more powers to the directors and making them more autonomous. But greater powers to the directors made it easier for them to exploit their situation for personal benefit.

Reform of SOEs

Weak performance led to economic reforms in 1979. The problem was first identified as over-protective government supervision and lack of managerial autonomy. So SOEs were granted autonomous powers and were allowed to retain part of the profits for company use. They were also allowed to respond to markets after meeting plan requirements. They were allowed to reward outstanding workers with bonuses and even salary increases, and were given more control over recruitment. This strategy seemed to work for a time, but soon problems emerged. As profits were shared with the government (in effect taxed at high and variable levels) profitable enterprises soon learnt to bargain with government and to absorb surpluses, for example in rewards to workers, promoting relatives, better housing, entertainment for managers and business guests, travel expenses and in other ways that reduced the declared profits. To avoid this, an enterprise tax law was introduced in 1983. The tax was fixed in advance and independent of profits.

The possibilities of success with this measure were already undermined by the growth of the township and village enterprises that were being encouraged by reduced tax levels. The SOEs continued to perform badly, for various reasons, some beyond their control such as their workers' housing and social security obligations. With other enterprises operating with considerable freedom to hire and fire, to take advantage of markets to buy and sell advantageously, the SOEs were not operating on a level playing field. This allowed the SOEs to claim that they were being discriminated against and could not be held responsible for their failures – SOEs continued to perform badly.

Experiments with the contract responsibility system (CRS) used in agriculture were tried with SOEs and in 1988 the State Council promulgated a law to implement this system for all SOEs. The contract listed the rights and responsibilities of the SOE and the relevant government department. Failure to carry out these by either party could, in theory, give rise to compensation. Under the previous system, the SOEs had exerted their rights but often failed to meet their responsibilities. It was expected that the new CRS would force SOEs to be responsible for their own profits and losses. Again, it worked well at the beginning, but soon problems emerged and SOE performance continued to be poor. The CRS contract normally lasted from three to five years. This encouraged short termism as companies might sacrifice the maintenance of fixed plant to be able to submit the agreed annual sum to the government. But also meeting the profit target could lead to increased demands from the government in the next contract. The incentive to minimise declared profit continued and moneys were diverted to earning a good reputation with the workers and the officials of the relevant supervising department. Problems accrued during one contract could be passed on to incoming directors. Departments were reluctant to bankrupt SOEs and preferred to merge profitable ones with badly performing ones. Workers had few fears of dismissal or redundancy and had strong expectations that in any case they would be looked after. This lowered standards of discipline and effort.

Reasons for failure of the contract responsibility system (CRS)

For these reasons it was eventually clear that the CRS could not solve the problems of the SOEs. First, the CRS could not restrain SOEs' directors acting as rentiers, exploiting their position. At each reform stage, the government emphasised the granting of autonomous powers to SOEs, in return, for their directors being made responsible for the entire management of the SOEs. But when directors of SOEs are granted extensive managerial powers without an effective system to inspect, supervise and restrain them, the result can be potentially disastrous. Directors of SOEs are fallible human beings with weaknesses including the inability to resist material temptations. Under the reforms so far, directors might be responsible for many things but not for financial risk. In effect, they remained in charge of state property under a notional contract system but in an environment where personal relations and networks remained most important. In such an environment it became all too easy for directors to sacrifice the state's property for their own private interests.

The CRS cannot force SOEs to take responsibility for management risk. The responsibility for management risk relates to the enterprises' financial credibility. Since the property of SOEs is owned by the State, SOEs themselves have no assets to be held against their losses. This partly explains why so many SOEs are in deep-triangle debts.[2] If a SOE is bankrupt, it does not have the right to liquidate the State's property. The utmost that the enterprise can do is to take limited responsibility by using its retained profit to pay its debt. If the debts are beyond its income, it can only pass the responsibility to the government. In such circumstances it is very difficult, if not impossible, to make SOEs responsible for their profits and losses. The effectivity of corporate governance mechanisms ultimately rests on the credible threat of market failure and a strong regulatory capacity. But, dominant state ownership has tended to erode this threat and the regulatory capacity of the state. In this view, sustainable improvements in corporate governance are unlikely without fundamental changes in ownership patterns (Tenev *et al.*, 2002).

China's Company Law and company system

When the CRS failed, the public company system was raised at the central government level again. Its perceived advantage was that once established, shareholders of a limited liability company, have rights defined by their shares and corporate law including that of limited liability. The company becomes a distinct legal person, owning its own property and therefore responsible for its own profit and loss. If SOE is transformed into a limited liability company, the state becomes an ordinary shareholder like other shareholders. In theory, the state has no right to interfere in the company's management. At the same time, the state does not carry unlimited liability for the companies. The company system was expected to reduce the problems associated with government interference in SOEs' management, based on state ownership of SOE assets.

On the other hand, the company system could also prevent company managers from misusing the state's assets. In a Chinese company, the shareholders' meeting is a decision-making organ which makes most important decisions, the board of directors executes the decisions made by the shareholders' meeting, and at the same time, is responsible for the company's daily management. Because of this management structure, decision makers and decision executors are separated. Theoretically, the company system could solve the problem that SOE directors were both decision makers and executors of their own decisions. Also, the law requires each company to establish a supervisory board, with the right to check the management and financial situation in the company in order to avoid the exploitation of executive managerial power by the board of directors.

In practice, Chinese companies not only face problems in corporate governance similar to those of Western corporations but also inherited problems from their centrally planned past. In some, state assets representatives, as majority shareholders, collaborate with directors to misuse the state assets. The shareholders' meeting and the supervisory boards are not functioning properly. Many Chinese commentators call these two organisations 'rubber stamps'. In some companies, one person is appointed as both chairman of the board of the directors and managing director leading to an over concentration of power.

Shareholders' meeting in China's Company Law

In accordance with the Company Law, the shareholders' meeting decides most important matters: determining the policies, investment plans and selecting and removing directors and supervisors; approving reports of the boards and so on.[3] But, the Law has no detailed provisions for the protection of the interests of the minority shareholders. This seemed unimportant when drafted in 1993. At that time, few Chinese people had private property or could afford to buy shares. The state became the majority shareholder. The state assets representatives[4] became the managers of the state assets in the company.

The Law has several drawbacks in protection of minority shareholders. For example, the Company Law states, 'a shareholder's right to vote at the shareholders' meeting shall be in proportion to the capital he has contributed.'[5] The principle of 'one share, one vote' was implemented in China. But as the state is still the majority shareholder in most companies the state assets representatives play a decisive role. Even if individual shareholders discover improprieties among these representatives and the directors, they have too few votes to remove them. Besides, there is no stipulation of derivative action in China's Company Law. Even if minority shareholders wanted to sue the state assets representatives on behalf of the company, it is quite difficult to find a legislative basis to support a case.

In practice few shareholders are interested in dividends. Over 80 per cent never attend a company meeting. They buy shares in the hope of capital gains in a stock exchange where sharp fluctuations in share values are common.

State assets representatives play a decisive role in both shareholders' meeting and the board of directors. In accordance with the statistics, 54 per cent of shares in a listed company are controlled by either the state or another company transformed from a SOE (Wu, 2001). The consequence is that the persons selected as state share representatives to be directors or majority shareholders in a company are either from the state assets management bureau, from different government departments or from another investor company. They do not behave like investors, individual or institutional, who are interested in the company's management, profit-earning ability and dividend distribution. They are more aggressive in making decisions on investment, expansion of production or establishment of subsidiaries. The reason behind the aggressive attitude is first, the company's interests and their personal interests are not closely connected. They are salaried employees working as state shareholder representatives or directors, so if the firm's results prove their decision a sensible one, they may be promoted. If the results are poor, their personal interests are little affected. The worst that can befall them is to be removed from the position of state assets representatives. If they have a good relationship with their superiors, they may continue as state assets representatives and simply be transferred from one company to another.

When state assets representatives are the majority shareholders in a company, they have decisive power in selecting the board and managers. This situation may mean that directors' decisions may not safeguard all shareholders' interests. Instead, it is possible for the state assets representatives as majority shareholders to collaborate with their selected directors to sacrifice the shareholders' interests for their own. In addition, as some of the state assets representatives in companies are from government departments, it is probably unavoidable that the government will still interfere in the management of the companies.

The board of directors in the Company Law

A company's board of directors is usually the most important organisation both in Western systems of corporate law and governance and in China. Subject to a unanimous informal resolution, directors in Common Law systems can only exercise their powers collectively by passing resolutions at a properly convened meeting of the board. Directors normally have no power to act individually as agents for the company unless articles of association of a company empower the board to delegate its powers to individual directors.

China's Company Law lists not only the detailed rights of the board of directors[6] but also those of the chairman of the board. For example, the chairman of the board should preside over the shareholders' meeting and chair the meetings of the board; inspect the implementation of resolutions of the board and sign share certificates and debentures.[7] The chairman also has the right to call for an interim board meeting, sign important documents on behalf of the company and exercise power as its legal representative.

It is open to argument that both in Western countries as well as in China, that a company's board of directors has considerable power that can easily be abused, whereas the power of the shareholders' meeting has shrunk despite attempts to entrench shareholder democracy. Therefore, all Company Laws in many countries emphasise a director's responsibilities to the company. But, as in China, a director's duty of care and skill is not mentioned in Company Law, our discussion focuses on director's fiduciary duties in law and its results in practice.

Although different Company Laws have different stipulations on duties of the company directors, the requirements of directors' duties in common law countries have significant impact on many other countries' corporate laws including that of China. In China, directors are legally required to perform the following fiduciary duties: comply with the articles of association of the company; perform their duties faithfully and not use their position to seek personal gain. Directors are forbidden to take bribes, accept other unlawful monies or misappropriate the property of the company.[8] Directors are not allowed to misappropriate or lend company funds to a third party, deposit the company's funds into their own account or under the name of other persons.[9] Directors are not allowed to take corporate business opportunities for themselves or disclose company secrets.[10]

Problems with the board of directors

With respect to the stipulation of directors' duties, China's Company Law has drawbacks. The director's duty of care and skill is not mentioned nor is there an equivalent to the US business judgment rule. But, more problems arise in the implementation of the Company Law. In companies transformed from SOEs, except for a few promoters who remain in directors' position after the transformation is completed, most of the directors are from former SOEs. 'Insider control' is serious. Management of these limited liability companies differs little from management of SOEs. Close relationships between the government and former SOEs continue and so government interference persists.

Directors, especially state assets representatives, show little enthusiasm for their work, as they are managing the state's assets rather than their own. They can easily collaborate with managers to loot the state assets in the company. In 1999, a company used forged accounts to impress a government department in order to be upgraded into the named listed companies. After listing, it issued shares to the public, its workers and staff. The capital collected through issuing shares was used, not for expansion of the production but for their own purposes. To cover their crime, they gave part of the shares intended for their employees as a bribe to the relevant government officers. The bribe was worth RMB 10,940,000 (Cheng, 2000: 194).

A company's performance and directors' personal interests and reward are not closely related. So directors can easily harm the company's interests in the pursuit of their own. Also the old egalitarianism is easily forgotten in companies transformed from SOEs. Directors' remuneration is considered in the shareholders' meeting in accordance with the Company Law.[11] But it is difficult for the shareholders, especially those state assets representatives who themselves are salaried employees to decide the directors' remuneration in accordance with the market standard. Based on a recent report, salaries of chairpersons and managing directors in a limited liability company average around RMB 40,000–50,000 and with a range from RMB 1,600 to 158,375. In some companies the senior management salaries are many times that of the workers while in others they are so low that a chairman or director may find it difficult to resist temptation to exchange power for money. This partly explains why it is so easy for a director to collaborate with managers to damage the company for their own advantage.

Due to the influence of the centrally planned economic system, some ex-SOEs are still managed in the old style. A 'keyman' is appointed as both chairman of the board of directors and managing director. He normally dominates the management of corporate affairs and the decision-making process is not transparent. With the presence of a keyman, it is difficult, if not impossible, for other directors to play their role in corporate governance.

Independent directors

To solve the problem of the 'inside controller', independent directors have been introduced – a normal practice in Common Law countries. Their presence is expected to reduce the risk of 'inside control'. Additionally, the use of a supervisory board is another measure intended to provide a system of checks and balances. This double measure exemplifies China's 'try it and see' approach in relation to the development of its corporate law and governance. The grafting of the concept of independent directors from the Anglo-American system onto what is a civil law two-tier board system is a novel concept.

Even in Common Law Jurisdictions, the concept of the 'independent non-executive director' (INED) is relatively recent – in terms of corporate governance. From large boards dominated by the CEO or Managing Director, the last 20 years has seen a reduction in the size of the boards, particularly in the US, there has been a move towards a 'majority independent' board of directors (Hamilton, 2000: 349). These developments have not been without difficulties of the sort, which no doubt will be encountered in similar form in China. Typical problems over the years in both the US and the UK have included a lack of satisfaction with the process of selection and appointment of INEDs (PRONED, 1992) and doubts about their contribution to firm performance. The empirical evidence is largely equivocal (Bhagat and Black, 1999: 921).

In terms of outside directors playing an important role in the board's monitoring role over management performance, the US has the advantage of a large public corporate sector. This means that outside directors are often current or former executives of other corporations, are familiar with board and management operations and bring considerable experience to their roles. The factors that have influenced the development of these governance trends are themselves continuing to develop and evolve, in particular the role of institutional investors and their approach to the exercise of 'voice' or relational investing. Yet all of these changes in corporate governance have not affected the basic power of corporate management to operate and manage the business of the corporation. Day-to-day management of the corporation and its business remains clearly vested in the CEO, the executives who report to him and the managers who report directly or indirectly to those executives. As the underlying theory of the modern monitoring board indicates, boards of directors of publicly held corporations are typically part time oversight boards having between eight and twelve meetings of the full board anually. The sub-committees meet even less frequently with perhaps the exception of the audit committee.

But the nagging question remains whether all of these developments can be shown to have had a positive impact on firm performance. A review of the empirical evidence shows that there is no convincing evidence that increasing board independence improves firm performance (Bhagat and Black, 1999: 921). Other reviews conclude that empirical data do not support either of the following propositions:

- that regardless of its composition, the board is ineffective because it is co-opted by management, or
- that a board composed of a majority of outside directors, who are independent from management, can always be relied on as an effective monitor of management decisions (Lin, 1996: 898).

There are some research reports tending to show that a professional board, one that is active and independent of management, leads to significant increases in profit (defined as operating earnings in excess of the cost of capital). So that while the results do not prove causation, corporations with active and independent boards *appear* to have performed much better in the 1990s, than those with passive, non-independent boards (Millstein and MacAvoy, 1998: 1283).

Whilst there have been considerable differences in the approaches of Common Law countries to the requirement for and role of INEDs, there continues to be a surge of recommendations as to how their role might be enhanced and made more effective in the context of corporate governance. The Canadians have rejected the concept of the INED as such, opting for a subtler concept of 'unrelated director' more appropriate to their often family-controlled publicly listed corporations (Toronto Stock Exchange, 1990, 2001). In the UK, the recent Higgs Report (2003) supports an enhanced role for INEDs and the development of a 'lead non-executive director' to help focus the work of the non-executives and liase with the Chairman on their behalf.

These developments are guaranteed to ensure that the debate over INEDs continues, perhaps with increased controversy. Possibly the most instructive lessons about INEDs comes from their introduction to Common Law jurisdictions like Hong Kong where, behind the corporate façade, quite different cultural norms and practices are at play. In particular, the very different nature of director interlocks in Chinese controlled, publicly quoted companies led to difficulties with the introduction of the concept (Lawton, 1996: 365–8).

There are two general warnings, about the introduction of independent non-executive directors in any context: INEDs will become socialised to the demands/needs of executive management (Brudney, 1982: 633) and the law is peripheral in nature and unlikely to have any direct impact on the processes by which corporate ethics and moralities are constructed in large public corporations (Stone, 1975: 67).

Problems in introducing independent directors in China

To guide independent directors, China's Securities Regulatory Commission (CSRC) promulgated *Guiding Opinions on Establishing the Independent Directors System in Listed Companies* (GOEID) (CSRC) in 2001. It requires that by 30 June 2002, no less than one-third of the boards of directors of listed companies should have independent directors who 'take no position other than as a board director and have no relationship with the company or its major shareholders that may affect independent and objective decision-making'. The purpose of issuing this regulation is to improve corporate governance of listed companies', protect the interests of minority shareholders and increase transparency in the listed companies.

In accordance with GOEIDS, independent directors have some independent power. Apart from their normal duties as board members, they are authorised to submit proposals to assemble shareholders meetings, recruit or dismiss accounting firms, invite independent auditors and offer independent financial reports.[12] Independent directors are also free to give independent opinions on major transactions with affiliated institutions, on assignment and payment of the managerial staff and to object in cases where the interests of the smaller shareholders might be hurt.

However, the real situation in listed companies is quite different from what GOEIDS expects. According to the report of *China Securities Journal*, '25 independent directors of 22 listed firms resigned their posts so far this year. Of the resigned, over 60 per cent are popular academics, professors and social activists' (CSRC, 2001). A publicised reason for the resignation of these independent directors is that they are too busy with their own research or academic work, therefore unable to spare time and energy to the listed companies. A second reason is that many independent directors are scholars in universities. When they are invited to be independent directors, they have to temporarily terminate their current duties if their work schedule as independent directors conflicts with their full-time job, for example, if they are frequently invited to go abroad as visiting scholars in foreign universities. A third reason is that some independent directors have to quit because their present roles have clashed with their other social identities, which may differ from their role as independent directors.

There are, however, some unmentioned reasons. One former independent director, a professor of law, explained the difficult position that the independent directors are in. Being an independent director, he said involves responsibilities for checking all the accounts and the relevant materials of a company. But if problems are discovered it is difficult to directly criticise the directors who pay his salary. To save directors' faces by refraining from pointing out their mistakes, the independent director takes risks himself. Sooner or later, he may lose integrity and good name because of his compromised position. If the case is serious, he could be fined or even imprisoned. Faced with these possibilities, the only choice left for an independent director is to resign (Ai-Jun, 2002).

That these risks are real is clear from the case of Mr Li Jian-Hao, a 71-year-old professor in Zhengzhou University. In 1994, he presented a paper on joint stock companies in a conference and impressed Li Fu-qian, former chairman of the board of directors of Zheng Bai-wen Corporate Group (ZBW).[13] In 1995, ZBW invited Professor Li to be its independent director. He agreed on condition that he would not involve himself in the company's daily management, and he refused any salary from ZBW. In fact, he was independent director only in name. Over six years, he may have attended only ten of the Board meetings. When ZBW was exposed as having offended against the law and was punished, Professor Li was fined RMB 100,000. He appealed, claiming that although he was an independent director, he had never received any payment from ZBW. Besides, he was not involved in making forged documents and making illegal decisions. His appeal was rejected on the grounds that as an independent director, he was to fulfill his duties. This case made independent directors realise their responsibilities and think twice about the possible risks before accepting appointment or continuing in position.

The independent director system was developed in Common Law countries where the unitary single board is the norm. The difference between companies under the Common Law system and the civil law system is that companies in Common Law countries only have shareholders' meetings and a single board. The board plays a decisive role in management. In order to ensure that the company's assets are not mismanaged and shareholders' interests are properly protected, independent directors are employed. These are normally retired managers or company directors of good reputation and experience.

In China, however, the situation is different. Companies are required to have share-holders' meetings, and two boards; the board of directors and the supervisory board. The function of the supervisory board is to examine the company's financial affairs and supervise the directors. Where independent directors are employed, they and the supervisory board exercise the same function, which can cause confusion and risks each shirking responsibilities. It resembles two cats chasing one mouse.

Comments on GOEIDS

GOEIDS requires that in a listed company, independent directors comprise more than a third of the board. All listed companies had to revise their articles of association and invite suitable personnel to be independent directors before June 2002. This was not practical. There are few qualified independent directors in China. In Western countries like England and America, the company system has existed for over a hundred years. Many retired directors and managers with decades of management experience are available. But, in China, the company system only began in the late

1980s. Few retired directors and managers are available. Most listed companies nowadays invite law or economics professors to be independent directors. Though knowledgeable in their research fields they are seldom experienced in company management or skilful in detecting fraud.

Independent directors' independence

Article 5 of GOEIDS has granted independent directors not only the powers endowed by the Company Law but also others listed in GOEIDS such as proposing accountants as auditors. Independent directors' independence, however, can be affected by the term of office and the remuneration.

In accordance with GOEIDS, 'the tenure of an independent director shall be the same as that of any other director of the listed company, with the maximum term of no more than six years.' A director's normal term is three years according to the Company Law. If an independent director is allowed to work in the same company for six years, in the context of China's culture, his or her independence may be compromised. Chinese people prefer 'he qi sheng cai', which means that people work together preferring to praise each other and save each other's faces rather than criticise. A refusal by an independent director to save the face of an internal director or the chairman at a board meeting may invite retaliation. The director or chairman may make the same independent director 'chuan xiao xie' meaning he will be put in an awkward situation (literally 'forced to wear small shoes'). Given this background it is not unlikely that an independent director would exchange his independence for an easy life in the company. The level of remuneration may also play a part in compromising independence. Article 8 of GOEIDS requires appropriate compensation for independent directors. But this is not defined. A professor of law once complained that he was invited to be an independent director of a listed company. He was issued an employment letter with no mention of remuneration. He attended several board meetings, but no one from the company ever discussed his remuneration or salary, with him, which gave him the impression that he was working for the company free of charge (Luo, 2001: 24). Such an impression is unlikely to encourage enthusiastic performance of the director's tasks.

Supervisory board

The Supervisory Board is another important organ of a limited liability company and the Company Law grants it important rights such as power to examine the financial affairs of the company, to supervise the work of directors and managers. Considering the realistic situation in Chinese companies, such an organisation parallel to the board of directors is necessary to restrain the board of directors from misusing its power to sacrifice state assets for their own gain and to ensure that shareholders' rights are being properly protected. But, due to omissions in the Company Law, their performance has been rather lacklustre. The Company Law has not granted the supervisory board the right to select directors or to bring derivative lawsuits on behalf of the company. Without these two important rights, the supervisory board cannot fulfill its duties. From the perspective of the board of directors, supervision of the supervisory board is something they can accept if they want to, or refuse if they do not. China's Company Law has no instruction on what the supervisory board should do if the board of directors refuses their suggestions. As a result, it is no surprise that the supervisory board in a company is commonly called 'a decoration' or 'a rubber stamp'. Also, members of the supervisory board often lack appropriate qualifications and experience in accounting and management, which makes for more difficulties in terms of completing their mission. An investigation of 33 joint stock companies transformed from SOEs found that most of the directors and managers in these companies were directors of the former SOEs and representatives of majority share-holders. Members of the supervisory board were formerly members of the trade union or the members of the CPC[14] in the former SOEs (Hu, 1999: 30). They are likely to be in difficulty if, in their role as supervisory board members, they have to criticise the directors who used to be their bosses.

Furthermore, members of the supervisory board are not properly rewarded. As their work is not closely connected with a company's profit, normally, the members of the supervisory board receive a minimal salary. They are unlikely to dedicate themselves or risk their careers to fight directors in the company's interest for so little a reward. The salaries that chairmen of the supervisory board receive range from RMB 1,600–160,000 (Lin and Dong, 2000: 228).

The supervisory board is subject to the board of directors' power to provide or reject financial support to the supervisory board. Even if the supervisory board considers it necessary to invite an outside audit firm to check the company's accounts, without the board of director's financial support, the supervisory board has no ability to make such a decision.

Suggestions to improve the roles of independent directors and supervisory boards

Clearly it is important to clarify the responsibilities of the supervisory board and the independent non-executive directors. For example, in companies transformed from SOEs, the state is, and is likely to remain, the majority shareholder for quite a long time. In 2003, plans to sell off large parts of the states' holdings in listed companies that were formerly SOEs were put on hold. In these companies, although the super-visory board has the right to examine the financial affairs, according to the Company, they have no voting power. If the supervisory board objects to the decisions made by the board of directors regarding selection of managers or a manager's remunera-tion, the maximum that the supervisory board can do is to make a belated criticism. It is up to the board of directors to accept or ignore the criticism. In this respect, the independent directors' role is quite different. They can attend the board meetings and have voting powers in making important decisions. If they consider that the suggestions made by internal directors are not proper, they can dispute them before decisions are made. On the other hand, independent directors cannot work full time in a company. It is therefore quite difficult for them to acquire the information needed to control the company's management. In this respect, the supervisory board can help, as it's members are full time. If the independent directors and the supervisory boards can share views and, where useful, join forces they could be a more useful check on the behaviour directors.

Protection of minority shareholders

On 11 November 2001, 'Guideline on the Governance of Listed Companies' (Drafted for Soliciting Opinions) (hereafter GGLC) was published. This guideline put more emphasis on protection of shareholders, especially minority shareholders. Article 3 of GGLC emphasises that 'Shareholders shall enjoy equal rights and bear corresponding obligations in accordance with the types of shares they hold' (preference shares, ordinary shares, etc.). China's Company Law contains some provisions on shareholders' rights such as requiring that an affirmative vote of the shareholders representing at least two-thirds of the shareholders is required for important decisions. But, the Company Law has no detailed stipulation in encouraging minority shareholders' participation in corporate governance. The GGLC improves on this by requiring a listed company to formulate rules of procedure for a shareholders' meeting with complete contents including the convening, constitution and conduct of meetings and related matters.[15] The GGLC also requires a listed company to use modern information technology to encourage more shareholders to attend the shareholders' meeting, on the premise of guaranteeing the legality, effectivity and safety of shareholders' meetings.

As mentioned earlier, minority shareholders are normally not interested in a company's corporate governance, due to a lack of awareness of their role in corporate affairs. In order to ensure that the shareholders' meeting is not manipulated by a few majority shareholders, the GGLC encourages institutional investors to 'exercise functions in such aspects as selection and appointment of directors, encouragement and supervision of operators, decision-making on important matters, etc'.[16] There are some examples of this happening. One such is the Tangshan Shanyou Alkalinity Industry Limited Liability Company (hereafter TSAILLC) where encouraging institutional investors' involvement in corporate governance proved successful and benefited the company. Four companies joined together to establish a corporate group called TSAILLC. Although the four major shareholders of TSAILLC are all institutional investors with the state holding a majority of shares in their companies, in order to defend their own interests they have to keep a keen eye on each other. Due to the active role of the shareholders' meeting in TSAILLC, the company has developed rapidly and the 'inside controller' problem has been largely eliminated (Su, 1997).

Regulating proprietary shareholders in a listed company

In China, majority shareholders who are also called proprietary shareholders in the GGLC, play an important role in limited liability companies. Proprietary shareholders are defined as 'any company group, authorized investment institution and actual controlling party'.[17] Since the Company Law has not particularly mentioned majority shareholders' responsibilities to a company, the GGLC improves this by requiring the proprietary shareholders to bear the obligation of good faith to the company and other shareholders, and not to seek extra benefits by their special status.[18] The Company Law states that the shareholders' meeting has the right to 'elect and remove members of the board of directors and supervisors'.[19] In practice, the proprietary shareholders have controlling power. In many companies, they can easily decide to appoint someone they prefer without considering minority shareholders' interests. The GGLC emphasises that the proprietary shareholders 'shall not perform the approval procedures for decisions on election of shareholders' meetings and decisions on appointments of board meetings, and shall not appoint and remove high-position managerial personnel of a listed company without the consent of shareholders' meetings and the board of directors.'[20] Furthermore, the GGLC also emphasises that the proprietary shareholders shall neither intervene directly in the decision-making and production and operation activities developed according to law of a listed company, nor damage interests of the listed company and other shareholders.

The Company Law has not clarified whether one person can serve concurrently as a managing director and a general manager. In practice, it is common in China that one person is appointed as both managing director and general manager. In light of the problem of majority shareholders' domination in a company, the GGLC emphasises that 'personnel and management of a listed company shall be independent of its proprietary shareholders'.

Encouraging minority shareholders to sue majority shareholders if their interests are affected

The Company Law makes provision for minority shareholders to sue majority shareholders if a resolution of the shareholders' meeting or of the board of directors violates the law or infringes the lawful rights and interests of the shareholders. The minority shareholders can apply for an injunction in a people's court to terminate the violation or infringement. But it is unclear whether the shareholders can get compensation if they file lawsuits against the majority shareholders or the board of directors. If they cannot get compensation, shareholders are unlikely to be keen to sue majority shareholders and defend the interests of the company. The GGLC improve this by emphasising that if 'decisions of shareholders' meetings or the board of directors of a listed company 'violate laws...and cause damage to the company accordingly, shareholders shall have the right to claim for compensation'. Shareholders are encouraged to obtain the compensation by means of instituting civil proceedings 'in accordance with the relevant provisions of laws and regulations.'[21] However, the GGLC has not mentioned the introduction of a derivative action or equivalents to other jurisdictions' statutory remedies available to minority shareholders to protect the company's as well as their own interests.

The La Porta et al.'s proposition that strong protection of minority shareholders' rights is essential for the development of deep and liquid capital markets is an important issue for China and SOE's in particular (Porta et al., 1997: 1131, 1998: 1113, 1999: 471). This issue has also arisen in more developed jurisdictions where PPCs are common such as Malaysia and Hong Kong. Despite various attempts to increase the proportion of shares offered to the public on initial listing in the latter jurisdictions concentration of shareholding remains the norm and the use of minority shareholder actions relatively minimal. The essence of the La Porta *et al.*'s thesis is that in the absence of strong minority shareholder and investor protection, shareholders can only protect themselves through the accumulation of power associated with block-holdings to the detriment of an equity culture. In China the respective roles of the state and the private sector are central to the reform process. The development of minority shareholders' rights in China, particularly in relation to former SOEs would represent a dilution of the role of the state in controlling productive enterprise. If the La Porta *et al.*'s thesis is correct and a successful privatisation programme by means of public securities markets requires strong minority rights then there are serious implications for the Chinese state's role as controlling shareholder in listed companies. But is there much substance to the La Porta *et al.*'s thesis? Let us pose the question by looking at some key differences between the US and the UK in this respect.

The US and UK compared: shareholder actions, derivative and class actions

In terms of enforcing directors' and officers' duties there are two categories of suits in the American system. These are derivative actions brought by the shareholders on the corporation's behalf and direct actions, brought by shareholders in their own right, either individually or as a class. It is important to bear in mind that the procedural requirements differ, and more hurdles are placed before plaintiffs in derivative suits. These differences in procedure have important financial ramifications that bear on the incentives for parties to settle even frivolous claims. In particular, in most states, payments in settlement or judgment of a derivative suit cannot be reimbursed and indemnification is instead limited legal expenses. Liability insurance for executives may cover losses that cannot be indemnified. There are limits imposed by the courts on the ability of insurers to avoid payment.

The combination of differential indemnification rights, insurance policy exclusions and plaintiffs' counsel as the real party in interest creates powerful incentives for settlement. Studies indicate that lawsuits are nevertheless a relatively infrequent occurrence for the public corporation. Whereas most suits settle, they provide minimal compensation and the principal beneficiaries of the litigation appear to be the attorneys. There is also little evidence of deterrence effect and the evidence of indirect benefits from litigation serving as backup monitoring of management is mixed. Evidence that lawsuits function as an alternative governance mechanism for the board is weak though they do tend to be useful for owners of blocks of shares. Inside ownership seems to serve as a successful alternative monitor for negligence but not for conflicts of interests. There are, however, benefits from a judicial decision clarifying the scope of permissible conduct. In particular, the benefit is not simply deterrence but also in the light of the contractual nature of the corporation, identification of a rule around which the parties may transact. But many lawsuits are needed to produce a particular rule (Romano, 1991: 55).

There have been calls for the legal process to be changed in order to put realistic limits on lawyers' fees in shareholder actions, particularly derivative actions (Loewenstein, 1999: 24). In this respect, it is also important to remember the role of contingency fees in the US. Without them many actions, especially the more frivolous in nature would never even be started. The UK does not have an equivalent situation in relation to shareholder actions. Also, unlike the UK, the US normally makes each side bear its own legal expenses, with the result that plaintiffs are spared the prospect of fee shifting against them of the typically greater legal expenses incurred by corporate defendants. According to some commentators, these three elements – the class action, the contingent fee and the American rule on fee shifting – have created in the US (but basically nowhere else to any equivalent degree) an entrepreneurial system of private law enforcement. Again at the level of public enforcement the Securities Exchange Commission (SEC) is generally regarded as the premier public enforcer in the area of corporate and securities law. Given lower private and public enforcement thresholds in other jurisdictions these commentators take the view that one must look beyond law to social norms to explain the very different performance of firms in Scandinavia, German, French and Common Law countries (Coffee Jr, 1987: 877, 2001: 111).

In the UK, the economic equation in relation to shareholder actions is very different to that of the US (Miller, 1998). There are comparatively very few derivative actions. The claimants must take the risk of incurring their own legal expenses. If they lose they also have to pay the 'taxed' costs of the defendant and the company (which as part of the derivative action process must be joined as co-defendant); and, if they win, any order is for the benefit of the company, which remains under the control of the wrongdoer! Gaining an indemnity from the company to cover costs is difficult. Most minority shareholder actions are brought under statutory remedies designed for the smaller private company, such as unfair prejudicial conduct and just and equitable winding up.[22] In the US, a large part of the second volume of the American Law Institutes 'Principles of Corporate Governance' is devoted to the governance aspects of derivative actions. In the UK one major derivative action brought by an institutional investor resulted in the law being restated by the Court of Appeal in a manner not in the best interests of minorities.[23] In another attempt by institutional investors under the unfair-prejudice remedy nothing was achieved.[24] The UK law gives little protection for minority shareholder interests in public listed companies in terms of its being translated into action. This leads some commentators to suggest that in the US, management is disciplined by minority actions whilst in the UK, the market for corporate control is a much more effective means of disciplining poorly performing managements (Miller, 1998).

As argued earlier, in China, minority-shareholder protection is relatively minimal and in its infancy, nor has a market for corporate control developed to any great extent, the large numbers of mergers having been part of the SOE reform process (Shu, 1998; Hu, 2000; Walter and Howie, 2000), although in early 2004 the Chinese media announced mergers between Shanghai's large retailers based on a share for share exchange.

Corporate scandals in developed and emerging markets indicate that there is no perfect model in corporate governance. But good corporate governance is critical to the development of a modern and competitive corporate sector in China. Corporate governance reforms must form an integral part of the broader process of the country's reform at both institutional and economic levels. This includes reform of other sectors such as the banking, finance and social security systems as well as the development of high professional standards in areas such as law, accounting, government and the media. Simply adopting structures from other models such as the German and the Anglo-American ones have not worked as was intended. Competitive markets for corporate control and managerial manpower are lacking. There are also important issues of information asymmetry and misalignment of incentives. But according to some commentators the failure to date is attributable to trying to impose an idealised corporate governance model that is not appropriate to China's present conditions (Kit, 1999). In April 2004, the National People's Congress (NPC) was scheduled to review a new securities law intended to revise rules on corporate governance, public offerings, share issuance by SOEs and the relationship between banks and securities markets. The new law had been delayed by conflicts between the Ministry of Commerce responsible for the Company Law and the CSRC. The committee responsible for the development of the new laws included representatives from the National Development and Reform Commission, the People's Bank of China and the China Banking Regulatory Commission. This will hopefully give the proposed reforms a comprehensive integrity and reasonable level of coherency. Subject to the outcome of the current debate and departmental quibbling, the new rules will allow for more flexibility, particularly in terms of the classes of shares that a company can issue to reflect the varying rights and obligations of different shareholders (Collier, 2004).

Wheareas there are many views on the nature of the Chinese economy as it moves away from central planning, for the foreseeable future that economy is likely to remain mixed, the state-owned sector has begun a 'corporate revolution'. This has resulted in a hierarchy of principal–agent relationships in which the agents enjoy a great deal of discretionary authority. A layering of information asymmetries has made it difficult for the state owner to effectively monitor and regulate the managers. Control has shifted from state bureaucrats to enterprise managers. To the extent that the reform of the SOE sector has produced a form of corporatisation without privatisation, there are parallels with shifts that occurred in the US and other western economies in the late nineteenth and early twentieth centuries. A 'managerial revolution' in a Chinese context could well follow. Whilst the state still owns a substantial part of China's economy, its hold on individual SOEs has been weakened. It cannot exercise direct leverage and cannot effectively monitor, almost assuming a passive role. Unlike the individual investor in such circumstances, the state rarely enjoys a dividend in the good times and cannot sell in the bad times. Until the state is willing to implement a path towards some degree of privatisation it is stuck with the worst of both worlds (Wedeman, 2004).

Impact of SOE reform on the private sector and the privately owned publicly traded corporation

The reform of the state sector shows that the self-interest of officials has often blighted the process of reform and taken resources and financing away from the private sector. 'Red Capitalists' often asset-stripped their SOE's taking advantage of their connections to grow their now privatised business (O'Niel, 2003, 2004). At the same time the private sector has encountered difficulties in obtaining finance and faced considerable problems in dealing with the bureaucracy of officialdom in ways that are not dissimilar to those considered in the historical introduction to this chapter. SOEs could not lead China's export drive. Once Zhao Ziyang,[25] realised this, and opened the door to rural China, network capital from Hong Kong and Taiwan flooded the coastal countryside in search of cheap labour and colluded with local officialdom to evade regulations governing joint ventures and foreign trade. Other complex forces were also at work in the drive to develop and almost inevitably internationalise China. The existence of, often opaque regulation, whose main effect was to create rents fostering a bureaucratic culture based on regulatory constraints was problematic. This was because personal relations (GUANXI), bribery or bureaucratic fiat usually determined access to the global economy and foreign access to the domestic economy (cf. Zweig, 2002). Much the same applied to internal matters affecting access to finance and capital markets where preference was often given to corporatised SOEs. Private business encountered enormous difficulty in terms of raising capital for expansion either by way of bank loans or access to the securities market by way of listing.

Just as the mandarins had been the guardians of and simultaneously determiners of, what was virtuous in a society based on Confucian norms, the modern state bureaucrat had been imbued with an ideology which was, at least in public expression, often hostile to concepts of private property and private business.[26] Traditional Confucian ideas suggesting that entrepreneurs should act in the interest of state and society under a measure of control, which often led to exploitation, were harnessed to ensure integration in a corporatist way into existing structures. Entrepreneurs were to conform to paternalistic socialist concepts showing themselves to be patriotic in the sense of identifying themselves with the political system and its values. They were also to play a useful role in China's adaptation to the global economy. But this approach left little room for the innovative nature of the entrepreneur and his family-orientated business. All of this required their enterprises to be very closely linked with local authorities and the good social connections that these links engendered were often felt to be essential to running their businesses. This in turn has led to high costs in the form of corruption and 'donations'. Entrepreneurs see the need for better legal protection and political participation as very important. In this sense, they are an engine for social change in addition to being a major contributor to economic change and development. As a result the debate in China concerning the role of entrepreneurs is becoming increasingly positive. However, private businessmen, entrepreneurs and others who might form a middle class are not yet safely embedded in the social establishment of power, prestige and income (Heberer, 2002).

Recently, the opening of membership of the communist party to entrepreneurial businessmen and women and recent amendments to the constitution recognising private property (cf. Ching, 2004) have cleared the way to a more even playing field. But it is probably the internationalisation of China that will have the greatest impact in the coming years. Many Chinese enterprises can now seek a listing on Asian capital markets such as Hong Kong and Malaysia where the privately held, publicly quoted corporation is the norm rather than the exception (Lawton, 2001). Others have also sought listings as far away as London and New York. The latest attempts to reform the SOE sector and to continue to attract FDIs will in turn help to spur reforms to the banking system where, post-WTO accession, overseas banks such as HSBC are taking stakes in mainland banks and helping with reform. Once these banks are able to offer loans at interest rates based on objective risk appraisals backed by security over corporate assets, finance for the private sector may ease.

Similar reforms for the securities markets in China could also help the development of PPCs. The guiding ideology behind the development and regulation of the stock markets has been 'to help state enterprises solve their problems'. It has been suggested that this should become 'help the state enterprises realise management by the people' (Zhang, 2003: 231) but as yet no one has openly voiced the idea that stock markets 'help the people share in private business'. Until there is a sea change in this regard, the stock markets will remain closed to the private enterprise.

The impetus to maintain FDI by selling off shareholdings in chosen sectors' corporatised SOEs could also add renewed vigour to the rule of law in the corporate sector. But whether this will be enough to convince mainland Chinese private family controlled business to corporatise and push for the right to a stock market listing, only time will tell. Much more is needed in terms of the development of legal protection, less interference in the running of their businesses by official fiat and a recognition of their often innovative role in the development of China's economy. The next decade will prove interesting in this regard. Regulators may recognise that more can be earned (in terms of tax revenues) by facilitating and abetting exchanges rather than impeding and blocking them. Entrepreneurs and more far-sighted leaders may persuade those with vested interests in the ambiguously and semi-regulated trade to give up their controls and provide an acceptable level of legal protection for those involved in private business enterprise from the rapacious demands of local officials. Otherwise, a form of gangster and crony capitalism will prevail in which the privately held business will veer more towards secrecy and keeping a low profile, and not towards the openness of a market listing.

Notes

1 Residual claimancy and residual control are important aspects of bona fide property ownership. The latter is the prerogative to do what one pleases with an asset except for that which is specifically forbidden by law or contract. Residual claimancy is the right to any income generated by an asset which has not been specifically assigned by law or contract. For a consideration of the relationship between the nature of the firm and ownership, residual control and residual claimancy, see Alchian, A. and Demetz, H. (1972) 'Production, Information Costs, and Economic Organization', *American Economic Review* 62: 777.

2 Triangle debts refer to the debts among several SOEs. Enterprise A supplied some products to Enterprise B but B failed to pay A, due to its internal problems. In order to survive in the market, Enterprise B had to purchase some raw materials from Enterprise C without paying money to C, because A had not paid the money back to B. Enterprise C had to do the same thing to Enterprise D. Therefore, increasing numbers of SOEs were involved in these chain debts.

3 Article 38, China's Company Law.

4 Since most of the assets in the limited or joint stock companies transformed from SOEs are state-owned, state assets management bureaux are established in all provinces and cities in China. The bureaux have the right to select and send state assets representatives to

companies where the state holds shares in order to be responsible for the maintenance and increase of the state assets.

5 Article 41, China's Company Law.
6 Article 46, China's Company Law.
7 Article 114, China's Company Law.
8 Article 59, China's Company Law.
9 Article 60, China's Company Law.
10 Articles 61 and 62, China's Company Law.
11 Article 38, China's Company Law.
12 Article 5, China's Company Law
13 Zheng Bai-wen is a corporate group, which is also a listed company. ZBW forged its accounts to get the government's approval to be a listed company. Later ZBW also published false information to mislead shareholders. ZBW claimed that from 1986 to 1996, its sale value increased 45 times. In 1996, its sales value reached RMB 4100 million. Because of its achievement, it was listed as one of the top 100 listed companies in China. In 1999, ZBW lost a profit of RMB 980 million, which made ZBW, the company with the highest deficits in Shanghai. One of its accountants later said that ZBW was not qualified to be a listed company at all. In order to become a list company, the only way was to forge its accounts to impress the government and the public. ZBW later was sanctioned by China's Securities Regulatory Commission. For details, see 'Securities Wants to Protect ZBW and Reorganize ZBW' on 23 May 2002. http://www.gog.com.cn/xb/x0204/ca161974.htm and 'From Case of Lu Jia-hao to See Independent Director System', 20 November 2002, http://www.peopledaily.com.cn/GB/news/8410/20021120/870745.html
14 The CPC refers to the grass-root organisation of the Communist Party of China in a company.
15 Article 5, 'Guideline on the Governance of Listed Companies' promulgated on 9 November 2001.
16 Article 12, 'Guideline on the Governance of Listed Companies' promulgated on 9 November 2001.
17 Article 13, 'Guideline on the Governance of Listed Companies' promulgated on 9 November 2001.
18 Article 13, 'Guideline on the Governance of Listed Companies' promulgated on 9 November 2001.
19 Article 38, China's Company Law.
20 Article 15, 'Guideline on the Governance of Listed Companies' promulgated on 9 November 2001.
21 Article 24, 'Guideline on the Governance of Listed Companies' promulgated on 9 November 2001.
22 See Companies Act 1985, ss 459–61 (unfairly prejudicial conduct) and Insolvency Act 1986, s 122(g) (Just and Equitable Winding Up).
23 *Prudential Assurance Co.* v *Newman Industries* [1981] Ch 257, CA.
24 Re Astec (BSR) plc [1998] 2 BCLC 556.
25 Zhao Ziyang was Premier of the PRC from 1980 to 1987 and General Secretary of the CPC from 1987 to 1989. Zhao was one of the first high-ranking Chinese leaders to call for economic reform but was stripped of all of his positions and placed under house arrest because of his support for students' demands for political reform in the Tiananmen Square incident in 1989.
26 For an example of the problems this can cause, see A Chiu, 'Millionaires misfortune after rich-list appearance' SCMP, 22 October, 2003. For an example of the winds of change, see the case of Peng James discussed by R. Tomasic (1995), 'Company Law and the Limits of the Rule of Law in China', *Australian Journal of Corporate Law*, 4: 370–487. Australian businessman James Peng was abducted from his Macau hotel room by Shenzen authorities in 1993 to be jailed on fraud and corruption charges two years later. He obtained a Hong Kong High Court order in 2004 for the return of shares in Shenzen Champaign Industrial Corp. which were found to have been illicitly transferred into the name of Deng Xiaoping's

niece, Ding Ping. James Peng sought her aid in dealing with his difficulties with the Shenzen bureaucracy. The court stated that the opportunity to acquire potentially massive profitable shareholdings in any new company played a highly significant part in what Ding Ping and the officials did. Mr Peng's ability to enforce his judgment in Shenzen remains to be seen as it is fraught with practical difficulties but it will be an interesting test for the rule of law in the context of corporate affairs in China, cf. Jane Moir 'Peng Takes his Fight to Shenzen' SCMP Monday, 2 February, 2004.

References

Ai-Jun (2002) 'Why many independent directors want to resign?', Available at http://www. peopledaily.com.cn/GB/news/8410/20020930/835056.html (accessed 30 September 2002).

Alchian, A. and Demetz, H. (1972) 'Production, information costs, and economic organization', *American Economic Review*, 62: 777.

Bhagat, S. and Black, B. (1999) 'The uncertain relationship between board composition and firm performance', *Business Law*, 54: 921.

Bowen II, J. R. and Rose, D. C. (1998) 'On the absence of privately owned, publicly traded corporations in China: the Kirby puzzle', *Journal of Asian Studies*, 57: 442.

Brudney, V. (1982) 'The independent director – Heavenly City or Potemkin village', *Harvard Law Review*, 95(597): 633.

Cheng, Xiang-long (2000) 'Discussion of corporate governance of a joint stock company – amendment of China's Company Law', in Guo-Feng and Wang Jian (eds), *Discussion of Amendments of the Company Law*, Beijing: Legal Publishing House, p. 194.

Ching, F. (2004) 'Fine tuning the constitution', *SCMP*, 17 March 2004.

Coffee, C. Jr (1987) 'The regulation of entrepreneurial litigation: balancing fairness and efficiency in the large class actions', *University of Chicago Law Review*, 54: 877.

Coffee, C. Jr (2001) 'The rise of dispersed ownership: the roles of law and the state in the separation of ownership and control', *Yale Law Journal*, 1: 111.

Colli, A. and Rose, M. B. (1999) 'Families and firms: the culture and evolution of family firms in Britain and Italy in the nineteenth and twentieth centuries', *Scandinavian Economic History Review*, 47: 24.

Collier, A. K. (2004) 'Revised securities law is scheduled to come under NPC Scrutiny', *SCMP*, 17 January 2004.

CSRC (2001) 'Guiding opinions on establishing the independent director system in listed companies', promulgated by China Securities Regulatory Commission in May 2001. Available at http://english.peopledaily.com.cn/200208/27/eng20020827_102181.shtml

Hamilton, R. W. (2000) 'Corporate governance in America 1950–2000: major changes but uncertain benefits', *Journal of Corporation Law*, 25: 349.

Heberer, T. (2002) 'The role of private entrepreneurship for social and political change in the People's Republic of China and Vietnam', in T. Menkhoff and S. Gerke (eds), *Chinese Entrepreneurship and Asian Business Networks*, London: RoutledgeCurzon.

Higgs, D. (2003) *Review of the Role and Effectiveness of Non-Executive Directors*, London: DTI.

Hu, Wen-Tao (1999) 'Reinforce functions of the supervisory board of joint stock companies in China', *Economy Research*, 6: 30.

Hu, Xiaobo (2000) 'The state enterprises and society in Post-Deng China', *Asian Survey*, XL: 641.

Jamieson, G. (1921) *Chinese Family and Commercial Law*, Shanghai: Kelly & Walsh.

Kirby, W. C. (1995) 'China unincorporated: Company Law and business enterprise in 20th century China', *Journal of Asian Studies*, 54: 43.

Kit, On Tam (1999) *The Development of Corporate Governance in China*, Cheltenham: Edward Elgar.

Lawton, P. (1996) 'Berle and means, corporate governance and the Chinese family firm', *Australian Journal of Corporate Law*, 6(348): 365–8.

Lawton, P. and Tyler, E. L. G. (eds) (2001), *Division of Duties and Responsibilities between Directors and the Company Secretary in Hong Kong*, Hong Kong: HKICS, p. 122.

Lin, L. (1996) 'The effectiveness of outside directors as a corporate governance mechanism; theories and evidence', *Northwestern University Law Review*, 90: 898.

Lin Lin and Dong Hong (2000) 'Management structure and achievements of listed companies with characteristics of high technology', in Guo-Feng and Wang Jian (eds), *Debates in Amendments of China's Company Law*, Beijing: Law Press, p. 228.

Loewenstein, M. J. (1999) 'Shareholder derivative litigation and corporate governance', *Delaware Journal of Corporate Law*, 1: 24.

Luo, Pei-xin (2001) 'Critical comments on independent directors', in JinRong Fayuan (ed.), *Economic Law Research Field*, 12: 24.

MacNeil, I. (2002) 'Adaptation and convergence in corporate governance: the case of Chinese listed companies', *Journal of Corporate Law Studies*, 2: 289.

Miller, G. (1998) 'Political structure and corporate governance: some points of contrast between the United States and England', *Columbia Business Law Review*, 51.

Millstein, I. M. and MacAvoy, P. W. (1998) 'The active board of directors and performance of the large publicly traded corporation', *Columbia Law Review*, 98: 1283.

O'Niel, M. (2003) 'Mainland tries to reign in blatant asset stripping', *SCMP*, 29 December 2003.

O'Niel, M. (2004) 'The king of Xingjiang: business genius or carpetbagger', *SCMP*, 17 January 2004.

Porta, R. L., Lopez-de-Silanes, F., Shleifer, A. and Vishny, R. (1997) 'Legal determinants of external finance', *Journal of Finance*, 52(3): 1131.

Porta, R. L., Lopez-de-Silanes, F., Shleifer, A. and Vishny, R. (1998) 'Law and finance', *Journal of Political Economy*, 106(6): 1113.

Porta, R. L., Lopez-de-Silanes, F., Shleifer, A. and Vishny, R. (1999) 'Corporate ownership around the world', *Journal of Finance*, 54(2): 471.

PRONED (1992) *Research into the Role of the Non-Executive Director*.

Romano, R. (1991) 'The shareholder suit: litigation without foundation', *Journal of Law, Economics and Organisation*, 7: 55.

Ruskola, T. (2000) 'Conceptualizing corporations and kinship: comparative law and development theory in a Chinese perspective', *Stanford Law Review*, 52: 1599.

Shu, Y. Ma (1998) 'The Chinese route to privatisation: the evolution of the shareholding system option', *Asian Survey*, XXXVIII: 379.

Stone, C. (1975) *Where The Law Ends: The Social Control of Corporate Behaviour*, New York: Harper and Row, p. 67.

Su, Xiao-mei (1997) 'TSAILLC is prosperous due to multi-shareholders – visiting TSAILLC', *Economic Work Report*, No. 24.

Tenev, S., Zhang Chunlin and Brefort, L. (2002) *Corporate Governance and Enterprise Reform in China: Building the Institutions of Modern Markets*, Washington, DC: The World Bank.

Toronto Stock Exchange (1990) *The Day Report 'Where were the Directors?'*

Toronto Stock Exchange (2001) *Corporate Governance in Canada: Ten Years to the Day*.

Walter, C. E. and Howie, F. J. T. (2000) *Privatising China: The Stock Markets and Role in Corporate Reform*, Singapore: John Wiley & Sons (Asia), p. 16.

Wedeman, A. (2004) 'Corporate capitalism and socialist China', in E. T. Gomez and H. H. M. Hsiao (eds), *Chinese Enterprise, Transnationalism, and Identity*, London: Routledge.

Whitley, R. (1992) *Business Systems in East Asia: Firms, Markets and Societies*, London: Sage.

Wilson, J. F. (1995) *British Business History, 1720–1994*, Manchester: Manchester University Press, pp. 153–6, 176–8, 182–94, 201–3.

Wu, Jing-lian (2001) 'Behaviour of majority shareholders and a company's corporate governance'. Available at http://www.cnstock.com

Zhang, Weijing (2003) Beijing University reproduced in C. E. Walter and F. J. T. Howie (eds), *Privatising China: The Stock Markets and Their Role in Corporate Reform*, Singapore: John Wiley and Son (Asia), p. 231.

Zweig, D. (2002) *Internationalizing China: Domestic Interests and Global Linkages*, New York: Cornell University Press.

4 Identifying ultimate controlling shareholders in Chinese public corporations

An empirical survey

Guy S. Liu and Pei Sun

Having classified controlling shareholdings on the basis of the principle of the ultimate ownership, we find that, by 2001, 84 per cent of Chinese quoted companies were ultimately controlled by the state, compared with 16 per cent of private-owned ones. The Chinese official shareholding classification, by contrast, is ambiguous for identifying ultimate owners, and this has misled many previous studies on the performance impacts of shareholding classes for Chinese corporations.

Introduction

In the latest empirical survey of the ownership structure of large corporations in 27 wealthy countries, La Porta *et al.* (1999) find that the presence of ultimate controlling shareholders is a rule rather than an exception in most of the world.[1] Moreover, they also provide a detailed account of the various means the controlling shareholders can use to maintain and extend their de facto control in downstream firms. The most common, the pyramid shareholding scheme is frequently applied by the controlling shareholders to create a set of control chains, within which a publicly listed company (PLC) may be controlled by another one, whose controlling shares in turn lie, directly or through several such similar chains, in the hands of the ultimately dominant shareholder group. So, the immediate ownership data from public corporations is not, in principle, adequate to present an accurate picture of the exact control pattern in these firms. The tracing of the ultimate shareholding structure is crucial to our understanding of ownership and control in modern corporations.

Among numerous types of controlling shareholders, extensive state control has been found in a number of countries such as Austria and Singapore in La Porta *et al.*'s sample. Unfortunately, China was not included in their dataset, but the issues of ownership and control in China are extremely important. How does the government in China, the most populous country and rapidly developing country in the world, manage to maintain control over most of the PLCs during its economic transition? What are the characteristics of the means by which the Chinese government seeks to retain its ultimate control? Answers to these questions are worth exploring not only for the understanding of the corporate ownership and control in general, but also for that of corporate governance mechanisms in emerging markets and transition economies in particular.

Following the principle that control lies with the ultimate owners, we first cast doubt on the methodological validity of previous literature on the relationship between ownership structure and corporate performance, based on the Chinese official shareholding classification. Then in this chapter, we, for the first time, reconstruct a reformed ownership controlling structure on the basis of the ultimate ownership principle for Chinese corporations. This will enrich our understanding of the corporate ownership and control around the world. Concluding remarks and suggestions for future research are provided at the end of the chapter.

Shareholding structure in Chinese public corporations

As shown in Table 4.1, the shares on the Chinese stock market are officially classified as non-tradable state shares, legal person shares, employee shares[2] and tradable public shares. While state shares are those directly held by government agencies, such as the state asset bureaus, legal person shares are those owned by domestic institutions, such as the state-owned or the non-state-owned corporations or other economic entities with a legitimately institutional status.

One problem of the official classification is that it fails to identify the ownership identity of the legal person shares, and it is unclear whether these legal entities are state-owned or non-state-owned institutions. It is quite possible that the owners of the legal person shares are enterprises or institutions, ultimately controlled by the

Table 4.1 Distribution of the official shareholding classes in Chinese PLCs (%)

	1997	*1998*	*1999*	*2000*	*2001*
Total non-tradable shares[a]	65	66	65	64	65
State	32	34	36	39	46
Domestic legal persons	30	27	25	23	17
Overseas legal persons	1	1	1	1	1
Employee	2	2	1	1	0.5
Total tradable shares[b]	35	34	35	36	35
A-shares	23	24	26	28	25
B-shares	6	5	5	4	3
H-shares	6	5	4	3	6

Source: China Securities Regulatory Committee (http://www.csrc.gov.cn).

Notes

a *State shares* are directly held by government agencies, such as state asset bureaus. *Legal person shares* are owned by domestic institutions, be they enterprises or other economic entities enjoying legal person status. *Employee shares* are offered to workers and managers of a listed company usually at a substantial discount.

b The tradable public shares can further be broadly classified as A-shares, B-shares and H-shares:

A-*shares* are the ordinary equity shares mostly held and traded by individual investors in RMB on the domestic stock exchanges.

B-*shares* refer to those that were once exclusively traded by foreign investors denominated in foreign currencies until 2001, when domestic investors can also hold these shares.

H-*shares* in the general sense concern the shares issued by Chinese corporations to foreign investors through listings on Hong Kong, New York and London Stock Exchanges. Since most of the shares are listed on Hong Kong, the H designation is used in this context.

central or a local government. If so, grouping the legal person shares to an independent shareholding class at par with the state shares and tradable public shares would be inappropriate, since the state controls the legal person who in turn controls the firm. Thus the ultimate owner of the firm is the state, and not the legal person itself. Unfortunately, previous empirical studies on the performance impacts of different shareholding classes, for example, Xu and Wang (1997, 1999), Chen (2001) and Sun *et al.* (2002), are almost invariably based on such *ad hoc* classification.

One example of such *ad hoc* classification is the Inner Mongolia Mengdian Huaneng, a thermal power corporation listed on the Shanghai Stock Exchange. Figure 4.1 shows this state asset bureau, as the third largest equity holder that directly controlled 7.5 per cent stocks in 2001, whereas the two largest shareholders were the Inner Mongolia Electricity Company (59.5 per cent of shares outstanding) and the Huaneng Group Corporation (12.5 per cent of the total shares). If we strictly follow the official classification of the state shares and the legal person shares, the firm should be regarded as to be under the control of the legal person – the Inner Mongolia Electricity Company, since it is the majority shareholder of the firm. A closer inspection, however, reveals that the firm is actually controlled ultimately by the state, because its two largest legal person shareholders, the Inner Mongolia Electricity Company and the Huaneng Group Corporation themselves are solely

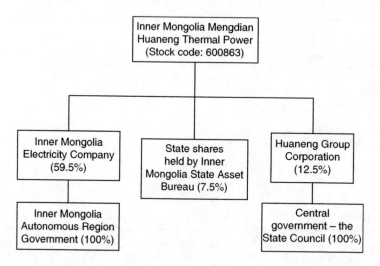

Figure 4.1 Inner Mongolia thermal power corporation.

Notes
Apparently, the ultimate owner of the company is Inner Mongolia Autonomous Region Government that owns entirely the non-listed company, Inner Mongolia Electricity Company, which in turn holds 59.5 per cent of the quoted company in the top box. Overall, the Inner Mongolia Thermal Power Corporation is controlled ultimately by the state that holds 79.5 per cent (59.5 + 7.5 + 12.5 per cent) shares in the total, rather than the legal person of Inner Mongolia Electricity Company that is regarded by the official shareholding classification as an independent entity at par with the state.

controlled by the Inner Mongolia local government and the central government (the State Council) respectively. Hence, the ultimate voting rights the state has in the thermal power corporation seem to amount to 79.5 per cent (59.5 + 12.5 + 7.5 per cent) rather than only 7.5 per cent as shown in the official record. If we are misled into uncritically accepting the state stockholding size of 7.5 per cent, the exact magnitude of state shareholding and the state's control would be underestimated. Given only the crude official data on shareholdings, an unbiased assessment of the relationship between shareholding structure and firm's performance would be hard to obtain.

Another example is the Shenzhen Nan-Guang Group PLC (Figure 4. 2), which is a diversified corporation involved mainly in tourism, real estate and the building industry, listed on the Shenzhen Stock Exchange. The largest stockholder of the company is the Shenzhen subsidiary of China National Aero-Technology Import & Export Corporation (CATIC), holding more than a quarter of the total shares. And the next two large shareholders are the Shanghai Xinya Group Company and the China New Era (Xin Shidai) Holding Group Company respectively. Each of these companies holds approximately 10 per cent of the shares. Once again, the three holding institutions are found to be subject to the ultimate control of the central and the local government. Specifically, the CATIC is owned by two parts of China Aviation Industry Corporation (AVIC), which is in turn under the direction of the State Council. The Shanghai Xinya Group was established by the Shanghai Municipal Government, with a major interest in the hotel industry and tourism, and the New Era Group is a diversified firm ranging from high-technology business to real estate development, also fully controlled by the central government. But ironically, the state shareholding level in the Shenzhen Nan-Guang Group is reported as zero in the official record! Obviously, the real scale of state control in the group should at least take into account the legal person shares held by the three state-controlled companies.

The misspecification of the state and the legal person shares pervades most of the previous literature. For instance, on examining the relationship between ownership structure and corporate performance, Xu and Wang (1997, 1999) found a positive correlation between the fraction of the legal person shares and the firms' profitability, and a negative correlation between the fraction of the state shares and its profitability. They interpreted the results by equating the legal person shares to institutional shares, and so ascribed all the merits of institutional shareholders in industrial countries to the Chinese legal persons. The interpretation of the legal person shares in this way is inconsistent with China's institutional context, because the legal person shares could represent a degree of state control via an indirect control form, as shown in our three cases, in which they are fundamentally different from the widely held institutional shareholders in Western economies, such as insurance companies, mutual funds and pension funds etc.

Another type of misspecification can be illustrated by the case of the Beijing Ufsoft Computer Software Co. Ltd, which was floated on the Shanghai Stock Market Exchange in 2001. Figure 4.3, shows the five largest shareholders of the company, labelled as legal person shareholders in the official record, collectively control

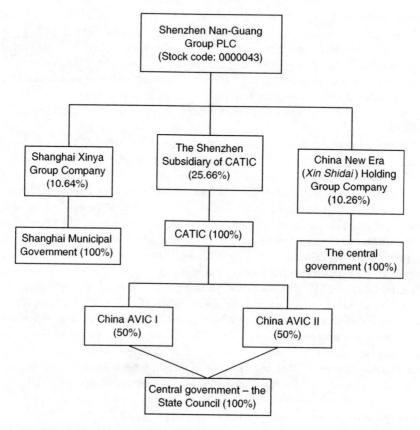

Figure 4.2 Shenzhen Nan-Guang Group PLC.

Notes

The company in question is ultimately owned by the central government, the State Council, since the Council controls respectively 100 per cent of China AVIC I and II, and each of these two companies owns 50 per cent of CATIC, in which CATIC owns 100 per cent of its Shenzhen subsidiary company that is the top shareholder (25.6 of shares) of the Nan-Guang Group PLC. In contrast, the 2000 statistical data of the official shareholding classification reported that the state shares of the company are zero, implying that it would be a non-state controlled company.

threefourths of the total stocks in the firm. Unlike the first case, it is further found that the five holding companies are not ultimately controlled by the government, but by an entrepreneur named Wang Wenjing. In fact, Wang Wenjing controls the downstream company by acting as the dominant shareholder of the five 'legal persons' in the intermediate control chain. Hence, it can be easily seen from the two cases that, since the legal person shares in the two public companies are qualitatively different (with different classes of ultimate-controlling shareholders), it would not be meaningful to pool all these legal persons shares as an independent

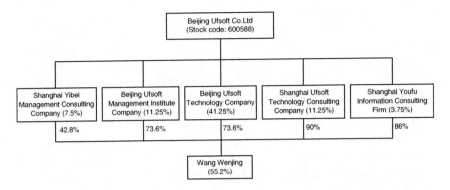

Figure 4.3 The Beijing Ufsoft Computer Software Co. Ltd.

Notes
In this case, the five legal person shareholders which in total hold 75 per cent of the company shares are not controlled by the government, but are in effect by an individual person. The entrepreneur Wang Wenjing ultimately holds more than half of the company's equities by holding the controlling stakes in the five holding companies of the listed firm (numbers shown beside the first control chain). His ultimate cash flow rights in the public company can be obtained as follows: $42.8 \times 7.5 + 73.6 \times 11.25 + 73.6 \times 41.25 + 90 \times 11.25 + 86 \times 3.75 = 55.2$ per cent.

shareholding class when studying the performance impact of the shareholding structure in China.

But this is precisely the course followed by Sun *et al.* (2002) whose study pools the state holding and the legal person holding into one class parallel with other classes in a comparative performance study. The study proposed indifference between the state shareholders and the legal person shareholders in Chinese public corporations, so that they regressed the sum of state shareholdings and legal person shares, as a proxy of government control, with performance measures of Chinese PLCs. Clearly, the work is arbitrary or biased since it overestimates the exact shareholding size of the state in their firm sample, since the class of legal person entities still consists of 16 per cent of the quoted companies that are non-state-controlled, as will be demonstrated in the following section.

Ultimate controlling shareholders and the pyramid structure in Chinese corporations

Identifying ultimate controlling shareholders through pyramid shareholding schemes is not easy, especially in the Chinese context. According to La Porta *et al.* (1999), an ultimate controlling shareholder can be identified via the pyramid structure in which at least one PLC lies between the downstream firm and the ultimate owner in the chain of 20 : 10 per cent voting rights. If the intermediate company happens to be a non-listed firm, however, the case does not enter their sample, primarily because the exact ownership data of the non-listed firm is hard to collect, while the intermediate listed companies have the obligation to disclose their shareholding information to the public.

Unfortunately, this practice does not work in China, since most of the holding companies of the public corporations are not quoted on the stock market. As will be shown later in our survey, only 19 firms that are the controlling shareholders of the public corporations are themselves listed companies. Therefore, we relax the strict specification of pyramid by including unlisted holding companies in our survey, and we believe such a relaxation is instrumental in obtaining the real picture of the ultimate shareholding structure in the Chinese public corporations. But, due to poor information disclosure in emerging markets and in China in particular, it is tremendously difficult, if not impossible, to get detailed ownership data for these holding companies. Nevertheless, we have made every endeavour to identify the real behind-the-scenes controllers of these companies through a careful study of company prospectuses and annual reports, press releases, company insider information, interviews with government officials, securities analysts and so on. Table 4.2, for the first time, reveals the identity of ultimate controlling shareholders in Chinese public corporations and how these ultimate controllers use different classes of shareholdings as 'control instruments' to direct the listed companies.

Not surprisingly, the shareholding structure in Chinese public corporations is still characterized by the state predominance,[3] in that the state is in the ultimate and absolute control of approximately 84 per cent of our firm sample. Furthermore, the state is by no means an integrated monolithic entity in China. Rather, it extends its ownership from direct control to indirect control via its pyramid shareholding scheme. Besides the straightforward government direct control, where government agencies act as the controlling shareholders in 8.5 per cent of the total companies, the pyramid structure is prevalent in 75.6 per cent of our sample companies. Within the category of government indirect control, intermediate companies used in the control chain include: state solely owned companies (32.6 per cent of the total firms, like the Inner Mongolia Electricity Company in case 1), state-controlled non-listed companies (40.6 per cent), state-controlled PLCs (1.4 per cent) and state-owned academic institutions (1.1 per cent). The four types of intermediate companies are the key parts of *the Chinese-styled pyramid shareholding schemes*, which extends La Porta *et al.*'s pyramid concept to the context of China's enterprise reform.

On the other hand, rather surprisingly, private and foreign forces have already controlled over 170 public companies on the Chinese stock market via their own pyramidal structure. Among them, 83 companies are controlled by domestic private firms, which are in turn in the hands of individuals or families (like the Beijing Ufsoft Technology Company in case 2); 77 companies are found to be under the control of collective firms and Township and Village Enterprises (TVEs). Although we lack exact data, anecdotal evidence clearly indicates that on many occasions private firms choose to register themselves as 'collective' to avoid government's unfavourable treatments in China's unique transitional environment. Finally, due to China's policy constraint, there are few involvements of foreign capital on the domestic capital market: only ten listed firms are indirectly controlled by foreign firms.

Table 4.2 Who ultimately controls China's PLCs in 2001?

Status of the largest shareholder of a publicly listed company	Number of companies as % of the total number listed in the market	Average shares held by the largest shareholder as % of total shares issued[a]
State as the ultimate controlling shareholder		
Direct Control		
Government departments or agencies	8.5 (94 firms)	39.6 (16.1)
Indirect Control		
State-owned enterprises (SOEs)	75.6 (836 firms)	47.3 (17.6)
In which of the SOEs:		
(1a) State-controlled public-listed firms	1.4 (15 firms)	52.3 (20.8)
(2a) State solely owned companies[b]	32.6 (360 firms)	49.7 (16.7)
(3a) State-controlled non-listed companies[c]	40.6 (449 firms)	45.4 (17.9)
(4a) State-owned academic institutions	1.1 (12 firms)	39.0 (14.1)
Total of state-controlled companies	84.1 (930 firms)	46.5 (17.6)
Non-state firms/families as the ultimate controlling shareholder		
(1b) Non-state-controlled publicly listed firms	0.4 (4 firms)	37.7 (24.9)
(2b) Non-listed collective firms & TVEs	7.0 (77 firms)	38.3 (16.9)
(3b) Non-listed domestic private firms	7.5 (83 firms)	33.3 (11.6)
(4b) Non-listed foreign private firms	1 (10 firms)	25.8 (6.5)
Total of non-state-controlled companies	15.9 (174 firms)	34.8 (14.7)
Grand total of number of firms in the sample	100.0 (1105 firms)	44.6

Notes

a Theoretically, being the largest stockholder in a company does not necessarily mean absolute control of the firm if there exist sufficient large stakes held by the other large shareholders, but the situation is less likely to appear in Chinese corporations in which the largest shareholder always owns a sufficiently large number of shares, as shown in the table, to guarantee control.

b This is a special type of company after the corporatization in China, since there is no shareholders' meeting in these firms, while the board of directors are directly appointed by state department or state-authorised investment institutions.

c Comparative to state solely owned companies, the general state-controlled non-listed companies shall have the shareholders' meeting because various state departments may have different levels of stakes in these companies, and it even could be the case that some domestic or overseas non-state companies hold some minority shares in the firms. In the same vein, all the fundamental decisions concerning merger and dissolution etc. should be at least formally decided upon in the shareholders meeting.

According to China Securities Regulatory Committee, the number of companies listed in December 2001 was 1160, in which 95.3 per cent of the total listed companies have responded to our survey on the economic status of their largest shareholders in 2001.

Brackets beside the percentage of shares are standard deviation of the average shares.

Concluding remarks

Based on the principle of the ultimate ownership and control suggested by La Porta *et al.* (1999), this chapter establishes a new analytical framework for the shareholding structure of the Chinese quoted companies and finds that the main feature of their structure is the state dominance both in terms of the number of firms listed on the stock market which are ultimately controlled by the state and the proportion of the voting shares. On the other hand, although the proportion of corporations ultimately controlled by private firms is small at present, only 16 per cent in 2001, it still raises a question that needs further scrutiny: is the current state-dominant shareholding structure in the Chinese public companies transitional or likely to endure? The dynamics of the evolution in corporate ownership and control in China, a unique post-communist country featured by gradualist transition, would be a fascinating agenda for future research.

In contrast to the shareholding classification proposed in the chapter, the Chinese officially reported shareholdings of the state and the legal persons are ambiguous in identifying ultimate owners of corporations. The absence of state shares shown in a company's annual report does not necessarily indicate the non-existence of the ultimate control by state. And the class of legal person shares is just a veil of various identities of ultimate owners including both the state and the private shares. This ambiguity has misled many previous studies in assessing the impact of shareholding classes on performance to varying degrees. Therefore, their empirical findings on the relationship between state shareholding and firm's performance, whether the unambiguous negative correlation (Xu and Wang, 1997, 1999) or the U-shaped correlation (Tian, 2001)[4] or even the inverse U-shaped one (Sun *et al.*, 2002), must be treated with a pinch of salt, if not deemed as outright spurious.

The avenue for future research would naturally lie in the examination of the complex performance impacts induced by different types of controlling shareholders, such as the state and the family. And an even more uncharted territory could be the empirical investigation on whether there are any significant performance impacts of various control mechanisms applied by the dominant shareholders. For instance, do different pyramidal structures, such as different classes of shareholding identities in the intermediate control chain, tend to be associated with different firm performance, despite the ultimate controlling shareholders remaining identical?

Acknowledgements

We are grateful for Mr Zili Pu's research assistance to our survey of Chinese quoted companies, and to Shanghai University of Finance and Economics for financial support.

Notes

1 Their methodology has been subsequently applied in the analysis of the corporate ownership structure in East Asian economies by Claessens *et al.* (2000) and in West European economies by Faccio and Lang (2002), with similar empirical results.

2 It should be recognized that non-tradable does not necessarily mean non-transferrable, since the state and the legal person shares can be transferred among various institutions subject to the approval of the China Securities Regulatory Committee (CSRC), but the crucial point here is that after the transfer, these shares still remain non-tradable and cannot be directly transacted on the market.

3 This is due to the Chinese government's policy of incorporating/listing the SOEs while maintaining at least indirect control and avoiding mass privatization since the early 1990s.

4 Although Tian (2001) attempted to deal with the ambiguous shareholding classification of the legal person shares by strictly applying La Porta *et al.*'s pyramid concept, he only defined those whose largest shareholder is also a publicly listed state-controlled corporation to be state controlled. Hence, he missed a large number of corporations under the control of non-listed state-owned/controlled companies. As a result, either his study is biased by defining the missing part of the corporations as non-state controlled, or unrepresentative of the population since its pyramid sample of 19 companies (and 4 of 19 are non-state controlled) was too small to be adequate.

References

Chen, Jian (2001) 'Ownership structure as corporate governance mechanism: evidence from Chinese listed companies', *Economics of Planning*, 34(1–2): 53–72.

Claessens, Stijn, Simeon Djankov and H. P. Larry Lang (2000) 'The separation of ownership and control in East Asian corporations', *Journal of Financial Economics*, 58(1–2): 81–112.

Faccio, Mara and Larry Lang (2002) 'The ultimate ownership of Western European corporations', *Journal of Financial Economics*, 65(3): 365–95.

La Porta, Rafael, Florencio Lopez-de-Silanes and Andrei Shleifer (1999) 'Corporate ownership around the world', *Journal of Finance*, 54(2): 471–517.

Sun, Qian, Wilson Tong and Jing Tong (2002) 'How does government ownership affect firm performance? Evidence from China's privatization experience', *Journal of Business Finance & Accounting*, 29(1–2): 1–27.

Tian, Lihui (2001) 'Government shareholding and the value of China's modern firms', William Davidson Institute Working Paper 395, University of Michigan Business School, Ann Arbor, MI.

Xu, Xiaonian and Yan Wang (1997) 'Ownership structure, corporate governance and corporate performance: the case of Chinese stock companies', World Bank Policy Research Working Paper 1794, June, The World Bank, Washington, DC.

Xu, Xiaonian and Yan Wang (1999) 'Ownership structure and corporate governance in Chinese stock companies', *China Economic Review*, 10(1): 75–98.

5   Corporatisation of China's state-owned enterprises and corporate governance

Jean Jinghan Chen

China's state-owned enterprises (SOEs) are notorious for low efficiency and profitability. It is argued here that it is their corporate governance structure that causes much of their inefficiency. There are agency problems with the SOEs. For most of them, governance seems to be characterised by insider control, soft budget constraints, managerial slack and a sheer lack of competent managers. Turning them into joint stock companies by issuing their shares on stock markets has not improved their performance, largely because it has failed to deal effectively with the agency problems associated with public ownership. Reforms so far have failed to grapple effectively with the problems of creating adequate incentives and monitoring systems for the directors to create value for the owners. To create an effective corporate governance mechanism, the country needs to develop market-oriented institutions. What precise structure should be adopted is difficult to say. But we argue that for former SOEs, a neo-corporatist approach with a two-tier board structure may have advantages over a neo-liberal approach with a single board. The key issue for China is not to adopt a fixed set of governance models to copy, but to develop institutions that lead to effective corporate governance in the context of China's economic and social environment.

Introduction

Most literature on the reforms of Chinese SOEs reported specific SOE efficiency problems – declining profitability and increasing loss making (McKinnon, 1994; Nolan, 1995; Sachs and Woo, 1997; Jefferson and Singh, 1999; Cook *et al.*, 2000; Lin and Zhu, 2001). Faced with mounting losses in the state sector, in the mid-1990s, the Chinese government began to shift the focus of SOEs reform from piece-meal measures to privatisation of small SOEs and corporatisation of larger ones. Research has shown that it is not realistic to entirely privatise all SOEs considering the important roles they have played in the national economy and the social respon-sibilities they have undertaken (Jefferson and Singh, 1999; Cook *et al.*, 2000; Liu, 2000; Chen and Wills, 2002). The government hoped that corporatisation could be an achievable and effective way to improve the performance of large SOEs. The aim is to turn SOEs from entirely publicly owned companies to shareholding companies, which previously controlled by industry-specific government agencies at various administrative levels, could now be transformed into companies that are, at least in theory, independent of the state in decision-making and, through the issue of shares, diverse in ownership.

This chapter discusses the effectiveness of the current corporatisation programme in terms of the governance structure of SOEs, and addresses the institutional requirement for creating effective corporate governance. It attempts to answer the following questions:

- Has the current share issuing corporatisation worked as a way to improve SOEs' performance?
- What are the essential institutional factors that China needs to create effective corporate governance?

The remainder of this chapter is organised into four sections. The first section reviews the agency problems in Chinese SOEs before corporatisation. The second investigates the effectiveness of the current corporatisation programme as a means to improve the firms' performance with particular reference to corporate governance. The third discusses the institutional requirements for an effective governance mechanism and suggests what China needs to do to meet these requirements. The fourth concludes by drawing implications from the findings.

Pre-corporatisation: SOEs' inefficiency and corporate governance

Before the introduction of corporatisation of SOEs in China, low efficiencies and increasing losses were often attributed to excessive welfare burdens (Broadman, 1996; Hu, 1996; World Bank Country Study, 1997), increasing competition (Jefferson and Rawski, 1999) and, more importantly, the built-in agency problems associated with public ownership in a centrally planned economy (Qian, 1996; Chen and Wills, 2002). As the Chinese economy has become increasingly market oriented, it is natural to expect that the artificial profit for SOEs as guaranteed by the planning system in the past would decline due to increasing competition. Since the late 1990s, measures have been taken to release SOEs' welfare burdens by privatising housing and medical benefits and laying off workers. But, these measures have not necessarily improved the intrinsic efficiency of SOEs. Rather, they have been at the expense of the workers and society without being accompanied by measures addressing SOEs' agency problems. The size of the pie has not increased; it has only been redistributed. Moreover, the effort to 'break the iron rice bowl' has backfired because it has caused tremendous uncertainty among workers about their future job security and hence, has depressed consumption demand. The depressed consumption would not help improve the profitability of SOEs. China still lacks a social security system to deal with these social burdens. These reforms simply shifted social costs from SOEs to tax payers.

Both the theory and the empirical evidences have suggested that the most important reason for the increasing losses in pre-corporatised SOEs was due to the agency problems (Qian, 1996; Chen and Wills, 2002). The agency problems with SOEs were twofold: on the part of enterprise managers, on the one hand, and on the part of government bureaucrats, on the other hand. SOEs, in principle, were owned by the state, but control rights were divided or shared between government bureaucrats and enterprise managers.

Although the bureaucrats were supposed to act as owners, they were not legally entitled to be the residual claimants of profits as owners of private enterprises would normally be. It was this lack of real owners combined with an inadequate governance structure that distinguished a traditional SOE from a Western-style public corporation and made the agency problems with SOEs far more serious.

Red tape, soft budget constraints and corruption were all manifestations of the agency problems on the part of bureaucrats. A particularly serious agency problem with the bureaucrats was in their choice of managers. Personal connections, seniority, political loyalty and factors other than management ability were often the criteria used for the promotion of SOE managers.

The agency problems in SOEs resulted in a monitoring problem, managerial slack and a lack of competent managers. Owners and managers lacked authority and incentives and there were no proper reward systems for managers or workers. The result was opportunistic behaviour by managers, workers and public officials to take more from the enterprise than they gave. The effect was persistent losses and a corporate governance structure characterised by insiders' control, managerial slack and lack of competent managers. This was the fundamental reason for SOEs' inefficiency.

Has corporatisation improved corporate governance of the firms?

It can be seen that the most difficult and fundamental task for reforming SOEs is to address the agency problems. The question, therefore, is: has corporatisation established effective corporate governance for the firms to overcome the agency problems associated with the public ownership resulting from a centrally planned economy.

China's corporatisation programme

Corporatisation of SOEs in China started in the mid-1990s. The central goal of corporatisation is to establish a system in China, through share-issuing privatisation, featuring corporate governance structures that separate the state from enterprises. Public listing of SOEs in domestic stock exchanges is a key measure of corporatisation. Indeed, the vast majority of China's publicly listed companies are formerly SOEs, mostly large and better-performing ones (Lin and Zhu, 2001). It is hoped that corporatisation will:

- change the ownership structure of the SOEs that features both state and non-state institutional shareholders in addition to small individual shareholders;
- separate the state from business operation for enterprises to achieve full autonomy not only in business structure but also in operational decisions and for the state to limit its liabilities to the enterprises, hence hardening the budget constraints;
- improve managerial incentives by installing shareholders with incentives and abilities to monitor the managers.

Ownership

Share-issuing privatisation has been one of the major forms of privatising SOEs around the world since the 1980s with many successful cases in developed countries (Megginson and Netter, 2001). Evidence from the developed countries indicates that corporate governance has a significant impact on the performance of public listed firms (Jensen and Meckling, 1976; Shleifer and Vishny, 1986, 1997). The objective of such an action in China is also expected to introduce elements of corporate governance that facilitate improvements in a firm's performance. But, it should be noted that China's case is different from that of the developed countries. It is neither the market, nor the motivation to obtain private benefits that determines the presence of shareholders. Ownership structures are largely determined by the government. At the time of listing, a significant proportion of shares are held back by the government (state owned), and a large proportion of shares are transferred to state-owned investment trusts and asset management companies owned by legal persons. The distinction between the state and the legal person shareholders is in many cases superficial because the legal persons are mainly government authorities. The state- and the legal persons-owned shares account for about 70 per cent of the total share issuance (Table 5.1). Institution share holding, according to the Western definition is rare, therefore, it is hard to see what the transfer from the state to the legal persons would have done for the potential monitoring effect. The public-listed shares are dispersed and minorities have little legal protection. Whether a company can make an initial public offering (IPO) is still determined largely by an administrative process rather than the market process seen in developed economies. When an SOE wants to go public, it must seek permission from the local government and/or its affiliated

Table 5.1 Development of China's stock market

	1992	1993	1994	1995	1996	1997	1998	1999	2000
Total number of listed firms	53	183	291	323	530	745	851	949	1088
Capital raised (billion yuan)	9.4	31.4	13.8	11.9	34.1	93.4	79.5	100	142.8
Market capitalisation (billion yuan)	104.8	353.1	369.1	347.4	984.2	1752.9	1950.6	2647.1	4809.1
Market capitalisation/ GDP(%)	3.9	10.2	7.9	5.9	14.5	23.4	24.9	32.3	54.0
Number of investors (million)	2.2	7.8	10.6	12.4	23.1	33.3	39.1	44.8	58.0
Total book value of assets (billion yuan)	48.1	182.1	330.9	429.5	635.2	966.1	1240.8	1610.7	1796.0
State share as a % of total shares	41.4	49.1	43.3	38.8	35.4	31.5	34.3	36.1	38.9
Legal person shares as a % of total shares	27.9	23.1	23.5	25.0	28.4	32.7	30.4	27.7	24.5

Source: CSRC (1999) *China Securities and Futures Statistics*, China Finance and Economic Publishing House, Beijing and its CSRC Official Web site http://www.csrc.gov.cn/CSRCSite/deptlistcom/ stadata.htm

central government ministries, which receive an IPO quota from the China Securities Regulatory Committee (CSRC).

This shows that corporatisation has not fundamentally changed the ownership structure of corporatised firms. The state still retains a majority shareholding. Unless the state is a passive owner, it is not clear how the state can be truly separated from enterprises. If the state indeed withdraws its control over corporatised firms, currently, there is no mechanism in place to prevent enterprise managers from abusing their newly acquired power. In fact, many managers of the corporatised SOEs tend to use their new independence to pursue reckless operations or engage in self-seeking activities (He, 1998). For example, the CEO of one of the largest department stores in Zhejiang Province caused huge losses to the company by 'blindly providing credit guarantees' without the consent of the board of directors due to the lack of monitoring and supervision (*Beijing Youth Daily*, 1997). Neither the employees as shareholders nor the board of directors had the ability or motivation to exercise any control over major business decisions and to monitor the chairman and the CEO of the company. A more serious misbehaviour by managers of corporatised SOEs is asset stripping, which for many is the quickest way to get rich. He (1988) provided several detailed cases that illustrate vividly some of the methods used by managers to divert state assets into their own pockets. In addition, if corporatised SOEs are not performing, the government will still bail them out, whereas in the developed countries they will go into bankruptcy.

Corporate governance structure

In developed economies, two broad types of governance structure can be distinguished (Shleifer and Vishny, 1997). One is the 'insider' or 'neo-corporatist model', such as the Japanese–Germanic model, that relies on large institutional stakeholders such as the banks for effective governance. The other is the 'outsider' or 'neo-liberal model', such as the Anglo-American model, that relies on capital market discipline and the legal system. China should not try to copy micro-level corporate governance models from the developed countries, whether neo-liberal or neo-corporatist. Nevertheless, it is argued that for former SOEs a neo-corporatist approach to the structure and composition of the board of directors, with a two-tier board structure, may have advantages over a neo-liberal approach with a single board, particularly when external monitoring devices, such as the stock market, are not well developed.

The two-tier board system of corporate governance, which is common in the European countries, is highly appreciated by the Chinese and is regarded as a means of enhancing internal unity and performance of the company. China has adopted this system since 1994 for publicly listed companies. The Chinese practice, however, is somewhat different from those found in Europe.

Shareholders' meeting

Compared with the normal function of a shareholders' meeting in European countries, such as passing resolutions on mergers, division, dissolution and liquidation, electing and removing directors and supervisors, and amending the articles of association of the company, a shareholders' meeting in China has a wider range of decision-making powers on financial matters, such as deciding policies on the business operation and investment plan of the company; reviewing and approving the annual financial budget, the final accounts and the plan of profits' distribution; and deciding on the increase or reduction of the registered capital of the company and the issuance of debentures by the company.

The principle of one share, one vote is included in the 1994 Chinese Company Law. Regarding the voting rights attached to different shares, there were different practices in Western countries. The Chinese remain silent on whether companies can issue non-voting shares or preferential shares and leave room for issuing special kinds of shares, if necessary. But, one of the legislative defects in China is that it fails to stipulate the quorum of shareholders at shareholders' meetings and the minimum holdings of shareholders. Therefore, theoretically, a shareholders' meeting can be held with any number of shareholders holding only one share. The state, even if only being a minority shareholder, can still take part in the shareholders' meetings and get involved in the decision-making process.

Supervisory board

In China, the members of the supervisory board are appointed by the shareholders' meeting. The board is obliged to submit their reports to the shareholders' meeting for review and approval. A supervisory board should have no less than three members. Among them, there should be an appropriate proportion of employee representatives, who are elected by the employees of the company rather then the shareholders' meeting. The board has powers to supervise the work of the directors and managers and to propose the holding of interim shareholders' meetings. In developed countries, Germany for example, supervisory board members include representatives of large institutional shareholders, such as banks that provide share capital as well as loans to companies. However, in China, independent institutional investors, including banks, are rare and they have not played this monitoring role in the system. Further, there is a lack of provisions for implementing the powers and duties. There are no provisions concerning rules of procedure, rules of voting, and rules of proposing and holding meetings of the supervisory board. Moreover, the board usually consists of quite a few government appointees who play a leading role in monitoring, while in Germany, government representatives on supervisory boards play a secondary role in monitoring to that of private shareholders. Therefore, in China, the supervisory function of the supervisory board in terms of monitoring management and reducing agency costs is very limited. The Company Law gives supervisory powers to supervisors, but does not prescribe how to exercise the power, or the liabilities of supervisors in case of breach of duty. In a country like China, where awareness of shareholders' rights is not well developed among the general public, it is even more important to provide a means of enhancing the supervisory capacity of the supervisory board.

Board of executive directors

Like the appointment of members of a supervisory board, in China, members of an executive board are also appointed by the shareholders' meeting, and the executive board is also required to submit the reports to the shareholders' meeting for review and approval. It is worth noting that the board of executive directors of a Chinese company is an organ of decision-making for day-to-day business operations, but not an organ for carrying out daily business operations. A manager who is normally appointed by the central government carries out the tasks of daily business management. The board of executive directors together with this appointed manager comprises the managerial capacity of the company. This characteristic distinguishes the board of directors of a Chinese company from that in the European systems where the board of directors is the management organ of a company. Moreover, the board of directors has fewer powers in a Chinese company than it has in the European systems. For example, in Germany, the management board has power over all matters regarding business operations. The shareholders' meeting can deal with those matters only if the management board requests it to do so. In comparison, only the board of directors in China has the power of formulating business and investment plans. The power of approving the plans is in the hands of the shareholders' meeting due to the lack of supervising capacity of the supervisory board. The main task of the board of directors is to implement resolutions passed at the shareholders' meeting. Considering the fact that the government is the major shareholder of the company, the two-tier board system in China clearly shows the government's intervention in day-to-day business operations. Furthermore, the Company Law states that the executive directors and the manager have the duty of upholding the interests of the company, but fails to address the directors' fiduciary duties, the duty of care or the business judgement rule. The absence of such provisions causes some inconvenience in practice (Zhang, 1998).

Managerial autonomy

Under such a governance structure, it is hard to see that a full managerial autonomy in the corporatised firms has been fulfilled. The problem of a lack of managerial autonomy and incentives has been manifested in the fact that the government bodies are still using their power as the 'owners' of firms to interfere with the operational decisions, typically through their control over investment, finance, personnel decisions and in making regulations. Many shareholding companies still operate like traditional SOEs, and their management teams are appointed by the government and often composed of government officials and the same senior managers from the pre-corporatised SOEs (He, 1998). China tried managerial stock options last year but quickly abandoned the attempt. This is because managerial stock options require stock prices to reflect the firms' true performance. An excessively speculative and poorly regulated stock market, such as China's, cannot serve this purpose.

China's financial markets and its legal and institutional environment

As a result of China's corporatisation drive, two stock markets, Shanghai Stock Exchange and Shenzhen Stock Exchange, began to emerge in the early 1990s and have developed rapidly since the late 1990s. At the end of the year 2000, 1,088 firms were listed on the two stock exchanges, with a total market capitalisation close to 5 trillion yuan (about US$0.6 trillion), or 54 per cent of China's GDP (Table 5.1). The stock market has also become an increasingly important means of raising capital for China's SOEs, resulting in more than 4,809 billion yuan new equity issuance in 2000 alone (Table 5.1). But, at present, China's capital markets are immature and have not been properly regulated. This is reflected by scandals of insider-dealing and large capital gains in secondary capital markets (He, 1998).

China's legal and institutional framework has become increasingly incompatible with a modern market economy. An immature and incomplete legal framework has been governing company operations. China's company law lacks specific rules governing the corporatisation of SOEs, the transfer of state assets and, particularly, rules clarifying the autonomous rights of companies, which would prevent arbitrary administrative interventions (World Bank, 1997). It is also ambiguous about debt-holders' rights. There are no specific rules about what debt-holders can do in the case of default. It is seriously flawed in giving shareholders and government agencies too much power in bankruptcy procedures. The law stipulates that liquidation teams be composed of 'relevant' shareholders, government agencies and professionals. Debt-holders are not given any rights of control in liquidation. There is also little legal protection for individual shareholders. Clearly defined private property rights and effective property rights markets for those minorities have not been established. Moreover, the enforcement of laws and regulations has been largely ignored or deliberately avoided. The judicial system is insufficiently independent of the party and the government. It is hard to see that shareholders' monitoring has led to any improvement of managerial quality.

There is a lack of the enforcement of bankruptcy law to protect both creditors and debtors. The country's financial sectors, such as banks, are still under the strong grip of the state and are largely insulated from market discipline. The bond market is undeveloped, and as a result of this, bankruptcy rules, even if enforced, they are largely ineffective. Also, key supporting institutions are lacking, such as efficient independent accounting and auditing systems for consistent and transparent information disclosure. China has carried out two accounting reforms so far – the 1998 and 2001 reforms. Listed companies are required to reconcile accounting earnings from Chinese Generally Accepted Accounting Standards (GAAP) to international accounting standards (IAS). This regulation is the most comprehensive effort so far at harmonising Chinese GAAP to IAS. But, to develop a good accounting system requires more than simply introducing good accounting standards. Harmonisation of accounting standards may not necessarily lead to harmonised accounting practices and comparable financial reports. There is a lack of mechanisms to ensure adequate incentives and discipline for standards to be implemented in practice. Chen *et al.* (2002) reported that the Chinese government's efforts have not eliminated the gap between Chinese and IAS earnings despite harmonised accounting standards. This is due to the lack of adequate supporting infrastructure, and is manifested in excessive earnings of management at the firm's level, preparers' low professional standards and low quality auditing. Furthermore, agency problems between the accountants and the listed firms prevail due to lack of monitoring systems. This may tempt companies to falsify statements of capital, budgets, costs and profits.

Empirical evidence

The analysis in the previous section suggests that the market and institutional conditions in China are very different from those in developed economies. Effective corporate governance has yet to be established by the current corporatisation programme in China. Agency problems within the former SOEs have not been effectively dealt with, and in some cases, they are even getting worse. The monitoring of management has not been effective, neither has managerial autonomy been really fulfilled, under the current corporate governance structure.

There is growing empirical evidence to support the argument. Wang *et al.* (2001) investigated the effect of public listing on performance in China. They argued that the effects of public listing on performance were not significantly affected by the percentage of shares held by the state or by large top shareholders within the current ownership structure. The overall poor effects of share issuing corporatisation in terms of improving performance suggested that ownership was not a major factor in improving firms' performance in the current process of corporatisation due to the fact that the corporate governance of listed companies was not effective. The result implies that the current corporatisation does not work as a way to reform SOEs. Wen *et al.* (2002) provided evidence on the relationship between the capital structure of Chinese listed firms and their corporate governance structure. It showed that only the board composition and the CEO tenure affected the firms' capital structure decisions rather than the board size and the fixed compensations of CEOs. This suggests that the corporate governance processes in Chinese listed firms are only partly working in the manner that might have been assumed on the basis of Western models. Chen (2004) studied the determinants of the capital structure of Chinese listed firms and found that none of the capital structure models derived from the Western settings provided convincing explanations for the financing decisions of the Chinese firms. The effects of tax and costs of financial distress were, therefore, not significant, which showed that the Chinese environment still kept some features of a centrally planned economy. This was attributed to the fact that the fundamental institutional assumptions underpinning the Western models of financial markets and the banking sector were not valid in China, and the corporate governance of either listed firms or banks was still inefficient. The study suggests that establishing effective corporate governance systems and improving the institutional environment to protect debtholders' rights and small individual shareholders' interest are crucial for the success of corporatisation in China.

What China needs to do

No governance structure is universally applicable. It is difficult either to prescribe what type of governance structure China should adopt or to predict what will actually emerge. What is common in countries that have more or less effective corporate governance is that they all have a system of effective institutions, in particular, a system of private property rights, and a relatively well-functioning financial market. For China, therefore, the most important issue is not to find a fixed set of governance models from which to copy, but to develop institutions that are conducive to effective corporate governance and enforce some basic rules of the market game. This section provides suggestions of what China needs to do to achieve this goal.

Establishing an effective monitoring system

It can be seen from the earlier analysis that the current corporatisation of SOEs has not served the purpose of diversifying ownership. The state's role in governance of corporatised SOEs must be limited. The state should act as an unbiased referee and regulator, and should not interfere in day-to-day affairs of business. But it will be only when the rule of law is properly established that the government can be truly separated from enterprises.

A real diversified ownership has an important advantage over concentrated state ownership. That is, no individual shareholder has the dominant control and hence all are prevented from abusing the power to reap private gains, but each shareholder has a stake that is significant enough to have both the incentive and the ability to monitor the firm's performance. Independent institutional investors would serve this purpose. The participation of independent large investors will promote information transparency, production efficiency and also bring liquidity to the market and sophistication to the business. They would also be important players in the monitoring system. These large independent investors should be able to hold large stakes in corporatised firms and be able to exert meaningful influence on enterprise managers.

China should encourage non-state institutional and individual investors to become important players in the market. Corporatisation in China has created many individual shareholders; most of them are inexperienced first-time buyers who do not have adequate knowledge about the stock market. Currently, they are left unprotected from expropriation by the large state shareholders. In order for both independent institutional investors and individual shareholders to be real players in the market and participate in governance of firms, the current securities law needs to include rules to protect their interests in the firm, and the law must be enforced. The securities law needs to clarify and define rights and responsibilities of each firm's claim-holders, such as independent institutional investors, individual shareholders and debt-holders, including their rights in liquidation, their voting rights, and the frequency and degree of information disclosure available for them.

An effective monitoring system relies on the motivation of managers of the business. To motivate them, their compensation must be tied to their performance and currently, most Chinese managers are provided with little contractual incentive. This makes corruption both inevitable and acceptable. It is more efficient to shift managerial incentives away from implicit or illegal benefits to explicit and legal forms of compensation. The key condition for the success of a two-tier board governance structure in corporatised firms would be the appointment and remuneration of the chief executive and other executive directors on the basis of competence and performance. Moreover, there must be mechanisms preventing the possibility of conspiracy between the supervisory board and the board of executive directors. For example, in Germany, there is a law that forbids managerial functions to be delegated upwards to the supervisory board. The board of executive directors should be given more powers over business operations in order to facilitate the separation of the state from the day-to-day business management.

An independent legal system is also crucial for effective corporate governance. It would help to deter misbehaviour by business managers, shareholders and government officials. Specifically, managers should be required by law to fulfil their fiduciary duty to shareholders. At the same time, enforcement of the anti-graft law should be strengthened to punish managerial corruption and self-dealing activities in business transactions. No governance system will work if business and bureaucracy lack a minimum degree of honesty. If the anti-graft law is strictly enforced, monitoring should be much improved. But, in addition, the judicial system needs to be independent and competent.

Regulating capital markets

The capital market is playing an increasingly important role in the corporatisation of China's SOEs and in sustaining the economic growth China has experienced. China must develop large and efficient capital markets. This is because domestic bank loans are unsustainable; capital markets provide not only an alternative corporate funding tool but also a mechanism for cleaning up problem loans. Large stock markets can promote bond markets, and thus promote the importance of corporate governance. Efficient stock markets are important for corporate control and as a compensation tool for corporate managers. Though it is still debatable, efficient capital markets may have decisive competitive advantages over banks or government financing in technological development, developing entrepreneurial growth and venture capital. Foreign direct investment, in particular, has been very important in China's economic development. Foreign capital is better channelled to the country through the capital market than through banks, because the former offers more efficient allocation of risks and rewards.

Currently, China's capital markets are still immature and the institutions are incomplete. Stock exchanges should set clear initial and ongoing listing requirements. The government should mandate additional disclosure and other rules by setting independent regulatory bodies, which are separated from business operations. China Securities Regulatory Committee (CSRC) is expected to serve this purpose. This committee is hoped to protect public and competitors, by regulating share pricing, service levels for utilities and transporting firms, but its role has yet to be enforced. Meanwhile enforcement of antitrust rules will promote competition and discourage collusion.

Establishing and enforcing supporting institutions

A governance system also involves legal regulatory features. An honest and independent auditing and accounting system is important for effective corporate governance. It is important for domestic shareholders, essential for foreign shareholders and perhaps most important (and difficult) for banks. Without reliable corporate information, effective internal governance, market discipline and law enforcement would be impossible to achieve. Developing the accounting system, however, is more than introducing good accounting standards. There must be mechanisms to ensure adequate incentives and discipline so that the standards will be implemented in practice. There is also a need for training accounting and auditing professionals.

Conclusion

This chapter has argued that the current share-issue corporatisation of SOEs in China does not work as a way to improve firms' performance because it falls short of addressing the critical issue of corporate governance. It has not dealt effectively with the agency problems associated with public ownership resulting from a centrally planned economy. Establishing effective corporate governance is the key issue for the success of reform of SOEs. The creation of an effective corporate governance structure requires the development of markets and institutions. China should learn lessons from the corporate governance systems in developed countries, particularly the European systems, to develop its own truly functioning and effective corporate governance in order to improve the efficiency of its corporations.

China's corporatisation scheme is apparently modelled on the Western-style public corporations. But what has been overlooked and poorly understood is the fact that in the West, the emergence of public corporations, characterised by the separation of ownership and control, is a result of an endogenous, evolutionary process based on voluntary exchanges of private property rights in pursuit of gains from specialisation (Fama and Jenson, 1983). In such a process, various governance mechanisms have been developed to safeguard owners' interests from managerial infringement. They include laws against self-dealing activities as well as economic mechanisms such as managerial stock options, independent auditing, bankruptcy and the market for corporate control (Hart, 1995; Shleifer and Vishny, 1997).

But, in addition, these governance mechanisms need to be supported by a well-functioning financial market and a sound legal system. Capital markets are essential for the emergence of nonbanking financial intermediaries and often these are needed to increase the holding of blocks of shares. The absence of a well-functioning capital market will also limit the effectiveness of corporate take-overs as a viable governance mechanism. In the mean time, the legal rights of investors and managers should be protected, and self-dealing activities must be effectively prosecuted. On the one hand, the governance function of bankruptcy requires that debt payment and the transfer of control rights upon bankruptcy be strictly enforced by law, and on the other hand, capital markets are developed so that firms have more choices in the means of financing.

The study has also argued that the micro-level adoption of a two-tier board structure in China by itself is no panacea for the macro-level problems addressed. In fact, discussing the implementation of such a structure serves to highlight issues such as the impotence of the banks, the paucity of private shareholders and the risk of inappropriate appointments of top managers, based on politics or cronyism. But as the macro-level institutional strengthening takes place, a truly effective two-tier board structure is expected to emerge and would be a more appropriate structure to benefit from them at the micro-level, than from a unitary board structure.

References

Beijing Youth Daily, 13 December 1997.

Broadman, H. G. (ed.) (1996) 'Policy options for reform of Chinese state-owned enterprises', World Bank Discussion Paper 335, The World Bank, Washington, DC.

Chen, J. J. (2004) 'Determinants of capital structure – empirical evidence from Chinese company panel data', *Journal of Business Research*, 57(12): 1341–51.

Chen, J. J. and Wills, D. (2002) 'Agency theory and corporate governance – the Chinese state-owned enterprises', in *Proceedings of the First International Conference of Corporate Governance*, 9 July, The Business School, University of Birmingham, Birmingham.

Chen, S., Sun, Z. and Wang, Y. (2002) 'Evidence from China on whether harmonised accounting standards harmonise accounting practices', *Accounting Horizons*, 16(3): 183–97.

Cook, S., Yao, S. and Zhuang, J. (eds) (2000) *The Chinese Economy under Transition*, Macmillan, Basingstoke.

Fama, E. F. and Jenson, M. C. (1983) 'Separation of ownership and control', *Journal of Law and Economics*, 26(2): 301–25.

Hart, O. D. (1985) 'Corporate governance: some theory and implications', *The Economic Journal*, May, 678–89.

He, Q. (1998) *The Trap of Modernisation* (in Chinese), Contemporary China Press, Beijing.

Hu, X. (1996) 'Reducing state-owned enterprises' social burdens and establishing a social insurance system', in H. G. Broadman (ed.), *Policy Options for Reform of Chinese State-Owned Enterprises*, World Bank Discussion Paper 335, The World Bank, Washington, DC, pp. 125–48.

Jefferson, G. H. and Rawski, T. G. (1999) 'China's industrial innovation ladder: a model of endogenous reform', in G. H. Jefferson and I. Singh (eds), *Enterprise Reform in China*, Oxford University Press, Oxford.

Jefferson, G. H. and Singh, I. (eds) (1999) *Enterprise Reform in China*, Oxford University Press, Oxford.

Jensen, M. and Meckling, W. (1976) 'Theory of the firm: managerial behaviour, agency costs and ownership structure', *Journal of Financial Economics*, 3: 305–60.

Lin, Y. and Zhu, T. (2001) 'Ownership restructuring in Chinese state industry: an analysis of evidence on initial organisational changes', *China Quarterly*, 16(6): 305–41.

Liu, M. (2000) 'Capitalist firms, public enterprises: ownership reform and privatisation of Chinese state-owned enterprises', in S. Cook, S. Yao and J. Zhuang (eds), *The Chinese Economy under Transition*, Macmillan, Basingstoke.

McKinnon, R. (1994) 'Gradual versus rapid liberalisation in socialist economies: the problem of macroeconomic control', in *Proceedings of the World Bank Annual Conference on Development Economics 1993*, The World Bank, Washington, DC.

Megginson, W. L. and Netter, J. M. (2001) 'From state to market: a survey of empirical studies on privatisation', *Journal of Economic Literature*, 39(2): 321–89.

Nolan, P. (1995) *China's Rise, Russia's Fall*, St. Martin's Press, New York.

Qian, Y. (1996) 'Enterprise reform in China: agency problems and political control', *Economics of Transition*, 4(2): 422–47.

Sachs, J. and Woo, W. T. (1997) 'Understanding China's economic performance', Working Paper 5935, National Bureau of Economic Research, Cambridge, MA.

Shleifer, A. and Vishny, R. W. (1986) 'Large shareholders and corporate control', *Journal of Political Economy*, 94(3): 461–88.

Shleifer, A. and Vishny, R. W. (1997) 'A survey of corporate governance', *Journal of Finance*, 52(2): 737–83.

Wang, X., Xu, L. C. and Zhu, T. (2001) 'State-owned enterprises going public: the case of China', Research Report, Hong Kong University of Science and Technology, Honkong.

Wen, Y., Rwegasira, K. and Bilderbeek, J. (2002) 'Corporate governance and capital structure decision of the Chinese listed firms', *Corporate Governance: An International Review*, 10(2): 75–83.

World Bank (1997) 'China's management of enterprise assets: the state as shareholder', World Bank Country Report, The World Bank, Washington, DC.

Zhang, X. (1998) 'Practical demands to update the company law', *Hong Kong Law Journal*, 248–9.

6 Insights into strategy development in China's TVEs

David H. Brown, Hantang Qi and Yong Zhang

Township and village enterprises (TVEs) have emerged to be a crucial element in China's economic development. In 2002, there were 21 million enterprises, employing 128 million and generating over 34 per cent of GDP. The majority of these TVEs employ less than five people, but a significant number is large and it is these TVEs that have seen the strongest growth. This research looks at the strategic development in two successful TVEs in the Zhejiang province from a process perspective. A framework, to explore the process of strategy formulation at the organizational level, is presented consisting of three perspectives: an environmental or outside-in perspective, a resource-based or inside-out perspective and an inter-organizational or network perspective. Two cases, which describe the underlying process of development, are presented: the first deals with the problems associated with ensuring effective R&D and the second with the problems of managing strategic coherence in a portfolio of enterprises. The research shows the importance of the environmental fit approach to both companies but that the commitment to a resource-based approach is less evident. The importance of networks as a mechanism for strategic development is confirmed and in particular the significance of inter-personal networks.

Introduction

From modest beginnings as commune and brigade enterprises (CBEs) the rurally based TVEs have emerged to be a crucial element in China's economic development. In 1984 when TVEs were formally established there were 6.06 million enterprises, employing 52 million rural residents and generating 171 million RMB. Some 15 years later, on the completion of the ninth-year plan in 2000 there were 20.84 million enterprises, employing 128.12 million and generating a total output of 11.62 billion RMB – representing over 34 per cent of GDP (*China Statistical Yearbook*, 1990, 2001). Throughout this period annual growth rates have varied from 8 to 40 per cent and typically have averaged 19 per cent. It is against this background of remarkable growth that the chapter explores the reality of how this has happened from one particular perspective. Although originally a poor relation to state-owned enterprises (SOEs) in terms of their interest to academic researchers the last ten years has seen increasing attention paid by scholars to TVEs to help understand their success (e.g. Byrd and Gelb, 1990; Naughton, 1992; Dong and Putterman, 1997; Jefferson, 1999; Luo, 1999; Tong, 1999; Fu and Balasubramanyam, 2003). Mainly these significant contributions are predominantly economic analyses concerned with aggregations of enterprises. However, in this research we were interested in *the individual organization as the unit of analysis*, and in particular the processes within the enterprise that help explain their strategic development. To do this the chapter is organized into five sections. In the following section some additional background, including a historical perspective, on TVEs is given. The sections on Approach and Theory explain the approach to the research and the theoretical framework. The section on Case narratives 5 describes the individual narratives for each of the three case organizations. Finally, in the penultimate and concluding section we provide the interpretation of the narratives in theoretical terms and some issues for the future.

TVEs – a recap

The change from CBEs to TVEs was formalized in 1984 in the Party Central Committee's 'red-titled' documents, which gave the green light to TVE development after many years of ambivalence and defined the general policy (TVEB, 1987: 111–13). The definition of TVE has always been problematic. Typically, an enterprise is classified by size or by ownership but the concept of TVE is not consistent with either of these, since it includes all forms of non-SOEs. Hence all enterprises within the purview of township and village governments are TVEs (i.e. those below county level), but only those run by the township and village are collectively owned. There are others run by partnerships (effectively private TVEs often with complex ownership arrangements) and those run by individuals. These differences are more than semantic since regulations differ for the various categories of TVEs (for a fuller discussion of TVE classification and ownership see Byrd and Lin, 1990; Weitzman and Xu, 1994; Brown and Qi, 2000).

The subsequent expansion of the sector was emergent rather than planned but was dramatic nevertheless. Over the 20 years, 1980–2000, growth rates have averaged 19 per cent and the profile of the TVE sector at the end of 2000 is shown in Table 6.1.

Of the very large total of TVEs some 86 per cent are officially classed as 'individual enterprises'; the remaining 2.86 million are organizations that are either collective or private in ownership terms. The clear trend has been for the larger TVEs to grow more rapidly. In 2000, there were approximately 53,000 with a turnover exceeding 10 million RMB, and of these 4,100 exceeded 100 million RMB. In total, these

Table 6.1 Overall profile of TVE sector 2000

	Unit	Total	Collective TVEs	Private TVEs	Individual enterprises
No. of TVEs	Unit	20,846,637	802,106	2,060,621	17,983,910
No. of employees	Person	128,195,720	38,327,882	32,525,396	57,342,442
Total output	Billion yuan	11,615	4,028	3,235	4,352

Source: Bureau of TVEs 2001, p. 95.

enterprises accounted for 24 per cent of total gross output for the TVE sector and had significantly greater growth rates. TVEs were aided in recent years by the decisions taken at the Fifteenth National Congress in 1997, which openly acknowledged the contribution of the non-state sector. Since then the constitution has been revised to equate the state and non-state sectors, and as recently as July 2002 the government stated its intention to expand party membership to incorporate 'new elements of society', including private entrepreneurs (US embassy, 2002). Together, these signalled further legitimising of the new ownership structures. In the year 2000, 188,000 TVEs restructured into either joint stock co-operatives (163,000) or share-holding companies (25,000). We were interested in understanding the strategic development of some selected TVEs against this background, and in the next section we outline the approach.

Approach

Strategic issues are inherently contextual and hence it is important to link the strategic development of TVEs with their general and relevant contexts and environments. Case studies are appropriate for the analysis of process and are focused on what there is and how it gets there, but without the limitations from specific hypothesis testing (Bennett, 1991). There are issues around generalizability in the statistical sense but case studies are capable of developing and refining concepts and frames of reference (Pettigrew, 1985b). The research reported here is based on two selected cases. The criteria for selection were guided by the review of TVEs given earlier. We were interested in established and successful enterprises that had lived through the economic and ideological changes of the past 20 years and were differ-ent in both size and sector. We also recognized that it would not be possible to uncover the 'whole strategic story', or even to try to – this would be far too complex and in essence is not recoverable in a literal sense. Rather we set out to focus on a strategic issue that would emerge from the research enquiry process. The two selected companies were both situated in Zhejiang province – itself highly committed to TVEs. The province has 1.03 million township enterprises that account for about 84 per cent of the province's entire industrial output. The first case is Zhejiang Shanfeng Industrial Holdings and the strategic focus was 'developing an R&D capa-bility'. Our second case is the China Hengdian Group Corporation and here 'central-izing the strategic role' became the focus. In each enterprise semi-structured interviews were the main data source and were held with all levels of relevant man-agers, including the general manager. Data from other sources such as financial data, market data and business plans were also collected. An average of ten days were spent in each company on the initial field visit. Several months later these were followed up with shorter visits to fill in gaps and to check understanding.

Theory

In Mintzberg's (1987) metaphor, strategies walk on two feet – one deliberate and one emergent. The deliberate foot equates to the strategic intent of the strategy.

The emergent foot is then the aspect of unanticipated change and adaptation that becomes part of the realized strategy as events unfold. However, as noted by Webb and Pettigrew (1999), there is a tendency in the strategic literature to focus on strategy typologies, which only depict strategy in static terms. Strategic research therefore tends to be ahistorical, aprocessual and acontextual (Pettigrew and Whipp, 1991; Pettigrew *et al.*, 1992). Ideally, strategic development is best made sense of when it is observed longitudinally. The resulting strategic formulation and re-formulation can usefully be viewed from three inter-related dimensions – process, content and context (Pettigrew, 1988).

This processual perspective on strategy enables the researcher to examine strategy as an unfolding organizational process driven by individuals and groups. Within this perspective, strategy *process* is defined as how strategies emerge, including decisions and actions taken by the actors involved. Strategy *content* is then defined as the objectives/outcome of the strategy. Finally, strategy *context* is defined as the set of circumstances that influence process and content.

In terms of strategy formulation three distinct approaches can be identified which characterize the strategy process itself: outside-in; inside-out; and networks. Within any given organization these may overlap to some extent but conceptually can usefully be separated (see Brown and Qi, 2000).

Outside-in is the perspective that largely informs 'conventional' strategic analysis and tends towards prescription. From the starting point of a statement of purpose (mission or objectives) the approach puts emphasis on a thorough assessment of the external environment, including competitors, to determine opportunities and risks. Taking into account organizational capabilities and internal values, strategic alternatives are then identified, selected and implemented. The notion of environmental fit is central to this perspective. There are multiple texts which describe or complement this approach: Ansoff (1965), Porter (1980), Wheelen and Hunger (1998), Johnson and Scholes (1999) are just a few and illustrate the longevity of this analytical tradition.

Inside-out is essentially a resource-based perspective. The underlying notion is that an organization's competitive position can be better sustained by exploiting its core competencies. Prahalad and Hamel (1990), in an influential article defined these in terms of the organization's collective learning, especially the co-ordination and integration of production and technology skills. Kay (1993), in an extended analysis, developed the resource approach using the idea of distinctive capability – architecture, reputation, innovation and strategic assets.

Networks our third perspective, is an approach to the strategy process which places a premium on understanding, managing and influencing the set of actor–resource relationships within which the organization transacts its business. The emergence of network theory has been an important development alongside our understanding of markets and hierarchies (Thorelli, 1986; Powell, 1990). Although 'networks' have always existed, for example, the on-going relationships within a vertical supply chain, the recognition of networks as a distinct organizational form, amenable to analysis and theoretical development is more recent (Miles and Snow, 1986;

Jarillo, 1988; Axelsson and Easton, 1992; Snow *et al.*, 1992; Sydow, 1992; Grandori and Soda, 1995; Provan and Milwood, 1995). Aldrich and Glinow (1992) further classify networks into personal and social networks and provide a basis for understanding the role of network as a broker within a set of relationships. This is a useful perspective within this research and other authors have also contributed specifically within the Chinese context of *guanxi* – the relationships or social connections based on mutual interests and benefits (e.g. Yang, 1994; Davies, 1995; Lee *et al.*, 2001).

Case narratives

Since we were interested primarily in a development perspective, the two case narratives are described chronologically. Because of their central importance to the process of development wherever possible we have included the roles played by individuals. We have mainly presented the narratives without comment and leave the interpretation until the next section. Table 6.2 summarizes the general information for the two enterprises.

Case A: Shangfeng Industrial Holding Company – strategic focus: developing an R&D capability

Zhejiang Shangfeng Industrial Group Company has grown out of a village enterprise, namely Shangyu Pneumatic Machinery Factory, which was established in 1974 with only seven people, a factory building of 90 square meters, and a capital of ¥2,000. The enterprise now has over 850 staff and workers, fixed assets of ¥210 million and an industrial output of over ¥600 million. The company, which specializes in the production of pneumatic machinery and air-cooling equipment, ranks second in its sector in terms of various technical and economic indicators. The company's products have won more than 30 honours at provincial, ministerial and national levels. Growth has been financed from earnings and from a wide range of generous local and national grants and investments.

Table 6.2 General information on the case enterprises

	Shangfeng	Hengdian
Year of founding	1974	1975
Founders	Village	Township
Current ownership	Shareholding	Shareholding
Industrial sector	Machinery	Conglomerate
Main products	Air-cooling equipment	Magnetic materials
Output value	570 million	4.99 billion
Turnover	510 million	4.60 billion
Profit before tax	82 million	1.12 billion
Fixed assets	210 million	4.79 billion
Employees	858	17,361
Strategic issue	R&D capability	Centralizing strategy

The founder and present Chairman and General Manager, Xu Can'gen, is a largely self-taught engineer who took courses at Shanghai Jiaotong University. In 1985, he was given the title of engineer and was promoted to senior engineer in 1990. In 1992, his 'Outstanding Contribution' was recognized by the Ministry of Machine-Building and Electronics Industry. Xu Can'gen is now a deputy to the National Peoples Congress and managing director of the Chinese TVE Association. Whenever asked to explain the success of the Shangfeng company, he attributes this to a combination of management and the introduction of advanced technology through continuous R&D. How to achieve this effectively was, and remains, a major strategic concern and is the focus of the case.

The company's development was in four main stages:

1. Starting point The company's predecessor was a white cement factory, which was on the verge of bankruptcy after operating for less than three years. This was because of its outmoded production methods and the low technology content of its products. Because of this, Xu Can'gen became aware that the potential for purely labour-intensive production was limited. He could not, however, see a way out of this dilemma. An answer was provided in 1974 when Mr Ren Shiyao, a staff member at Shanghai Jiaotong University, returned to his hometown, Shangpu township, to recuperate after an illness. Mr Ren was able to tell Xu Can'gen that, although research under his leadership into low noise and energy-saving fans had been successful, he had been unable to find a factory for trial production of the new machinery. Xu Can'gen realized that it could be a promising product, and the co-operation between the factory and the university began. He invited Mr Ren to become the technical supervisor of the factory and organized seven peasants, who were completely ignorant of what the industrial fan was, to build a workshop in a small temple with only ¥2,000. There, they produced the first electricity-saving, low-noise-specialized fan for cooling towers in China.

Early trials of the products by the factory's customers were highly successful. The products started to sell well, and the factory gained in reputation.

2. Being friends From the outset, following his discussions with Ren Shiyao, Xu Can'gen recognized the importance of collaborating with Shanghai Jiaotong University. In order to be an 'understanding friend' of the scientists and technicians, he attended the university from 1977 to 1978. He took and completed specialized engineering courses and was then able to use technical terms in communicating with the staff. To progress the collaboration he provided research equipment to the university, which could also be used in the development of his products. In 1985, although the company achieved an output of only ¥10 million and its profit of ¥2 million, it spent more than $60,000, accounting for nearly two-fifths of its profit, in meeting the university staff's request of introducing a new system from a US company. This was deeply appreciated by the staff. Despite many failures, they succeeded in developing the core technology and product designs for a range of advanced air-cooled fans.

3. Institutionalization The technological co-operation between Shangyu Pneumatic Machinery Factory and Shanghai Jiaotong University started at the people-to-people level. The move to a more formal institutional relationship was undertaken in two steps.

The first step was signing an agreement with Shanghai Jiaotong University for co-operation. Believing that new products needed to be developed continuously, and old products needed to be upgraded frequently, Xu Can'gen held that the co-operation with the university should be indefinite. He proposed that the proportion for the university's charges, excluding the research institutes' costs, which were met separately, should be one per cent of the turnover.

The second step was the establishment of a production and learning research institute. In 1987, the company, together with Shanghai Jiaotong University, set up a United Research Institute on the basis of the original factory-owned Research Institute. The company invested ¥2.25 million in an office building and laboratories for the institute, together with purchasing the instruments for experiments, calibration and testing. The institute was led and staffed by the university. The two parties shared equally the profit gained from the products developed by the institute. Under the current arrangement the university supplies 'software', the institute conducts the product design experiments and the company produces the products

4. *Going beyond* In addition to the technical support from Shanghai Jiaotong University, the company also constantly increased its investment in its own employees. Starting from the early 1980s the company had invested more than ¥2 million in the formal training of 700 workers and engineers. This practice was valued highly by the State Science and Technology Commission and State Education Commission, and greatly appreciated by their foreign counterparts. This also continuously strengthened the company's co-operation with the university and its widespread recognition as an example of successful co-operation between TVEs and institutions of higher learning.

Today the company produces 16 types and over 800 variations of pneumatic machinery and air-cooling equipment. All are of low energy consumption, low noise and high efficiency. Because all its products have reached, and some have surpassed, the current international advanced level, the company's products sell well not only in the domestic market but also in 17 other countries and regions, such as Japan, Australia, Europe, America and Southeast Asia. The board of directors, in addition to Xu Can'gen, consists of four vice general managers and two nominated village representatives. The two villages remain a major beneficiary of the company's success. There are ten functional departments in the organization. Product quality, based on the continuous upgrading of technology, is the main concern for Xu Can'gen, who is responsible for the overall strategic development. There is no formal written long-term planning. However, there is a rolling annual plan which is examined and approved by the general manager, and the vice general managers are responsible for its implementation.

Case B: China Hengdian Group Corporation – strategic focus: centralizing the strategic role

China Hengdian Group Corporation is the first TVE group-company. Set up in March 1993, with the official ratification by the Office of Economy and Trade under the State Council, it is now China's largest TVE conglomerate. It grew out of a commune-run silk plant situated in a remote and backward mountain area in the middle part of Zhejiang Province, where there were neither transport facilities nor enough resources. The Group is now an industrial corporation with 15 sub-groups or general companies in different trades. It controls 21 specialized subsidiary companies and main factories, 86 key close-linked enterprises, over 700 small enterprises run by families. In 1992, its gross value of industrial output was ¥602 million, and profits before tax reaching ¥62.8 million. By 2000, the value of industrial output had increased to ¥5.00 billion, with combined profits and tax of ¥600 million.

The Group is led by a Board of Directors. Xu Wenrong, the Chairman of the Board, was the original Party Branch Secretary of the Hengdian commune brigade. Today, he is also the President of the Group General Corporations and Chairman of the Group Economic Bureau – the most important decision-making body within the Group. From the outset, Xu Wenrong was concerned that the very many peasant family activities within the Hengdian township authority were not isolated endeavours, and that as far as possible development was 'coordinated', or at the very least was not random. This concern for a strategic perspective has remained, and as the complexity of the Group has grown strategy has become synonymous with centralizing the strategic role. This case outlines the business development of the Group and the efforts made to remain coherent.

The development was in three main stages:

1. The pioneering stage   Compared to many other places, the peasants in this part of Zhejing Province were even less well placed for economic development. The distance to urban centres, poor transport and communications, and the difficult farming terrain all combined to disadvantage the Hengdian locality. There was no dominant agricultural economy and incomes were mixed. Many of the peasants had family and friends working away from the village. In the late 1960s, in order to try to change their circumstances, a list of 208 villagers who worked elsewhere was drawn up. Using this list, the villagers contacted their 'distant cousins' for information and suggestions about products that were needed and which could possibly be produced in the Hengdian district. This was the origin of the Hengdian network. During the period 1971–8 the Hengdian peasants started a variety of non-agricultural enterprises including wood-carving, silk plant, bamboo weaving plant, cement manufacture, tea processing and even radio components. The lack of funds, expertise, technology and enterprise policies meant that many of these initiatives soon ceased. However, the experience of trying and failing produced significant learning. Among these early initiatives only silk products were listed in the State's purchasing plan and Xu Wenrong made the most of this opportunity. The Hengdian Silk Plant was successfully developed and later became the 'parent plant' of the Hengdian Group. At the end of the 1970s, when the central authorities began to encourage peasants to set up CBEs, Hengdian had already established a scale of advantage and had built up trading partners, government contacts and enterprise expertise.

2. Expansion and diversification   The network, based on the original 'folk relationships', continued to play a very important role in the development of the Hengdian enterprises. In 1980, for example, a Hengdian villager working at a large SOE in Northwest China, passed on some information and contacts about the potential of the magnetic materials industry. In response, the Hengdian Silk Plant invested in the first magnetic materials plant in Zhejiang Province – later to become the most important centre for this technology in China. By 1984, a further 20 enterprises had been 'assisted' by the parent silk company. Although these enterprises had 'blood relationships' in terms of their assets and governance they were different businesses, each doing things in their own way. For Xu Wenrong this 'guerrilla' model was unsatisfactory for further development and in November 1984 combined all the plants and enterprises to form the Hengdian Industrial Company. This brought a scale to the Hengdian operations rarely seen in rural enterprises anywhere in China.

In 1985, the advantage of this scale became quickly apparent. The state in order to protect SOEs from the growing competition from TVEs introduced tax and credit measures, which disadvantaged TVEs. By combining internal group funds Hengdian safeguarded the start of 11 new projects. That year the output value doubled, with profits increasing by 58 per cent. In 1987, the gross value of Hengdian's industrial output reached ¥110.09 million, making it the first '¥100 million Town' in Jinhua Prefecture. Similar internal tradeoffs and adjustments continued to be made to ensure the Group's further development.

Concurrent to the economic activity the relationship with the town government was significantly changed. The newly formed industrial company became the decision-making and investment centre for all the town's enterprise industrial activity. The town's industry office was disbanded, and other administration streamlined. Such radical and resisted reorganization was possible only through the personal standing of Xu Wenrong. This economic independence exerted far-reaching influence on the later development of the Hengdian Group.

3. Corporatization and growth   By 1990, Hangdian was the largest TVE-based group company in Zhejiang Province and was renamed Zhejiang Hengdian Enterprise Group Corporation. The ownership was notionally community but with complex shareholdings. Using the model of central control, and particularly of investment, the company doubled its industrial output each year. In 1993, it was the first TVE formally examined and approved by the State Council and was renamed the China Hengdian Group. It was during this period that the Group improved the financial structures and invested in skilled personnel. The Group adopted a new technology-orientated development strategy and one of the subsidiary company's, Donyang Magnetic Equipment Group, was authorized to invest 7 million RMB in advanced technologies in a single year. New technologies were also funded at the early research stage with universities. At the end of the decade the Group, despite the problems of 'managing' such a complex set of enterprises, had become the third largest and second most profitable TVE in China.

Today, the management of the Group remains separate from the township and there is no local government representation on the Board of Directors. The Group's constitution provides for the power of the Board to be the same as the Chairman. The Board and the President of the Group, through the policy-making centre and the Group Economic Bureau both based at the headquarters, are responsible for: overall Group direction;

investments for key projects; appointing and removing senior personnel; approving the exit or entry of member companies; control of Group's capital and funds; approving overseas travel; and, deciding the overall proportion of bonus against profits and the distribution of senior staff bonuses. The 21 subsidiary companies are profit centres and are responsible for raw materials, products and marketing; the 86 close-linked individual enterprises are cost centres and focus on reducing production costs.

Analysis and discussion

This research started with the aim of better understanding, both theoretically and practically, the strategic development of TVEs at the organizational level and from a process perspective. The two detailed cases are in no sense representative of the TVE sector – this is so heterogeneous that devising any sample frame would be problematic. However, they are indicative of a particular class of TVE, namely large (exceeding ¥100 million turnover), successful and with collective ownership/shareholding status – such TVEs are probably less than 0.02 per cent of the total. However, they account for a quarter of gross output of the TVE sector and enjoy the highest growth rates. This kind of organization is crucial to China since their growth provides re-employment opportunities from the SOE sector, and their size allows for engagement in the more advanced technologies.

Our two cases are both from the same province, started within 12 months of each other and share a commitment to advanced technology as a basis for their main products. However, there are important differences. Shangfeng is large within its particular niche and serves an industrial market; Hengdian is very large (between 10 and 20 times depending on the measure) and is active in many markets, both consumer and industrial. In terms of their strategic processes there are differences but also significant similarities. From the case narratives the processual based analysis summarizes our findings. These are presented in Tables 6.3 and 6.4, and are discussed in the following sections.

1. Strategic content In both companies the strategic content is defined in terms of long-term, overarching strategic concerns. For Shangfeng this was the need to ensure continuing access to advanced technology. In the case of Hengdian, the imperative was on-going strategic co-ordination for a complex and diverse group of enterprises.

2. Strategic context Both companies have experienced the same policy environment for TVEs throughout the 1980s and 1990s, which is part of the *strategic context* in the interpretive framework. This policy was highly ambivalent with contradictory messages from the state depending on the general economic conditions and the needs of SOEs. Despite these inconsistencies, the general economic growth provided a munificent environment and one that both companies took advantage of. Other aspects of the strategic context (the internal environment, in Pettigrew's (1988) term, were different. For Shangfeng, the personal link with Shanghai Jiaotong University was central to the company's development of technology and needs to be seen against a background of considerable difficulty for TVEs to access skilled technical resources. For Hengdian, the geographical isolation meant that people identified strongly with the area and each other. Self-sufficiency and experimentation led to a wide base of industrial activity.

Table 6.3 Characteristics of strategy process Shangfeng

Strategic content	Strategic context	Strategic process
Need to achieve parity with international technology standards Continuous stream of R&D required	Proximity to Shanghai provided customer base Increasing international competition, especially during 1990s	Early process was *outside-in* but opportunistic rather than deliberate No formal strategic planning but strong operations control Clear evidence of *inside-out* as company exploits quality reputation *Networks* important throughout the company's development. Initially personal links giving technology access, later institutional to institutional links become very significant

Table 6.4 Characteristics of strategy process Hengdian

Strategic content	Strategic context	Strategic process
Need to co-ordinate the highly diverse township enterprises	Industrial enterprise activity crucial for development of the township	Strong tendency to *outside-in*; early silk business developed to meet a 'gap' in national production
Requirement for control and investment prioritization	Extended personal network based existed throughout China from previous emigration	Later businesses, e.g. magnetic media derive directly from external links and market opportunities. Formal strategic planning but focuses on portfolio management
Separation of commercial and non-commercial activities within the township followed	Increased international competition, especially in the 1990s	Some evidence of *inside-out* as company exploits scale factors. *Networks* very important throughout the company's development, especially for new business development and for funding

3. Strategic process All three of the analytical perspectives – outside-in, inside-out and networks – are in evidence in both companies but with different degrees of emphasis. In Shangfeng the initial idea to produce industrial fans was entirely external and opportunistic – a clear outside-in or environmental perspective. Within the company no formal long-term strategy was written, although the 'pattern' of development in Mintzberg's (1987) terms was familiar, namely: the incremental adaptation of both technology and markets. The inside-out, or resource-based view was also evident (Grant, 1991). The distinctive competencies and capabilities included quality assurance and cost effective R&D. In Kay's (1993) terms, the network of research institutions is equivalent to a resource architecture from which real competitive benefits derive and hence can be seen as a distinctive strategic asset.

In Hengdian, the outside-in perspective is very important. The whole approach over 25 years is one of opportunity seeking often facilitated by its wide network of contacts. The original Hengdian TVEs were unusual in that their separation from the governance of the township occurred very early and meant that the needs of the enterprises were less likely to be compromised by the needs of the township. Such separation, although resisted by the township, was possible because individual enterprises acted as a group (through the leadership of Xu Wenrong). However, unlike Shangfeng the evidence of an inside-out perspective in Hengdian is less apparent. One possible factor for this is the much wider variety of enterprise activity, which mitigates against developing deep operational and market competencies. Throughout Hengdian's development, strategic planning at the enterprise level appears to have been subordinate to the Group view. The issue here has been one of the appropriate relationships between the centre and the subsidiary companies and close-linked enterprises. The model, at least with respect to the subsidiary companies, equates most closely to that of Goold and Campbell's strategic control (1987). Here, the centre not only prioritizes investment capital but also influences overall strategic direction – Hengdian does both of these things.

The aspect of strategic process that both Shangfeng and Hengdian share is the prominence of networks, and in particular the importance of personal networks. The broad term *guanxi* is used in China to describe interpersonal connections. The principles of interaction between individuals can be explained in terms of the different *guanxi* bases (Tsui and Farh, 1997). These are: family/kinship; particularistic (distant relative, classmates, same hometown, neighbour etc.) and strangers/acquaintances who share social characteristics. Another classification by Fan (2002) combines the second and third bases into 'helper *guanxi*' and adds a new third category of 'business *guanxi*', based on intermediary connections.

In Shangfeng, the founder Xu Can'gen built up his initial contacts entirely through his hometown contact. Later these were extended as he himself developed further particularistic ties within Shanghai Jiaotong University. With these *guanxi* ties Shangfeng was able to access a level of expertise that couldn't have been acquired by a small CBE any other way. With such favours and co-operation is the anticipation that they will be reciprocated and this was done by Shangfeng through financial support and other mechanisms. Over a period of ten years these personal links although still important were institutionalized through contracts and the creation of a joint research institute. Despite this formalization, the character of the relationship is still particularistic, rather than a business relationship that is viewed as temporary.

In network terms the genesis of the Hengdian Group is similar. The first *guanxi* ties were particularistic and based on neighbour and hometown factors and confirm the importance of these in a Chinese context (see also Fahr *et al.*, 1998). This loose Hengdian network, outside of the Zhejiang Province, continues to play an important role in informing the strategic possibilities. Even though these contacts are not direct business relationships they function as a bridge between otherwise disconnected social clusters (Burt, 1992).

Today, the inter-organizational interactions within the Hengdian Group have matured into two kinds. The 21 subsidiaries have disparate goals but have formal organizational relationships in respect of the inclusive goals of the Group. The 86 close-linked enterprises are similar but their formal links between each other, the subsidiaries and the centre is much weaker. In Ghoshal and Bartlett's (1990) terms the interactions would be classified as 'federative' and 'coalitional' respectively. For the remaining 700 enterprises, which are 'within' the Group network, the locus of authority is at the unit level. In Brown and Lockett's (2004) classification the subsidiaries broadly can be seen as a 'network' characterized by high structure and high integration, whilst the close-linked enterprises are 'associations' with high structure but lower integration. The significance is that over a period of 25 years the characteristics of the aggregated 'business units' within the Hengdian Group has changed, and will continue to do so, in relation to the governance between the centre and the units, and their integration. Managing this dynamic change remains the strategic concern of the Hengdian Group.

Conclusion

We looked in depth at two successful TVEs to understand better, their strategic development in process terms. We were not surprised that for both of these companies 'environmental fit', largely an outside-in perspective, was very important. Initially, this had been opportunistic but soon became deliberate. Planning regimes and mechanisms were also important especially at the operational level. In the Hengdian Group, the processes in place for the strategic co-ordination of the portfolio of enterprises was sophisticated, and well suited to the social environment that was collective TVEs. In contrast, the importance that the two companies afforded to a resource-based perspective was variable. This compares with many Western and Japanese companies that increasingly emphasize the significance of distinctive resources in highly competitive markets. The Hengdian Group may be particularly vulnerable to this as many of its products are open to international competition.

We expected the role of networks to be significant but the extent and longevity of their importance in both companies surprised us. Whilst the networks themselves can change, the commitment to managing relationships as distinct organizational forms and to the value of personal links within this process remains robust. A number of issues, practical and theoretical, arise from the latter observation and relate to the transferability of goodwill from the individuals to the institutions. In both of these companies single individuals, Xu Can'gen and Xu Wenrong, have had a disproportionate network influence. This, and their well-demonstrated leadership skills, will be difficult to replace in any *process* of strategy formulation. The problem is unlikely to be unique to Hengdian and Shangfeng – many of the other large and successful TVEs will also have benefited from similar *ad hominem* influences.

References

Aldrich, H. and Glinow, M. A. (1992) 'Personal networks and infrastructure development', in D. V. Gibbon, G. Kozmetsky and R. W. Smilor (eds), *The Technopolis Phenomenon: Smart Cities, Fast Systems, Global Networks*, Rowman and Littlefield, New York, pp. 125–45.

Ansoff, H. I. (1965) *Corporate Strategy: An Analytical Approach to Business Policy for Growth and Expansion*, McGraw-Hill, New York.

Axelsson, B. and Easton, G. (eds) (1992) *Industrial Networks: A New View of Reality*, Routledge, London.

Bennett, Roger (1991) 'How is management research carried out', in Smith N. Craig and Paul Dainty (eds), *The Management Research Handbook*, Routledge, London.

Brown, D. H. and Lockett, N. (2004) 'The potential of critical and applications for engaging SMEs in e-business: a provider perspective', *European Journal of Information Systems*, 13(11): 21–34.

Brown, D. H. and Qi, Hantang (2000) 'Strategic development in China's changing state and non-state enterprises', in R. Thorpe and S. Little (eds), *The Global Change: The Impact of Asia in the 21st Century*, Macmillan, London.

Burt, R. S. (1992) 'The social structure of competition', in N. Nohria and R. G. Eccles (eds), *Networks and Organizations: Structure, Form and Action*, Harvard Business School Press, Boston, MA.

Byrd, W. and Gelb, A. (1990) 'Why industrialize? The incentives for rural community government', in W. Byrd and Qingsong Lin (eds), *China's Rural Industry: Structure, Development, and Reform*, Oxford University Press, New York, pp. 358–87.

Byrd, William and Lin, Qingsong (eds) (1990) *China's Rural Industry: Structure, Development, and Reform*, Oxford University Press, New York.

China Statistical Yearbook 1990, 2001.

Davies, H. (1995) *China Business: Context and Issues*, Longman Asia Ltd, Hong Kong.

Dong, X. and Putterman, L. (1997) 'Productivity and organisation in China's rural industries', *Journal of Comparative Economics*, 24: 181–201.

Fahr, J. L., Tsui, A. S., Xin, K. and Cheng, B. S. (1998) 'The influence of relational demography and *guanxi*: The Chinese Case', *Organisation Science*, 9(4): 471–88.

Fan, Ying (2002) 'Questioning *guanxi*: definition, classification and implications', *International Business Review*, 11: 543–61.

Fu, Xiaolan and Balasubramanyam, V. N. (2003) 'Township and village enterprises in China', *Journal of Development Studies*, 39(4): 27–46.

Ghoshal, S. and Bartlett, C. A. (1990) 'The multinational corporation as an interorganisational network', *Academy of Management Review*, 15(4): 603–25.

Goold, M. and Campbell, A. (1987) *Strategies and Styles: The Role of the Center in Managing Diverse Corporations*, Basil Blackwell, Oxford.

Grandori, A. and Soda, G. (1995) 'Interfirm networks: antecedents, mechanisms and forms', *Organisation Studies*, 16(2): 183–214.

Grant, R. M. (1991) 'The resource-based theory of competitive advantage: implications for strategy formulation', *California Management Review*, 33: 114–35.

Jarillo, J. C. (1988) 'On strategic networks', *Strategic Management Journal*, 9: 31–41.

Jefferson, G. (1999) 'Are China's rural enterprises outperforming state enterprises? Estimating the public ownership effect', in G. Jefferson and I. Singh (eds), *Enterprise Reform in China: Ownership, Transition and Performance*, Oxford University Press, Oxford.

Johnson, Gerry and Scholes, Kevan (1999) *Exploring Corporate Strategy*, 5th edn, Prentice-Hall, London.

Kay, J. (1993) *Foundations of Corporate Success: How Business Strategies Add Value*, Oxford University Press, New York.

Lee, D. J., Pae, J. H. and Yong, Y. H. (2001) 'A model of close business relationships in China (guanxi)', *European Journal of Marketing*, 35(1–2): 51–69.

Luo, Yadong (1999) 'Environment–strategy–performance relations in small businesses in China: a case of township and village enterprises in Southern China', *Journal of Small Business Management*, 38(1): 37–52.

Miles, R. E. and Snow, C. C. (1986) 'Organisations: new concepts for new forms', *California Management Review*, 28(2): 62–73.

Mintzberg, Henry (1987) 'Crafting strategy', *Harvard Business Review*, July–August, 65(4): 66–75.

Naughton, B. (1992) 'Hierarchy and the bargaining economy: government and enterprise in the reform process', in K. Lieberthal and D. Lampton (eds), *Bureaucracy, Politics and Decision Making in Post-Mao China*, University of California Press, Berkley, CA, pp. 245–79.

Pettigrew, A. (1985) 'Contextualistic research: a natural way to link theory and practice', in E. E. Lawler, A. M. Mohrman, S. A. Mohrman, G. E. Ledford, T. G. Cummings and Associates (eds), *Doing Research that is Useful in Theory and Practice*, Jossey-Bass, San Francisco, CA, pp. 222–48.

Pettigrew, A. (1988) *The Management of Strategic Change*, Basil Blackwell, Oxford.

Pettigrew, A. and Whipp, R. (1991) *Managing Change for Competitive Success*, Blackwell, Oxford.

Pettigrew, A., Ferlie, E. and McKee, L. (1992) *Shaping Strategic Change*. Sage Publications, London.

Porter, M. E. (1980) *Competitive Strategy: Techniques for Analyzing Industries and Competitors*, Free Press, New York.

Powell, W. W. (1990) 'Neither market nor hierarchy', in B. M. Staw and L. L. Cummings (eds), *Network forms of Organisation in Research in Organisational Behaviour*, JA1-Press, Greenwich, CT.

Prahalad, C. K. and Hamel, G. (1990) 'The core competence of the corporation', *Harvard Business Review*, May–June, 79–91.

Provan, K. G. and Millwood, H. B. (1995) 'A preliminary theory of interorganisational network effectiveness', *Administrative Science Quarterly*, 40: 1–33.

Snow, C. C., Miles, R. E. and Coleman, H. J. Jr (1992) 'Managing 21st century network organisations', *Organisational Dynamics*, 21(4): 5–20.

Sydow, J. (1992) 'On the management of strategic networks', in H. Erneste and V. Meier (eds), *Regional Development and Contemporary Industrial Response*, Pinter, London.

Thorelli, H. B. (1986) 'Networks: between markets and hierarchies', *Strategic Management Journal*, 7: 37–51.

Tong, C. (1999) 'Production efficiency and its spacial disparity across China's TVEs', *Journal of Asian Economics*, 10: 415–30.

Tsui, A. S. and Farh, J. L. (1997) 'Where *Guanxi* matters: relational demography and *guanxi* in the Chinese context', *Work and Occupations*, 24: 56–79.

TVEB of Ministry of Agriculture, Animal Husbandry, and Fishery (1986) *Statistical Materials of TVEs (1978–1985)*, Mimeo, Xinhua Publishing House, Beijing.

TVEB of Ministry of Agriculture, Animal Husbandry, and Fishery (1987) *Selection of Policies and Statutes concerning TVEs, 1979–1985 (xiangzhen qiye zhengce fagui xuanbian)*, Xinhua Publishing House, Beijing.

US Embassy. Available at http://www.usembassy-china.org.cn/econ/smes2002.html

Webb, D. and Pettigrew, A. (1999) 'Temporal development of strategies', *Organisational Science*, 10(5): 601–21.

Weitzman, Martin L. and Xu, Chenggang (1994) 'Chinese township–village enterprises as vaguely defined cooperatives', *Journal of Comparative Economics*, 18(2): 121–45.

Wheelen, T. L. and Hunger, J. D. (1998) *Strategic Management and Business Policy: Entering 21st Century Global Society*, 6th edn, Addison-Wesley, Reading, MA.

Yang, Mayfair (1994) *Gifts, Favors, and Banquets: The Art of Social Relationships in China*, Cornell University Press, Ithaca, NY.

7 Value creation in Chinese and European business relationships

Ian Wilkinson and Kevin Yeoh

The strategic importance of business relations to a firm's performance and competitive advantage is being increasingly recognised but most of the research has focused on Western business contexts. Here European and Chinese business relations are compared in terms of a model of value creation. We briefly review the literature on Chinese business relations and compare it to the Western contexts. Then we develop, from a supplier's perspective, a model of value creation in terms of relationship functions. This model is tested using data from the Industrial Marketing and Purchasing (IMP2) database which gathered extensive data concerning the nature of business relationships in Europe as well as China. Rather than a common underlying model, different models emerge for the Chinese and the European samples. The results confirm the importance of trust and social bonding in facilitating relationship functions and value creation in both the Chinese and European contexts. Trust is particularly relevant in the fulfillment of indirect or network functions. The management implications of the results as well as the directions in future research are discussed.

Introduction

Western firms entering the Chinese market face various types of problems because business systems there do not necessarily operate in the same manner as they do in the West. These differences stem in part from the way the Chinese business has evolved from a centrally planned system to a more market directed one in which central and regional governments still play a powerful role and from the effects of cultural differences. Much has been written about the nature of Chinese business and its implications for foreign firms entering the market and other chapters review and discuss this literature in this book. Our focus here is on the nature and function of inter-firm buyer–seller relations in China, the extent to which they operate in similar or different ways to such business relations in the West and what this means for firms entering the Chinese market.

The role and impact of business relationships and networks on a firm's performance and competitive advantage have been subjects of increasing interest in business and marketing practice and research (e.g. Anderson *et al.*, 1994; Kanter, 1994; Dyer and Singh, 1998; Ford *et al.*, 2003). Longer term, cooperative relations with suppliers, customers, distributors, technological partners, complementors and even competitors are being recognised as being of strategic importance because they provide direct and indirect access to key resources, skills and knowledge controlled by others and because of the way valuable resources are co-created through business relations and networks (e.g. Axelsson and Easton, 1992; Håkansson and Snehota, 1995; Brandenburger and Nalebuff, 1997; Roy *et al.*, 2004). Such relations and networks provide sustainable resource advantages because they are difficult for competitors to appropriate or copy.

Most research on the role and impact of business relations has been conducted in the contexts of Western business and the question arises as to whether Chinese business relations operate in similar ways to the West? What is the role and importance of long-term cooperative relations between and with Chinese firms compared to the West. For example, Ambler and Styles (2003) examine the relevance of transactional vs relational approaches to marketing in a highly relational society like China and argue that both types can and do coexist. Do the same factors shape the development and functioning of relations in Western business contexts? The research reported here addresses these issues by comparing the results of a comprehensive study of buyer–seller business relations carried out in Europe and China.

The rest of the chapter is organised as follows. First, we briefly review previous research concerning the nature and role of relations and networks in Chinese business and compare this to the Western business contexts. Next, a model of value creation in business relations from a supplier's perspective is proposed, in terms of the types of functions relations can perform. Then the data base used to test this model in European and Chinese business contexts is described, followed by the results. We conclude by discussing the implications for research and management of our results.

Relations in Chinese business

Guanxi is a pervasive and important element of Chinese society and business (Redding, 1990; Kao, 1993; Davies, 1995; Luo, 1997). '*Guan*' means 'door' and 'to close up', while '*xi*' means to 'tie up'. If A has '*guan*' with B and B with C, contact is possible between A and C via introductions and favours are stored, remembered and returned when necessary. *Guanxi* functions like insurance as to the reliability and reputation of others through referrals and past interactions (Ambler, 1995) and is rooted in family, hometown, school or workplace ties (Jacobs, 1982; Kipnis, 1997). It creates indebtedness in terms of social obligations or *renqing*, which is a form of social capital (Yang, 1994; Yeung and Tung, 1996). *Guanxi* networks have been identified as a key reason for the success of overseas Chinese business empires (Wong, 1992; Chu, 1996). But, this may be changing as a result of the opening up of the Chinese economy and the increasing amount of interaction between Chinese and Western business (Wu, 1994).

Is *guanxi* unique to the Chinese? Much research on business relations in the West emphasises the important role played by personal and social relations (Kirkbride *et al.*, 1991; Wu, 1994; Bjorkman and Kock, 1995; Ambler, 1995). Davies (1995) compares *guanxi* to the old-boy network, although such personal networks can be seen as more problematic than advantageous in the West, as indicated in words like 'nepotism', 'pork-barrel politics' or 'jobs for the boys' (MacInnis, 1993).

In order to examine the extent to which Chinese and Western business relations function in similar or different ways, we develop a model of value creation in business relations which we test using a sample of European and Chinese business relations.

Value creation and the functions of business relationships

A transaction is an exchange of values for mutual advantage and a relationship involves a pattern of transactions over time in which the values exchanged may be understood in terms of the functions of the relationship for each party involved. Two types of relationship functions may be distinguished – direct and indirect (Anderson *et al.*, 1994; Håkansson and Snehota, 1995; Walter *et al.*, 2001). Direct value comes from the relationship itself in the form of profits, knowledge and resources. Indirect value comes from the way a relationship plays a role in a wider network of relations, such as a distributor providing access to particular customers and markets, or a relationship with a supplier or technology partner being a means of accessing particular technologies.

Here we focus on the value or function of relationships from a supplier's perspective, using a classification proposed by Walter *et al.* (2001). Whereas suppliers have to offer value to their customers in the form of competitive products and services in order to gain and retain them, they also need to gain benefits from the customer.

Four direct functions are identified. The *profit function* refers to customer relations contributing directly to profits because the revenue generated exceeds the costs to serve them. The *volume function*, is the contribution a customer makes to reducing a firm's overall costs by helping it to better utilise its capacity and achieve economies of scale. The *safeguard function* refers to customers maintained as an 'insurance against crises or difficulties with other customers' (Walter *et al.*, 2001), such as an outlet for excess stock and remaindered items, not necessarily on favourable terms.

The *innovation function* is when customers are a valuable source of new product, process and service ideas. This can arise directly from interactions with the customer as new problems are identified and products and services are adapted, particularly when the customer is a lead user (Von Hippel, 1986; Lilien *et al.*, 2002). It can also be an indirect or network function stemming from the way a customer is connected to other firms and information channels, such as the customers and markets for its own outputs.

A second indirect function is the *market function* when customers support the development of new markets and commercial relations for a supplier in the form of referrals or reputation effects. The third indirect function is the *scout function* in which customers are a source of market information as a result of their other relations and information channels, such as information about marketing strategies of competitors. The *access function* refers to the way a customer acts as a bridge or go-between to gain access to relevant organisations such as government agencies and financial institutions.

The study of inter-firm relations has identified a number of dimensions of relations that are likely to affect relationship, conduct and performance and impact on relationship functions. As relationships move through different stages, the relative importance of different functions will vary (Spencer *et al.*, 1996; Wilkinson and Young, 2001). Initially, business transactions may be small and a lack of trust may inhibit knowledge sharing. Here the customer is valuable because of actual or potential revenues accruing from their orders. Safeguard customer relations may never develop beyond this simple form even though the firms continue to do business periodically. As a relationship develops, indirect functions become more likely as trust and greater mutual understanding develops. A satisfied customer can be a source of innovative ideas, of market referrals and access to new markets (Reichheld and Sasser, 1990). Adaptations take place in products, services and operations leading to stronger activity links, resource ties and actor bonds resulting in further value creation through reduced costs and improved quality (Håkansson and Snehota, 1995). Here we focus on three dimensions of business relations that limit or enable the development of relationship functions and hence relationship value, that is, social bonds, trust and commitment.

Social bonds, the personal relationships that develop in business can play an important role in relationship development and success (Anderson and Weitz, 1989; Wilson and Jantrania, 1995). They add to the cooperative nature of a relationship, reducing opportunism (Morgan and Hunt, 1994), act as a switching barrier (Storbacka *et al.*, 1994) and promote relationship continuation (Naudé and Buttle, 2000).

Personal relations may be less important in business relations in the West. For example, Rodriguez and Wilson (1995) found that American managers viewed socialisation as 'unimportant' and of 'no purpose' in the development of long-term business relationships, whereas the importance of social interaction is often stressed in the development of close relationships in Chinese society (Goodwin and Tang, 1993). Mavondo and Rodrigo (2001) found that social bonding in Chinese relationships is central to the formation of a business relationship and was an antecedent of other relationship dimensions. Hence, it is proposed that social bonds directly affect trust and commitment as well as relationship functions.

Trust is an integral part of any long-term business relationship (Crosby *et al.*, 1990; Moorman *et al.*, 1993; Morgan and Hunt, 1994; Garbarino and Johnson, 1999) and may be defined as 'the perception of confidence in an exchange partner's reliability and integrity' (Morgan and Hunt, 1994: 23). Trust affects the level of cooperation and long-term orientation in relations (Ganesan, 1994; Morgan and Hunt, 1994; Iacobucci and Hibbard, 1999) which should translate into the development of a richer assortment of relationship functions.

Research suggests that the nature and role of trust in business relations may differ in Western and Eastern cultures. For example, Rodriguez and Wilson (1995) found that the emotional component of trust did not affect trusting behaviour in an individualistic culture like America, while it did for a collectivist one such as China. Sako and Helper (1998) found three dimensions of trust in a Japanese sample, that is opportunism, goodwill and competence-trust, but only one in the

United States. In China, a sharp divide exists between in and out groups in terms of who they trust (Redding, 1990; Fukuyama, 1995). Thus Leung (1988) finds that the Chinese from Hong Kong were more likely to sue a stranger than were Americans, whereas Li (1992) reports that, compared to the Americans, the Chinese regarded strangers as less likeable, less likely to be from the same group and less fair.

Commitment exists when parties are focussed on the continuation of the relationship and involves cognitive, affective and behaviour dimensions (Anderson and Weitz, 1992; Sharma *et al.*, 2001). Firms with a short-term orientation are more likely to focus on direct functions and to try to maximise profits in discrete transactions (Ganesan, 1994).

Eastern collectivist cultures are portrayed as more long-term oriented (Hofstede, 1994; Triandis, 1995) and Yau (1988) notes that *guanxi* incorporates elements of long-term orientation such as 'continuity' and 'past-time'. Conflict is to be avoided in relationships emphasising continuity through the reciprocation of favours and benefits. 'Past-time' refers to the shadow of the past that is difficult to break in an established relationship and to rebuild a broken relationship with Chinese (Mavondo and Rodrigo, 2001).

The resulting model of relationship value and its determinants is summarised in Figure 7.1.

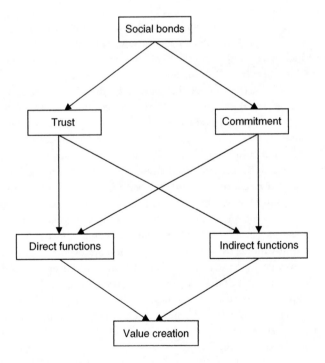

Figure 7.1 A model of value creation in business relations.

Methodology

The model was tested using a database of trade relations from Europe and the PRC developed by the Industrial Marketing and Purchasing (IMP) group as part of the IMP2 project. The IMP group comprises an international group of researchers whose contribution and history is described elsewhere (Håkansson and Snehota, 2000; Wilkinson, 2001; McLoughlin and Horan, 2002). A comprehensive, structured questionnaire was used to gather data on samples of international and domestic business relations in a number of countries.

Samples

In Europe, locally based researchers in various European countries conducted interviews with industrial suppliers about a self-defined important customer relationship. The resulting sample comprises 136 customer relations from firms in Germany, France and Sweden, spread over 7 customer countries (France 23.5 per cent, the Untied Kingdom 16.2 per cent, Germany 14 per cent, Sweden 14 per cent, Italy 13.2 per cent the United States 10.3 per cent and Japan 6.6 per cent). The supplier companies in the study belong to different industries, ranging from raw materials to equipment. Interviews were conducted with the marketing executive most responsible for the relationship.

The questionnaire was translated into Chinese and back translated to establish equivalence (Dawson *et al.*, 1997) and interviews were conducted with a sample of Chinese suppliers by the China Statistics Bureau. The sampling frame was based on the 'Third Industrial Census' and the 'First National Basic Business Census' developed by the China Statistics Bureau. For the purpose of sampling, the frame was stratified into Northern (Beijing as the center), Eastern (Shanghai as the center), Southern (Guangdong as the center) and Middlewestern (Sichuan and Chongqing as the representatives) regions and a target sample size of 100 was set-based on interview costs. Approximately 200 suppliers in each region were selected for the initial sample, including Sino-foreign joint ventures, large-sized industrial enterprises, and those involved in import and export. The specific respondent was determined by telephone pre-interview. Interviews continued until the target sample size of 100 was achieved. The weighted response rate was 15.7 per cent, which is to be expected, considering the extensive nature of the questionnaire, which took up to two hours to complete.

The Chinese sample comprised of 50 per cent state-owned firms, 35 per cent joint ventures, 4 per cent Chinese owned and 3 per cent foreign owned. Eight per cent did not specify their ownership structure. The sample was spread over 32 different countries, including the United States 14 per cent, Japan 10 per cent and Hong Kong 11 per cent. 49 per cent of customers were from the Asian region, 37 per cent from Western countries (including 19 per cent from Europe), 6 per cent were from South America and 8 per cent were unspecified.

It should be noted that the average duration of the European relationships is 22 years, compared to 5 for Chinese relationships. This is because Chinese firms have only been able to form direct relations with foreign counterparts since the opening up of the Chinese economy.

Measures

The items used to measure each construct are shown in Table 7.1 together with the alphas for the European and Chinese samples. Relationship functions were operationalised by asking respondents to rate their agreement with statements describing the importance of the customer using a five-point scale from strongly disagree (1) to strongly agree (5). Relationship value creation is measured in terms of the perceived profitability, given all costs and revenues, of the relationship over the last five years, using a scale from (1) very bad to (5) very good as in previous studies (Blankenburg *et al.*, 1996, 1999; Walter *et al.*, 2001). The relationship dimensions were measured in terms of respondent's agreement with various statements about the relationship, using a scale from (1) strongly disagree to (5) strongly agree. Items that did not have strong-item total correlations, were deleted.

In the Chinese data, the construct of commitment was not captured well. Commitment was also problematic in the translation of the questionnaire (Dawson *et al.*, 1997). The translation revealed that 'commitment' is translated as 'obligation,' which may in part account for differences in reliability.

Cases with large numbers of missing values were deleted from the sample. This gave final samples of 81 for China and 92 for Europe. Missing values were replaced with the mean value of similar items measured on the same individual (Hulland *et al.*, 1996).

Table 7.1 Measures of model constructs

Construct	Measures	Cronbach Alpha	
		Chinese	*Europe*
Social bonds	We usually make an effort to establish personal contacts with people in the customer's company We have excellent personal relations on a social level with people from the customer	0.74	0.84
Trust	We feel we can trust this customer completely We have full confidence in the information provided to us from this customer	0.67	0.93
Commitment	This customer is committed to a long-term relationship with us We are strongly committed to this customer	0.61	0.86
Innovation function	• Important partner in technical development • Source of product technology ideas for us	0.84	0.65
Market funtion	• Bridgehead for expansion in customer country • Bridgehead for expansion in other countries	0.86	0.70
Scout function	• Relationship enhances our image (standing) in *that* country • Relationship enhances our image (standing) in *other* countries	0.84	0.65
Access function	• Gives access to other organisations in *that* country • Gives access to other organisations in *other* countries	0.92	0.82

Results

First, we examined the equivalence of the measures used in each sample using methods described by Mullen (1995) and Singh (1995). Confirmatory-factor analysis (CFA) supports factor similarity in terms of the pattern of factor loadings. But, a comparison of results for models in which the measures are constrained to be equal or allowed to vary across the samples, shows that there are significant differences between the two samples. Further analysis shows that the measures of relationship dimensions are not equivalent but the measures of relationship functions do not differ significantly. This has to be taken into account in interpreting the results.

The original model has a poor fit for the Chinese sample, with a normalised fit index (NFI) of 0.43 (χ^2 = 29.81, df = 5, p < 0.001, GFI = 0.88). The modification indices suggested that the model would improve if direct paths were established with trust → value creation and social bonds → value creation. Both were considered as theoretically acceptable and the modified model, shown in Figure 7.2a, has a good fit (NFI = 0.93, χ^2 = 4.0, df = 3, p = 0.27; GFI = 0.88). Significant paths exist between trust and value creation, social bonds and trust, between commitment, trust and indirect functions and commitment and direct functions.

The original model is a very good fit for the European data (NFI = 0.92, χ^2 = 2.7, df = 43, p = 0.67; GFI = 0.99) and is shown in Figure 7.2b. None of the direct paths from the relationship dimensions to value creation are significant.

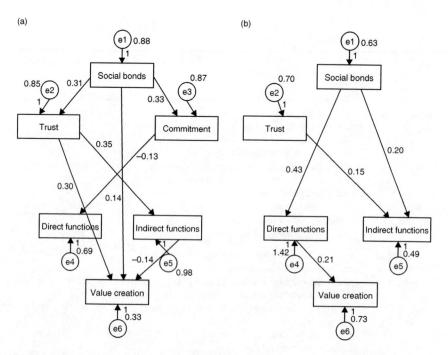

Figure 7.2 Final Chinese and European path models. (a) Chinese model and (b) European model.

The significant paths are between direct functions and value creation, direct and indirect functions and social bonding and trust and indirect functions.

Discussion

Social bonds are significant in the Chinese and European models, which goes against claims that managers in Western countries do not consider social bonding as an integral part of business relationships (Rodriguez and Wilson, 1995; Iacobucci and Ostrom, 1996). For the Chinese sample, social bonds directly relate to trust and commitment, which supports previous findings (Ambler, 1995; Mavondo and Rodrigo, 2001). Social bonds are also linked directly to value creation, which supports the role social bonds play in economic performance and is in accord with other results linking *guanxi* and business performance (Luo, 1997; Park and Luo, 1997).

In the Chinese sample social bonding is linked directly to value creation, while in the European sample, social bonding links to the fulfillment of relationship functions. This could be a sign of more collectivist goals in the Chinese sample (Chen *et al.*, 1998). Trust seems to play a more significant role in the Chinese sample and is linked to the fulfillment of indirect functions in both samples but not to direct functions. This makes sense because indirect functions require more intense collaboration and interaction between buyers and sellers, which make trust important.

While commitment was not significantly related to any other variable in the European sample, it was found to have a negative relationship with direct functions in the Chinese sample. This may be a spurious relation, reflecting the nature of the Chinese sample, which comprises more short-term relations. More recently developed relations may be the most valuable in terms of direct functions but commitment is still low because the suppliers have had less time to get to know their overseas customers who are still be considered as relative 'outsiders' (Fukuyama, 1995). Hence the relationship is more transaction-oriented. Older relations are not so profitable but there is more commitment.

Trust plays a more significant role in the Chinese sample, which could be due to the European relations being more established and is consistent with the results of research by Grayson and Ambler (1999). In a study of advertising agencies and their clients, they found that trust was less influential in longer term relationships. This may be because a long-term relationship requires the existence of a certain level of trust and therefore the amount of variance in trust in such relations is dampened. In the European sample, (mean duration 22.5 years), trust has already been established and hence is no longer an issue. Further, as the relationships have been established for a long time, commitment has no detectable impact on the relationship functions.

We considered adding duration to the model, as a proxy for stage of relationship development, but it is not highly correlated with any other variable in the Chinese sample, which is not surprising given the limited time that there has been for these relations to develop. In the European sample, this was also the case, except for direct functions, suggesting that the longer a relationship lasts, the more important are the direct functions. We also tried to match the two samples in terms of duration, but this was not possible due to non-overlapping distributions between the two samples.

Previous research has found that the direct and indirect functions both have significant and positive effects on value creation (Walter et al., 2001). Our results, for both samples, do not support this. In the European sample, direct functions have a significant effect on value creation but indirect functions have none. This is surprising because, given the established nature of the European relationships, it would be reasonable to assume that the indirect functions would be more important. The value-creation measure might be a problem and some have treated it as a measure of the direct profit function (Wilkinson and Young, 2001). Future research should seek to further define and clarify value creation and its measurement in order to capture both short-term and long-term value. Of course this result could reflect the short-term transactional motives or individualistic goals of Western business practices (Chen et al., 1998).

In the Chinese sample, the indirect functions were found to have a significant, but negative, relationship with value creation. This suggests that value in terms of profit, may be being sacrificed in return for the longer term benefits of indirect functions. This is plausible given the fact that Chinese firms are relatively new to international markets and may seek out and value more the learning and network development of their international relations more. Indeed, long-term orientation is a dimension added to Hostede's cultural dimensions as a result of including the Chinese people in his sample.

Conclusions

Our results confirm the importance of trust and social bonding in facilitating relationship functions and value creation. For managers this suggests the need to take steps to identify those Chinese counterparts who are capable of providing functions of strategic importance (particularly indirect functions) and to try to develop strong social bonds with them as a basis for cooperation. This is easier said than done because it is difficult to assess in advance the extent to which another firm will make a valuable partner and with whom a cooperative, trusting working relation can be established. For this reason potential partners are selected mainly from within existing networks of relations, including firms with whom some form of previous relationship exists or they are introduced via a trusted partner. Research in Chinese and Western contexts shows this tendency (Li and Rowley, 2002; Wong and Ellis, 2002).

Another problem is that selecting a partner is not just about choosing but also about getting chosen. Value creation is a two-way process and it is far easier to form a partnership with a firm that also wants to form a partnership with you! This depends on being able to convince a counterpart of the strategic value of your potential contribution to the relationship and demonstrating that you can be trusted and are cooperative, which reinforces reliance on existing networks of business and personal relations.

The long-term existence of a relationship requires both partners to understand the value-creating functions within their relationship and how to effectively share and balance value-creation with their partners and wider network. An unbalanced assortment of functions may undermine the long-term viability of a relationship, but there is little research addressing this issue. Most research tends to focus on relationship value from one partner's perspective only. More studies of value sharing (Wilson, 1995) and the 'functional balance' within a relationship (Young and Wilkinson, 1997) are required, especially of the way these develop over time in relations involving participants from different cultures.

Finally, firms face problems in developing a cooperative relationship with counterparts if their previous relations have been adversarial and opportunistic, even though these are the firms they are familiar with (e.g. Corbett *et al.*, 1999).

Even after strong bonds have been developed, ultimately trust is the most important relational variable. This implies that a successful ongoing relationship and greater access to the *guanxiwang* must be carefully nurtured. Managers shouldn't assume that simply singing a few songs at karaoke and drinking copious amounts of rice wine will ensure a successful and culturally sensitive relationship, it is also a matter of demonstrating cooperativeness and trustworthiness through business action over time.

Social bonds are linked to the fulfillment of direct and indirect functions in the European context. This is further evidence of the role and value of personal relationships as a means of enhancing business cooperation and trust, not just in the East, but also in the West. It is no surprise that trust is linked strongly to the fulfillment of indirect functions. The greater the trust, the more likely is a customer to engage in actions of potential value to a supplier, such as divulging market-sensitive information, introducing new customers, or even collaborating in innovation or product development.

While our research has provided some insights into the nature and role of relations in Chinese vs Western business contexts, there is much more that needs to be done. Our research is constrained by the measures contained in the IMP2 questionnaire, which were developed in a Western context and the sampling methods used. Thus, measures of relationship dimensions previously found to exist in Asian relationships, such as face and reciprocity (Mavondo and Rodrigo, 2001) were not included. Problems also exist in terms of measure equivalence between the samples for the relationship dimensions. This is an area requiring further attention. Although translation equivalence (Mullen, 1995) was broadly established, the concept of *commitment* was not captured well and was translated in terms of *obligation*, which is a potentially important dimension of Chinese business relations (Redding, 1990) and suggests the need to include an additional theoretical construct into the model (Dawson *et al.*, 1997).

It has been common in the relational literature for researchers to investigate international business relationships through the direct replication of Western constructs. However, this Western-centric approach is flawed as it fails to understand the true essence of international or cross-contextual factors (Mavondo and Rodrigo, 2001). Brislin *et al.* (1973) note that often an approach that is meant to be etic, is in fact emic or 'pseudo-etic'. For example, a Western researcher may unknowingly propose that universal measures of good relationships should include dimensions of openness, closeness and empathy. It is possible that cultures like Japan or China might find such openness, crude and insensitive (Dawson *et al.*, 1997). Cross-cultural researchers suggest that etic constructs be operationalised using emic concepts (Mintu *et al.*, 1994;

Sperber *et al.*, 1994) and future research should try to develop measures from a Chinese perspective.

Lastly, as noted, the value-creation measure is suspect and may be more a measure of the value of short-term direct functions only. Single item measures have also been used for the direct functions.

References

Ambler, T. (1995) 'The derivation of guanxi', *Marketing Management*, 4(1): 27.

Ambler, T. and Styles, C. (2003) 'The co-existence of transaction and relational marketing: insights from the Chinese business context', *Journal of Business Research*, 32: 633–42.

Anderson, E. and Weitz, B. (1989) 'Determinants of continuity in conventional industrial channel dyads', *Marketing Science*, 8(4): 310–23.

Anderson, E. W. and Weitz, B. (1992) 'The use of pledges to build and sustain commitment in distribution channels', *Journal of Marketing Research*, 29(1): 18–34.

Anderson, J. C., Håkansson, H. and Johanson, J. (1994) 'Dyadic business relationships within a business network context', *Journal of Marketing*, 58(4): 1–15.

Axelsson, B. and Easton, G. (eds) (1992) *Industrial Networks: A New View of Reality*, London: Routledge.

Bjorkman, I. and Kock, S. (1995) 'Social relationships and business networks: the case of western companies in China', *International Business Review*, 4(4): 519–55.

Blankenburg, Holm D., Eriksson, K. and Johanson, J. (1996) 'Business networks and cooperation in international business relationships', *Journal of International Business Studies*, 27(5): 1033–53.

Blankenburg, Holm D., Eriksson, K. and Johanson, J. (1999) 'Creating value through mutual commitment to business network relationships', *Strategic Management Journal*, 20: 467–86.

Brandenburger, A. M. and Nalebuff, B. J. (1997) *Co-opetition*, New York: DoubleDay.

Brislin, R. W., Lonner, W. J. and Thorndike, R. M. (1973) *Cross-cultural Research Methods*, New York: John Wiley.

Chen, C. C., Chen, X. P. and Meindl, J. R. (1998) 'How can cooperation be fostered? The cultural effects of individualism – collectivism', *The Academy of Management Review*, 23(2): 285–304.

Chu, P. (1996) 'Social network models of overseas chinese entrepreneurship: the experience in Hong Kong and Canada', *Canadian Journal of Administrative Sciences*, 13(4): 358–65.

Corbett, C. J., Blackburn, J. D. and van Wassenhove, L. K. (1999) 'Case study: partnerships to improve supply chains', *Sloan Management Review*, 40(4): 71–82.

Crosby, L. A., Evans, K. R. and Cowles, D. (1990) 'Relationship quality in services selling: an interpersonal influence perspective', *Journal of Marketing*, 54(3): 68–81.

Davies, H. (1995) 'Interpreting guanxi: the role of personal connections in a high context transitional economy', in H. Davies (ed.), *China Business: Context and Issues*, Asia: Longman, pp. 155–69.

Dawson, B., Young, L. C. and Wilkinson, I. F. (1997) 'Experiences in the linguistic and cultural translation of a business questionnaire into chinese', paper presented at the Sixth Symposium on Cross-Cultural Consumer and Business Studies, Honolulu: Hawaii.

Dyer, J. and Singh, H. (1998) 'The relational view: cooperative strategy and sources of inter-organizational competitive advantage', *Academy of Management Review*, 23: 660–79.

Ford, D., Gadde, L.-E., Håkansson, H. and Snehota, I. (2003) *Managing Business Relationships*, 2nd edn, Chichester: Wiley.

Fukuyama, F. (1995) *Trust*, London: Penguin.

Ganesan, S. (1994) 'Determinants of long-term orientation in buyer–seller relationships', *Journal of Marketing*, 58(2): 1–19.

Garbarino, E. and Johnson, M. S. (1999) 'The different roles of satisfaction, trust, and commitment in customer relationships', *Journal of Marketing*, 63(2): 70–87.

Goodwin, R. and Tang, C. S. (1993) 'Chinese personal relationships', in Michael Harris Bond (ed.), *The Handbook of Chinese Psychology*, Oxford: Oxford University Press, pp. 294–308.

Grayson, K. and Ambler, T. (1999) 'The dark side of long-term relationships in marketing services', *Journal of Marketing Research*, 36(1): 132–41.

Håkansson, H. and Snehota, I. (1995) *Developing Relationships in Business Networks*, London: Routledge.

Håkansson, H. and Snehota, I. (2000) 'IMP perspective on relationship marketing', in J. Sheth and A. Parvatiyar (eds), *Handbook of Relationship Marketing*, Thousand Oaks, CA: Sage: 69–93.

Hofstede, G. (1994) 'The business of international business is culture', *International Business Review*, 3(1): 1–14.

Hulland, J., Chow, Y. H. and Lam, S. (1996) 'Use of causal models in marketing research: a review', *International Journal of Research in Marketing*, 13: 181–97.

Iacobucci, D. and Hibbard, J. (1999) 'Toward an encompassing theory of business marketing relationships (BMRS) and interpersonal commercial relationships (ICRS): an empirical generalisation', *Journal of Interactive Marketing*, 13(3): 13–33.

Iacobucci, D. and Ostrom, A. (1996) 'Commercial and interpersonal relationships: using the structure of interpersonal relationships to understand individual–individual, individual-to-firm, and firm-to-firm relationships in commerce', *International Journal of Research in Marketing*, 13(1): 53–72.

Jacobs, J. B. (1982) 'The concept of *guanxi* and local politics in a rural chinese cultural setting', in S. Greenblatt, R. Wilson and A. Wilson (eds), *Social Interaction in Chinese Society*, New York: Praeger, pp. 209–36.

Kanter, R. M. (1994) 'Collaborative advantage: the art of alliances', *Harvard Business Review*, 72(4): 96–108.

Kao, J. (1993) 'The worldwide web of Chinese business', *Harvard Business Review*, 71(2): 24–36.

Kipnis, A. (1997) *Producing Guanxi: Sentiment, Self, and Subculture in a North China village*, Durham, NC: Duke University Press.

Kirkbride, P. S., Tang, S. F. Y. and Westwood, R. I. (1991) 'Chinese conflict preferences and negotiating behaviour: cultural and psychological influences', *Organizational Studies*, 12: 365–86.

Leung, K. (1988) 'Some determinants of conflict avoidance', *Journal of Cross-Cultural Psychology*, 19: 125–36.

Li, M. C. (1992) 'Cultural difference and in-group favoritism: a comparison of Chinese and American college students', [in Chinese] *Bulletin of the Institute of Ethnology, Academia Sinica*, 83: 153–90.

Li, S. X. and Rowley, T. J. (2002) 'Inertia and evaluation mechanisms in interorganizational partner selection: syndicate formation among U.S. Investment banks', *Academy of Management Review*, 45(6): 1104–19.

Lilien, G. L., Morrison, P. D., Searls, K., Sonnack, M. and von Hippel, E. (2002) 'Performance assessment of the lead user idea generation process', *Management Science*, 48(8): 1042–59.

Luo, Y. (1997) '*Guanxi* and performance of foreign-invested enterprises in China: an empirical inquiry', *Management International Review*, 37(1): 51–70.

MacInnis, P. (1993) '*Guanxi* or contract: a way to understand and predict conflict between Chinese and Western senior managers in China-based joint ventures', in D. McCarty and S. Hille (eds), *Research on Multinational Business Management and Internationalisation of Chinese Enterprises*, Nanjing: Nanjing University, pp. 345–51.

McLoughlin, D. and Horan, C. (2002) 'Notes on a unique understanding', *Journal of Business Research*, 55(7): 535–43.

Mavondo, F. T. and Rodrigo, E. M. (2001) 'The effect of relationship dimensions on interpersonal and interorganizational commitment in organizations conducting business between Australia and China', *Journal of Business Research*, 52(2): 111–21.

Mintu, A. T., Calantone, R. J. and Gassenheimer, J. B. (1994) 'Towards improving cross-cultural research: extending Churchill's research paradigm', *Journal of International Consumer Marketing*, 7(2): 5–23.

Moorman, C., Deshpandé, R. and Zaltman, G. (1993) 'Factors affecting trust in market relationships', *Journal of Marketing*, 57(1): 81–101.

Morgan R. M. and Hunt, S. D. (1994) 'The commitment-trust theory of relationship marketing', *Journal of Marketing*, 58(3): 20–38.

Mullen, M. R. (1995) 'Diagnosing measurement equivalence in cross-national research', *Journal of International Business Studies*, 26(3): 573–96.

Naudé, P. and Buttle, F. (2000) 'Assessing relationship quality', *Industrial Marketing Management*, 29: 351–61.

Park, S. H. and Luo, Y. (1997) '*Guanxi* and organizational dynamics: organizational networking in chinese firms', *Strategic Management Journal*, 22: 455–77.

Redding, S. G. (1990) *The Spirit of Chinese Capitalism*, Berlin and New York: de Gruyter.

Reichheld, F. F. and Sasser, W. (1990) 'Zero defections: quality comes to services', *Harvard Business Review*, 68(5): 105–11.

Rodriguez, C. M. and Wilson, D. T. (1995) *Trust me!!! . . . But how?*, Institute for the Study of Business Markets, Pennsylvania State University, Pennsylvania, PA.

Roy, Subroto, Sivakumar, K. and Wilkinson, Ian F. (2004) 'Innovation generation in supply chain relationships – a conceptual model and research propositions', *Journal of the Academy of Marketing Science*, 32(1): 61–79.

Sako, M. and Helper, S. (1998) 'Determinants of trust in supplier relations: evidence from the automotive industry in Japan and the United States', *Journal of Economic Behavior and Organization*, 34: 387–417.

Sharma, N., Young, L. and Wilkinson, I. (2001) 'The structure of relationship commitment in interfirm relationships', paper presented at the seventeenth Industrial Marketing and Purchasing Conference, Oslo, Norway.

Singh, J. (1995) 'Measurement issues in cross-national research', *Journal of International Business Studies*, 26(3): 597–619.

Spencer, R., Wilkinson, I. F. and Young, L. C. (1996) 'A cross country comparative study of the nature and function of interfirm relations in domestic and international industrial markets', paper presented at the International Conference on Relationship Marketing, Humboldt-Universitat to Berlin, 29–31 March.

Sperber, A. D., DeVellis, R. F. and Boehlecke, B. (1994) 'Cross cultural translation – methodology and validation', *Journal of Cross-Cultural Psychology*, 25: 501–24.

Storbacka, K., Strandvik, T. and Grönroos, C. (1994) 'Managing customer relationships for a profit: the dynamics of relationship quality', *International Journal of Service Industry Management*, 5(5): 21–38.

Triandis, H. C. (1995) *Individualism and Collectivism*, Boulder, CO: Westview Press.

von Hippel, E. (1986) 'Lead users: a source of novel product concepts', *Management Science*, 32(7): 791–805.

Walter, A., Ritter, T. and Gemünden, H. G. (2001) 'Value creation in buyer–seller relationships', *Industrial Marketing Management*, 30: 365–77.

Wilkinson, I. F. (2001) 'A history of channels and network thinking in marketing in the 20th century', *Australasian Marketing Journal*, 9(2): 23–53.

Wilkinson, I. F. and Young, L. C. (2001) 'Antecedents of relationship functions in international industrial markets: a cross cultural analysis', paper presented at *ANZMAC Conference*, Massey University: New Zealand, 3–5 December.

Wilson, D. T. and Jantrania, S. (1995) 'Understanding the value of a relationship', *Asia–Australia Marketing Journal*, 2(1): 55–66.

Wong, P. L.-K. and Ellis, Paul (2002) 'Social ties and partner identification in Sino-Hong Kong international joint ventures', *Journal of International Business*, 33(2): 267–89.

Wong, S. L. (1992) 'Business networks, cultural values and the state in Hong Kong and Singapore', paper presented at the meeting of the Third Soka University Pacific Basin Symposium, Singapore.

Wu, W. P. (1994) '*Guanxi* and its managerial implications for western firms in China: a case study', paper presented at the *International Conference on Management Issues for China in the 1990s*, University of Cambridge, Cambridge.

Yang, Mayfair (1994) *Gifts, Favors and Banquets: the Art of Social Relationships in China*, New York: Cornell University Press.

Yau, O. H. M. (1988) 'Chinese cultural values: their dimensions and marketing implications', *European Journal of Marketing*, 22(5): 44–57.

Yeung, I. Y. and Tung, R.L. (1996) 'Achieving business success in Confucian societies: the importance of *guanxi*', *Organizational Dynamics*, 3: 54–65.

Young, L. and Wilkinson, I. F. (1997) 'The space between: towards a typology of interfirm relations', *Journal of Business to Business Marketing*, 4(2): 53–97.

8 *Guanxi*, relationship marketing and business strategy

Yunyan Li, Martin F. Parnell and Nick Hawkins

The focus is on the practicality of turning *guanxi* into a more structured relationship marketing approach. The argument proceeds in five stages: (i) definition and analysis of relationship marketing, and *guanxi*; (ii) exploration of the relevance of, and connections between, the concepts and the reality of small- and medium-sized enterprises/township and village enterprises (SMEs/TVEs and private ones); (iii) combining the analyses of (i) and (ii) in the case study of JIDE Electrical Appliance Co. Ltd, and the household electrical appliances industry within which it operates, we focus on the relationship of *guanxi* to strategy; (iv) extrapolating from (iii): presentation of a new, broader, theoretical model combining *guanxi* and relationship marketing, emphasizing the centrality of market orientation and offering a justification of relationship marketing as the core element of future strategy; (v) the conclusion shows how one company, JIDE, in the context of sharper competition, has evolved through strategies of product orientation, production orientation to market orientation. The analytical framework developed clarifies the relationship between *guanxi* and relationship marketing, revealing the former's deficiencies and indicating the latter's advantages, not the least in identifying and cultivating long-term business relationships on a sustained, professional basis. The framework also provides support for (a) how serving customers well depends crucially on a company's capacity for learning and education and on (b) the necessity to develop new products for consolidating core competences.

Introduction

This chapter analyses the nature of the relationship between a general, ubiquitous phenomenon in the Chinese-speaking world *guanxi*, and the relatively new, specific phenomenon of relationship marketing. Such an analysis is pertinent for at least two reasons: first, to explore the extent of theoretical and practical links between what appear to be cognate terms. Normally, the concept of *guanxi* is translated into English as meaning relationships, personal connections, networks and networking and similar alternatives; however, the reality is much more complex: *guanxi* includes all these things and more. Second, this chapter represents an initial exploration of the relevance and possibility of transferring the very Western notion of relationship marketing to the very different business environment of China.

A first necessity, however, is to clarify the economic context in China, over the last 25 years, materially affecting a modern interpretation of *guanxi* in the business environment and its potential for enhancing, or indeed hindering, the introduction and application of relationship marketing in China. The context is the 'opening up' of China to the outside world since 1978. This process was inaugurated by the then new paramount leader, Deng Xiaoping, and has since been continued by his successors, primarily President Jiang Zemin and Premier Zhu Rong-ji. This historic development has been consolidated and made irreversible by China's accession to the WTO.

Moreover, further developments during this period have reinforced and enhanced China's opening up and the transformation of the economy and society, not least the emergence of so-called TVEs: township and village enterprises.[1] These may be loosely described as non-state firms in the public sector, as the majority of them appear to be owned by local or provincial authorities. But, unlike the state or private sectors, the TVE sector is hybrid and amorphous in which some enterprises may function like local government (department) enterprises, but the majority appear to have such operational freedom that many function more like co-operatives, others indeed more like private companies. The 'boundaries' between the central-government-owned state sector, especially given significant changes in capital and management structures over the last decade, and TVEs on the one hand, and between TVEs and private companies on the other, are fluid and osmotic.[2] The case study, which follows and forms a central part of this chapter, is based on an unambiguously private company.

Certain realities, however, still obtain in China, for example, a dominant state role, continues, for example, in continuing five-year plans (although these are becoming more indicative). Companies generally, but SMEs especially, lack modern management skills. How can this deficiency be rectified? Particularly, how are modern marketing principles to be adopted?; and most crucial for this study, is it appropriate to apply relationship marketing to the development and implementation of company strategy in China? Would the all-pervasive *guanxi* enhance or hinder this possibility?

To address these issues we focus on three related questions: does market orientation matter for China's SMEs? How do small- and medium-sized companies undertake a strategic orientation within the complex and constantly changing business environment? How do owner-managers of China's SMEs make the strategic marketing decisions that sell their products and maintain competitiveness? To answer these questions, the study employs as data collection methods: exploratory research,[3] a single case study of the Ningbo JIDE Electrical Appliances Co. Ltd, an in-depth interview, documentation,[4] mailed questionnaires and field interviews. The research findings offer a new model to define relationships between China's SMEs, relationship marketing and *guanxi*. Our final section outlines key conclusions for managers, including a framework for confronting the most central challenges.

Relationship marketing, market orientation and *guanxi*

Relationship marketing

One factor that brought the new concept of relationship marketing to the fore in the 1990s was a growing recognition that sustainable competitive advantage in the global economy increasingly requires one to become a trusted participant in some network or set of alliances (Morris *et al.*, 1998). The new relationship approach reflected the need to create an integrated cross-functional focus of marketing, one which emphasizes keeping as well as winning customers (Payne *et al.*, 1998). But, the precise meaning of relationship marketing remains to be clarified: the concept was first introduced by Berry in a service context to describe 'a longer-term approach to marketing' (cited in Payne, 1997: 42). Hunt (1995: 2) defines relationship marketing as 'all marketing efforts directed at establishing, developing and maintaining successful relational exchange'.[5] According to Morris *et al.* (1998), relationship marketing is a strategic orientation that both buyer and seller organizations adopt to look for long-term beneficial collaboration. This implies that relationship marketing involves senior management commitment on both sides, entails dynamic interaction between two parties and requires a high degree of co-operation, adaptation and interdependence (the latter being exactly like *guanxi*, see in the following sections).[6] Such ideas have now become part of the mainstream of contemporary marketing, integrated within the modern marketing concept, which is itself a cornerstone of the marketing discipline, perceived essentially as a business philosophy, an ideal or a policy (Grönroos, 2000).

Market orientation

The term 'market orientation' means the implementation of the marketing concept – market orientation is the very heart of modern marketing management and strategy (Narver and Slater, 1990) and considered a key element of superior corporate perfor- mance. More formally, market orientation refers to the organization-wide generation of market intelligence, dissemination of the intelligence across departments and organization-wide responsiveness to it (Kohli and Jaworski, 1990). Although, market intelligence may be the starting point of a market orientation, the latter may also be perceived as a corporate culture which creates the necessary behaviours to deliver value for its customers and to create superior performances for the business continuously (Narver and Slater, 1990). Superficially, at least, the structural change in China from a planned economy to a market economy should facilitate the adoption by mainland Chinese companies of a market-driven approach in general and of relationship mar- keting in particular. Key changes in the marketplace include 'consumers learning how to be consumers' (McDermott and Choi, 1997) and companies learning how to respond to increased competition and how to satisfy consumers' needs. The traditional values of Chinese society, however, change more slowly than such surface changes as those of company structure and legal environment. Tjosvold *et al.* (2001: 168) claim that 'China is transforming itself into its own version of an open, modern market- oriented society'. The term 'own version' implies something distinctively Chinese and also a compromise between the old and the new. Perhaps the most characteristic fea- ture of Chinese society that will endure in this context is the phenomenon of *guanxi*.

Guanxi

Guanxi is a cultural characteristic that has significant implications for interpersonal and inter-organizational dynamics in Chinese society, not least for business: the latter is not generally conducted with strangers, even though business with strangers is accepted – the preference is for people one knows and likes. Even in the so-called age of information, these personal relationships are likely to remain pivotal. Such relationships tend to be stable and form the basis of personal and social networks, that is, *guanxi* networks, the formation and maintenance of which are important tasks for top management, especially in marketing and sales. Business networks are a subset of wider social networks, the latter often being, for instance, more important than professional relationships and suppliers' competence. The so-called 'Liberation' of 1949 has not changed this. *Guanxi* refers to the concept of drawing on a web of connections to secure favours in personal and organizational relations. It is an intricate and pervasive relational network that contains implicit cultural obligations, assurances and understanding. It is critical for business in China, whether foreign or local, to understand and properly utilize *guanxi* in order to gain an edge over competitors (Park and Luo, 2001). *Guanxi* has been the lifeblood of personal relationships and business conduct in Chinese society; it has not become less important in very recent times, possibly even more important.[7]

Guanxi networks: In recent years, networks and relationship building have become critical for the success and survival of organizations around the world (see Park and Luo, 2001). Networks, for example, enhance competitive advantage by providing access to the resources of other network members, and are particularly important in respect of market entry, where their strategic role has been well-documented (see, for example, Davies *et al.*, 1995). This is precisely where a good *guanxi* network can prove invaluable, for example, as an important source of information on market trends and business opportunities. A *guanxi* network can also help a firm overcome the lack of resources to accommodate growth while alleviating substantial bureaucratic costs that would result from internalizing operations. Moreover, as market information is greatly distorted in a transition economy, the *guanxi* network becomes a reliable source of necessary information for the making of strategic decisions. Yet *guanxi* is not a panacea, even in network-based Chinese society: its effective utilization depends on its fit with institutional, strategic and organizational attributes (Park and Luo, 2001).[8]

Interim summary

The previous examination of various key concepts of relationship marketing yielded a distinctive, if 'unco-ordinated', terminology which, superficially, in many respects matched and seemed compatible with that of *guanxi*, namely: trusted participant; networks; longer term/long term; beneficial collaboration; high degree of co-operation, adaptation and interdependence; and relationship focus. But are the similarities merely a coincidence or evidence of a deep and significant overlap and mutual compatibility? The successful transference of relationship marketing to China would depend on the latter being true. However, differences in the social context are both great and fundamental: relationship marketing is a subset of marketing, which is a subset of business, which is a subset of the economy, which is a subset of society as a whole. *Guanxi*, on the other hand, is a concrete manifestation of Chinese social reality, a society which is relationship-based (*shehui benwei*); *guanxi* is an indispensable social institution.

The following case study is intended to illuminate, within the Chinese context, what *guanxi* may entail for the strategy of a manufacturing SME and for the potential to apply relationship marketing.

Case study methodology

A single case study is used as the main research strategy to collect qualitative and quantitative data. Case study observation included interviews, complemented by documentation and mailed questionnaires to JIDE's business customers. The methodology entailed in the research design subserved two primary objectives:

1 to explore how JIDE changed its strategic orientation from *guanxi* to product orientation and why JIDE should now change to market orientation;
2 to explore how and why a Chinese owner-manager, 'the proprietor', builds relationship marketing with his business customers, makes strategic marketing decisions and markets his products and maintains competitiveness.

The experience of the proprietor that is, the founder, owner and manager of JIDE, forms the main basis of this study. Long interview techniques were used to guide the interview (Siu, 2000), focusing on a series of open questions pertaining to *guanxi*, relationship marketing, production and market orientation of JIDE. A semi-structured questionnaire was used, permitting flexibility in discussion.

The semi-structured questions (33) centred on 8 areas general information about the company; company development; *guanxi* (relationships) and business; new product development; change and innovation; marketing, relationship marketing and market orientation; marketing education and training; company problems and planning. The interview, taking approximately three hours, was recorded and transcribed.

Mail methods the core business of JIDE is to manufacture plastic components used by the large-scale home appliance companies which are JIDE's target business customers. Accordingly, this research used the mail approach to these leading brand companies in order to learn about customers' attitudes to the home appliances market, *guanxi*, and marketing philosophies and also to learn about JIDE awareness, reputation and customer satisfaction. The data set consisted of 9 current business customers and 11 branded home appliance companies (Chinese and foreign). Twenty mail interview packages, consisting of covering letter, questionnaire in both Chinese and English, and return envelopes, were dispatched to 20 selected companies. After 2 rounds of reminders (over 3 weeks), 8 usable responses with complete information were received, representing a 40 per cent response rate. Almost all of the responses were from JIDE's business customers (the proprietor also being involved here – personal relationships or *guanxi* played an important role in this respect as well as in others in this research).

The questionnaire employed closed-end questions and scale-response questions (15), embracing 4 areas general questions; attributes of selected suppliers or Original

Equipment Manufacturers (OEM); attributes enhancing the relationships between the company and its suppliers; JIDE company awareness and customer satisfaction. Traditional telephone and field interviews with washing machine customers were also conducted.

Caveats (1) all the market research was conducted in three months; the 40 per cent response rate would not have been achieved without the proprietor's intervention; (2) the database: compared with the Western countries, it is difficult to obtain professional databases on consumers from government statistics; (3) organizational constraints: hard to obtain information from companies about their customers although abundant information has been accumulated; general issue of inaccuracy, scarcity and contemporaneousness of secondary data in developing countries (China, Taiwan and Vietnam being particularly problematic (Lassere, 1993)). Hence, the internal records of JIDE were considered more relevant than secondary data sources. Face-to-face structured interviews were replaced by mail methods.

JIDE, *guanxi* and market orientation

The JIDE company is part of a wider international phenomenon, that is, SMEs playing an increasingly important role in the modern economy. In China, the emergence of dynamic SMEs, making an indispensable contribution to the dramatic growth of the Chinese economy, is primarily a phenomenon of the last 25 years, with TVEs setting the pace in the 1980s, and private companies assuming more of the initiative in the 1990s, particularly in the later 1990s and the first years of this century. Critical, new issues have emerged for Chinese SMEs, however, whether TVE or private, especially lack of modern management knowledge, particularly in marketing. JIDE is a company attempting to address these challenges.

The JIDE Electrical Appliance Co. Ltd employs 200 people and specializes in manufacturing various kinds of plastic products. It was first established in 1980; it acquired its present name in 1996 and in 1998 invested £1.5 million in new plant and equipment, including many large plastic injection machines and other advanced mould precision processing facilities. It became ISO9002-registered in 1999, as part of achieving the company's aim to establish itself as a world-class manufacturer, in partnership with its customers. The company now has eight business customers, of which BSH (a joint venture (JV) of Bosch and Siemens in China), Meiling, Fedders, Electrolux and Weili are considered the leading ones (Fedders and Electrolux are also (JVs). In 2001, JIDE's main products were: washing machine and plastic injection products (such as plastic components and trash cabins).

According to the company's managing director, the proprietor,[9] JIDE experienced five development stages during its evolution. These stages are shown in Table 8.1.

Production orientation start of market orientation, but still based on product orientation. Clearly, the company has since evolved and developed much further than relying largely on *guanxi* for making progress. The MD believes that *guanxi* is, nevertheless, one of the key elements of doing business in China – without *guanxi* businesses can do nothing and it takes a long time, two-to-three years, to develop it with key outsiders, that is, with people not companies. He will need to enhance

Table 8.1 JIDE's five development stages

Periods	Stages	Strategic orientation
1980–1986	Exploring stage	*Guanxi* orientation 1
1987–1995	Capital accumulation stage	*Guanxi* orientation 2
1996–1998	New exploring stage	Product orientation
1999–2001	Company innovation stage	Production orientation
2002–future	New development stage	Market orientation

existing, and develop effective, new *guanxi* to help master the emerging challenges, for example, of differential growth of demand for various electrical appliance products, and increasing domestic and foreign competition.

As founder, owner and manager of JIDE, he confirms that good *guanxi* has been and remains very important to JIDE's development. He has good *guanxi* with local government departments, bank agents, business customers, suppliers, competitors, employees and so on. For developing new *guanxi*, honesty, generosity and adaptability are crucial: they facilitate the creation of trust. The most important facets of sustaining and developing *guanxi* further are trust, adaptation (i.e. adaptability) and favour/(mutual) benefit (*renqing*). The latter is compatible with, and partially explained by, Wong's conceptual model of *Guanxi* and Relationship Performance (see Appendix 2). The two preconditions for acquiring the aforementioned qualities and exploiting their business potential are: personal reputation, and the company's potential for further development. *Guanxi* played different roles in different stages of JIDE's development: (1) 1980–6 was the exploratory stage for JIDE, the company sought *guanxi* with state-owned manufacturers because at that time *guanxi* was the only way of doing business in China: in terms of establishing a company, finding raw materials, borrowing from banks and seeking business customers. (2) 1987–95 was the family factory stage where accumulating capital was critical and *guanxi* was continuing to be built and enhanced. JIDE was a supplier to large companies and totally dependent on them, for example, the Yangzi group; good *guanxi* also continued to be cultivated with other Chinese business customers, local government departments and banks. It was at this time that he first prioritized product quality for achieving customer satisfaction, a commitment maintained ever since. (3) 1996–8 was a new exploratory stage. JIDE had become over-dependent on Yangzi which withdrew its custom when it merged with BSH – this loss of business suddenly plunged JIDE into crisis, one involving its very survival. The good *guanxi* with local government and the banks proved to be JIDE's life-line, for example, in acquiring land, plant and (from the banks) capital; this even allowed expansion of productive capacity, but *guanxi* did not suffice when seeking new customers. Indeed, lack of marketing knowledge induced him to invest in two new products (between 1996 and 1998) which both failed. The main way forward then, it seemed, was to forge a relationship with BSH, but on this occasion through relationship marketing.

In the early period of relationship marketing, JIDE's relationship with BSH was quite different from the *guanxi* relationship with Yangzi: there was, indeed, overlap in respect of co-operation, trust, company reputation and image, but now product and service quality, company production and technology and company management acquired vital significance. BSH was a foreign company and establishing a successful relationship marketing with them would demonstrate JIDE's capacity to succeed in accessing its new target market of globally famous companies. Nevertheless, despite these initial developments, overall, the third stage in the company's evolution was that of production focus, leaving open the vital question of how to improve sales generally. He came to recognize at this time that full market orientation offered the best way forward and also to believe that there were no insuperable, internal company barriers to adopting a market orientation.

The fourth stage (1999–2001) was characterized by three components, (i) company innovation, technically and administratively; (ii) the beginning of market orientation: satisfying customer needs, building competitive advantage and improving profitability; (iii) a continuing product orientation. This latter was demonstrated in his decision to invest massively in a new washing machine product; fortunately, a major new customer appeared, Weili, a large private company which had been seeking OEM suppliers. But relying on chance was no longer an option: it was time for JIDE to become fully market-oriented.

The fifth stage of JIDE (2002–future) is that of New Development – Market orientation and Relationship Marketing. JIDE's 2002 marketing plan contains the following growth strategies:

- market penetration strategy: improving market share with current business customers;
- market development strategy: to develop international markets for its plastic trash cabin and washing machine;
- product development: a new washing machine model will be produced as well as hotel products;
- diversification: satisfying customer needs by establishing a new centre for making plastic injection moulds.

He realizes that the most important issue in fulfilling these strategies is people: they are the key element in the company's development; hence, company learning, marketing education and training have become critical.[10]

The proprietor and his main staff had travelled up a crucial learning curve together, an experience which, in principle, can be replicated throughout China. JIDE had been reflecting at microlevel the macrolevel changes in the Chinese economy in transition from production- to customer-orientation. A market-based economy mandates priority for the marketing 'function', a precondition for the emergence and consolidation of relationship marketing – what the latter means for (Chinese) companies in general can be captured in model form.

A new model

Although the phenomenon of *guanxi* (in the sense of important personal contacts) is not unique to Chinese society, existing to some extent in every human society, what is special about China is that *guanxi* is an inherent, structural feature of Chinese society, deeply and widely anchored in long-held cultural values which, in China's fast-changing environment, and contrary to some academic opinion, has become even more entrenched, with strong and direct implications for contemporary social attitudes and business practices. However, *guanxi* alone, as has been established, cannot be viewed as a panacea – *guanxi* alone will not make customers buy a company's products (Figure 8.1).

According to the case study, market orientation does matter for company development. As was also the Western experience, the Chinese market is going through the stages from product orientation, production orientation, selling orientation to market orientation, which is not decided by one company alone. This trend is doubly significant for SMEs which must stake out their own futures, innovation being one key to corporate survival, not least in the form of company learning, marketing

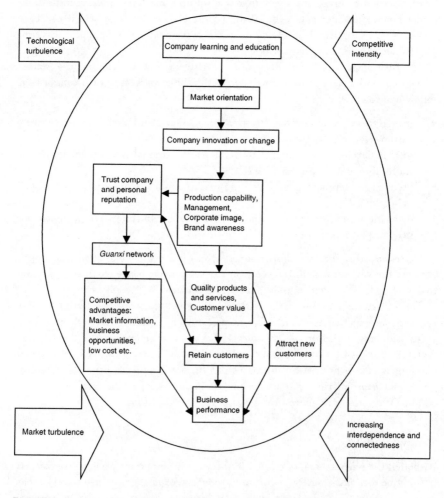

Figure 8.1 A new model: *guanxi*, relationship marketing and strategy.

education and training, for example, learning from developed countries (including Hong Kong and Taiwan). It is possible to attempt to define, encapsulate and partially explain the relationships which determine a Chinese company's capacity to evolve, innovate and survive in a (new) model based upon the research findings, that is, the case study findings, combined with an interpretation of current research in the field (primarily by Narver and Slater, 1990; Jaworski and Kohli, 1993; Deng and Dart, 1994; Hunt, 1995 (see also Appendix 1)).[11]

The model structures the relationships of market orientation, relationship marketing and *guanxi* in such a way that a modern focus of marketing management and strategy can be described (for Chinese companies) and used as a tool for a particular company to enhance corporate performance. It focuses primarily on market orientation, which can improve company innovation or change; company innovation mediates the relationship between market orientation and performance. Innovation and change are the keys for company survival within a turbulent environment, not least in enhancing employee adaptability through appropriate education and training.

Conclusion

We have sought to define the relationships between business performance, market orientation, relationship marketing and *guanxi* for China's SMEs. It has been established that despite the centrality and indispensability of *guanxi*, it 'may not be enough' for China's SMEs, especially when looking for new customers: *guanxi* alone does not suffice. Relationship marketing would appear to be needed because of the changing nature of competition to network competition in many industries; it may also provide a comparative advantage in resources when seeking a competitive position in the marketplace and superior financial performance. Market orientation, additionally, has been found to have a significant impact on business performance.

JIDE has shown that building a good relationship with customers by employing a relationship marketing strategy will be more suitable for looking for new customers than relying on *guanxi* strategy. The company is building long-term relationships with its primary customers: Meiling, Fedders, Electrolux and, above all, with BSH. The study finds that market orientation does matter for China's small- and medium-sized manufacturers, confirming that such market orientation is to be considered both as corporate culture and a key element of superior corporate performance. Acquiring ISO9002, for example, illustrates JIDE's innovation in terms of technical and administrative improvement in order to satisfy customer needs, to build competitive advantage and to improve profitability.

It seems also to have been established that company innovation mediates that relationship between market orientation and performance. Technical and administrative innovations have improved JIDE's corporate image (CI), production capability and management. With such improvements, JIDE now provides quality products and services for its customers: retaining existing customers, attracting new ones and improving company performance. The final, provisional finding is that company learning and education will help the company become further 'market oriented' – this will be increasingly true for Chinese companies generally, as the market economy takes hold; they are learning that people are a key resource, as elsewhere in the world.[12] JIDE's progress manifests the kind of adaptation which Chinese companies can and must make in order to meet the competitive challenges entailed in China's full membership of the WTO.

Appendix 1 – relationship marketing

Hunt (1995) identifies the scope of relationship marketing, which includes: supplier partnerships, lateral partnerships, buyer partnerships and internal partnerships (Figure 8A1.1). He also claims that there are two reasons for engaging in relationship marketing: the changing nature of competition to network competition in many industries; and providing a comparative advantage in resources which facilitates acquisition of competitive advantage and of superior financial performance.

Appendix 2 – *guanxi* models

Of various *guanxi* models developed in recent years, it would seem that Y. H. Wong's have currently acquired the widest currency. Figure 8A2.1 represents a conceptual model linking *guanxi* and relationship performance. The figure attempts to illustrate the correlation between constructs and performance indicators.

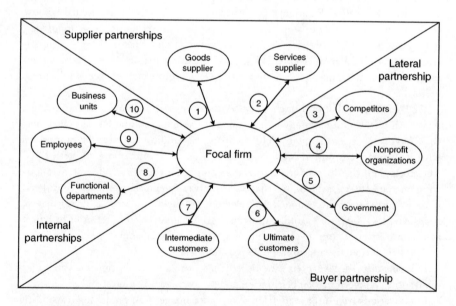

Figure 8A1.1 The relational exchanges in relationship marketing.
Source: Hunt (1995: 4).

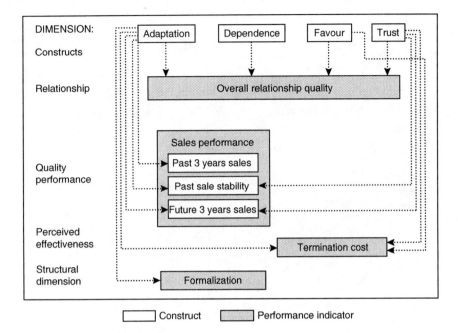

Figure 8A2.1 A conceptual model of *guanxi* and relationship performance.
Source: Wong (1998: 30).

Table 8A2.1 *Guanxi* and outsider–insider dichotomy – perceptual positioning

Process	Outsider	Insider
A1 Availability	Bargaining	Belonging
A2 Association	Experiment	Experience
A3 Acceptance	Clarifying	Compromise
A4 Affectiveness	Fitting-in	Fine-tuning
A5 Affordability	Accommodation	Assimilation
A6 Affirmation	Trial	Trust
A7 Assurance	Convergence	Commitment
A8 Adaptation	Fiancé	Friend (Old)

Source: Wong and Chan (1999: 115).

Regarding the *guanxi* building process itself, this model can be developed further to incorporate the apparently crucial insider/outsider distinction. Effective interaction, for example, requires adaptation, see Table 8A2.1 and Figure 8A2.2.

The model incorporates further dichotomies: *yin/yang* and Heart/Mind. Such models attempt to capture an essentially Chinese propensity for making (management) decisions according to certain social values which themselves are a distinctive cultural

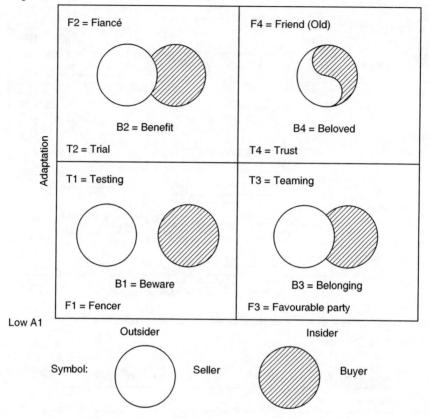

Figure 8A2.2 FBT *guanxi* model.

Source: Wong and Chan (1999: 117).

artefact. Such representations purport to contrast a holistic, 'human' Chinese approach with a one-sidedly rationalistic and formalistic Western approach.

Notes

1 Known as collectives in the larger urban areas – not to be confused with the earlier collectivization of agriculture via communes.
2 Most TVEs are SMEs – this fact is intrinsically significant, but it is also important in that the emergence and development of these enterprises provided a kind of training ground for China's new breed of private entrepreneurs. With the concomitant introduction of a so-called socialist market economy, TVE–SMEs provided an experience of non-state market activity which represented an invaluable learning curve for the new players in China's unique 'market economy'. In recent years, most TVEs have been 'privatized' (see Seitz, 2000: 383, 397–8).
3 See the section on Case study methodology.

4 See the section on Case study methodology.

5 See Appendix 2 for a more detailed presentation of Hunt's views.

6 The relationship marketing concept also encompasses various complementary perspectives: emphasis on long-term customer retention, shift from a transaction focus to a relationship focus; the development of relationships with external markets (such as supplier, recruitment, referral and influence markets) as well as internal markets; and alignment quality, customer service and marketing activities (Payne, 1997).

7 A number of necessary conditions obtain for the establishment of *guanxi*:

- a *guanxi*-base: *guanxi* operates in concentric circles, with close family members at the core and with distant relatives, classmates, friends and acquaintances arranged on the periphery according to the distance of the relationship and the degree of trust;
- *ganqing*/affection: determines the degree of closeness between two people; *ganqing* is a measure of the emotional commitment of the parties involved; it may involve gift-giving (not bribery);
- trust: willingness to rely on an exchange partner in whom one has confidence; personalized trust through networks is particularly crucial to the conduct of business in China;
- *mianzi* (face): an individual's public image, gained by performing one or more specific social roles that are well recognized by others, face as an intangible form of social currency and personal status.

8 See Appendix 2 for one approach to diagrammatic representation of *guanxi* (business) networks, namely that of Y. H. Wong, Hong Kong.

9 What follows represents a synopsis of the views of the proprietor, henceforth referred to as 'the MD' or 'he'.

10 Training for employee skill development is, however, very much in its infancy in China.

11 For details of Jaworski and Kohli, 1993 and Deng and Dart, 1994, see bibliography, other authors here are already referred to in the text.

12 The authors accept that these conclusions might have been modified if greater time and resources had permitted (i) by a wider range of semi-structured interviews with managers, engineers, supervisors and shop-floor workers in the case company; (ii) given that different types of manufacturers have different market environments, a multiple case study would have been desirable.

References

Aaker, D. A., Kumar, V. and Day, G. S. (1997) *Marketing Research*, 6th edn, John Wiley & Sons, New York.

Barnes, J. G. (1994) 'Close to the customer: but is it really a relationship?', *Journal of Marketing Management*, 10: 79–88.

Bruton, G. D., Lan, H. and Lu, Y. (2000) 'China's township and village enterprises: Kelon's competitive edge', *Academy of Management Executive*, 14(1): 19–29.

Burns, A. C. and Bush, R. F. (1998) *Marketing Research*, 2nd edn, Prentice-Hall, Englewood Cliffs, NJ.

Buttery, E. A. and Leung, T. K. P. (1998) 'The difference between Chinese and Western negotiations', *European Journal of Marketing*, 32(3–4): 374–89.

Chetty, S. (1996) 'The case study method for research in small- and medium-sized firms', *International Small Business Journal (Incorporating European Small Business Journal)*, 15(1): 73–83.

China Household Electrical Appliances Association (2002) *Statistics of Electrical Home Appliances*. Available at http://www.cheaa.org/public/tongji/index.asp

China Statistical Yearbook (1990–1996).

Chinese Private Company (2002) Available at http://www.chinatech.com.cn/htmortxt/jsjg/jsjg4.htm

Chisnall, P. M. (1995) *Strategic Business Marketing*, 3rd edn, Prentice-Hall International (UK) Ltd, Hertfordshire.

Christie, M., Rowe, P., Perry, C. and Chamard, J. (2000) 'Implementation of realism in case study research methodology', in *Proceedings of the Annual Conference*, International Council for Small Business, Brisbane.

Chu, G. C. and Ju, Y. (1993) *The Great Walls in Ruins: Communication and Cultural Change in China*, Albany, New York.

Churchill, G. A. Jr (1996) *Basic Marketing Research*, 3rd edn, The Dryden Press, Chicago, IL.

CIM. Available at http://www.cim.co.uk

Czinkota, M. R. and Ronkainen, I. A. (1994) 'Market research for your export operation: part 1 using secondary sources of research', *International Trade Forum*, 3: 22–33.

Davies, H., Leung, T. K. P., Luk, S. T. K. and Wong, Y. (1995) 'The benefits of "Guanxi": the value of relationships in developing the Chinese market', *Industrial Marketing Management*, 24: 207–14.

Day, S. G. (1999) *The Market Driven Organization: Understanding, Attracting and Keeping Valuable Customer*, The Three Press, New York.

Deng, S. and Dart, J. (1994) 'Measuring market orientation: a multi-factor, multi-item approach', *Journal of Marketing Management*, 10: 725–42.

Dibb, S., Simkin, L., Pride, W. H. and Ferrell, O. C. (1997) *Marketing Concepts and Strategies*, 3rd European edn, Houghton Mifflin, Boston, MA.

Dyer, G. and Wilkins, A. (1991) 'Better stories, not better constructs to generate better theory: a rejoinder to Eisenhardt', *Academy of Management Review*, 16(3): 613–19.

Eisenhardt, K. (1989) 'Building theories from case study research', *Academy of Management Review*, 14(4): 532–50.

Eisenhardt, K. (1991) 'Better stories and better constructs: the case for rigor and comparative logic', *Academy of Management Review*, 16(3): 620–7.

Fu, G. and Saunders, J. (1994) 'China's regulated marketing mix: the role of the state administration bureau for industry and commerce', *Journal of Marketing Management*, 10: 655–66.

Giaoutzi, M., Nijkamp, P. and Storey, D. J. (1990) *Small and Medium-size Enterprises and Regional Development*, Edited, Reprinted, Routledge, London.

Grönroos, C. (2000) *Service Management and Marketing*, John Wiley & Sons Ltd, Chichester.

Gummesson, E. (1999) *Total Relationship Marketing*, Butterworth-Heinemann, Oxford.

Han, S. L., Wilson, D. T. and Dant, S. P. (1993) 'Buyer-supplier relationships today', *Industrial Marketing Management*, 22: 331–8.

Harris, S. and Dibben, M. (1999) 'Trust and co-operation in business relationship development: exploring the influence of national values', *Journal of Marketing Management*, 15: 463–83.

Horng, S. C. and Chen, C. H. (1998) 'Market orientation of small and medium-sized firms in Taiwan', *Journal of Small Business Management*, July, 79–85.

Hunt, S. D. (1995) 'Seven questions for relationship marketing', *Handout of MEG Conference Guest Speech*, July, University of Ulster, Coleraine.

Hussey, J. and Hussey, R. (1997) *Business Research: A Practical Guide for Undergraduate and Postgraduate Students*, McMillan Press Ltd, London.

Jaworski, B. J. and Kohli, A. K. (1993) 'Market orientation: antecedents and consequences', *Journal of Marketing*, July, 57: 53–70.

Kalwani, M. U. and Narayandas, N. (1995) 'Long-term manufacturer-supplier relationships: do they pay off for supplier firms?', *Journal of Marketing*, 59(1): 1–16.

Kohli, A. K. and Jaworski, B. J. (1990) 'Market orientation: the construct, research propositions, and managerial implications', *Journal of Marketing*, 54(2): 1–18.

Kotler, P. (1999) *Marketing Management*, 9th edn, Prentice-Hall, Engelwood Cliffs, NJ.

Kotler, P. (2000) *Marketing Management*, Millennium edn, Prentice-Hall, Englewood Cliffs, NJ.

Kumar, N., Scheer, L. and Kotler, P. (2000) 'From market driven to market driving', *European Management Journal*, 18(2): 129–42.

Kumar, V., Aaker, D. A. and Day, G. S. (1999) *Essentials of Marketing Research*, John Wiley & Sons Inc., New York.

Lassere, P. (1993) 'Gathering and interpreting strategic intelligence in Asia Pacific', *Long Range Planning*, 26(3): 56–66.

Lehmann, D. R., Gupta, S. and Steckel, J. (1997) *Marketing Research*, Addison-Wesley Educational Publisher Inc., Reading, MA.

McDermott, M. C. and Choi, T. C. L. (1997) 'The distribution of fast-moving consumer goods in the People's Republic of China', *Journal of Marketing Management*, 13: 195–217.

Malhotra, N. K. and Birks, D. F. (2000) *Marketing Research: An Applied Approach*, European edn, Prentice-Hall, Essex.

Ministry of Foreign Trade and Economic Cooperation, PRC (2000) Available at http://www.moftec.gov.cn/moftec_cn/tjsj/wztj/2000_9-22-7.html

Moore, N. (2000) *How to do Research: The Complete Guide to Designing and Managing Research Projects*, 3rd edn, Library Association Publishing Ltd, London.

Moorman, C., Deshpande, R. and Krishnam, R. (1993) 'Factors affecting trust in market research relationships', *Journal of Marketing*, 57(1): 81–101.

Morris, M. H., Brunyee, J. and Page, M. (1998) 'Relationship marketing in practice: myths and realities', *Industrial Marketing Management*, 27: 359–71.

Narver, J. C. and Slater, S. F. (1990) 'The effect of a market orientation on business Profitability', *Journal of Marketing*, 54(4): 20–35.

Neuman, W. L. (1997) *Social Research Methods: Qualitative and Quantitative Approach*, 3rd edn, Allyn and Bacon, Boston, MA.

Park, S. H. and Luo, Y. (2001) 'Guanxi and organizational dynamics: organizational networking in Chinese firms', *Strategic Management Journal*, May, 22: 455–77.

Payne, A. (1997) *Advances in Relationship Marketing*, Reprinted, Kogan Page Ltd, London.

Payne, A., Christopher, M., Clark, M. and Peck, H. (1998) *Relationship Marketing for Competitive Advantage*, Reprinted, Butterworth-Heinemann, Oxford.

Peng, M. and Heath, P. S. (1996) 'The growth of the firm in planned economies in transition: institutions, organizations, and strategic choice', *Academy of Management Review*, 21: 492–528.

Seitz, K. (2000) *China: Eine Weltmacht kehrt zurueck*, Siedler Verlag, Berlin.

Shapiro, B. P. (1998) 'What the hell is "Market Orientation"?', *Harvard Business Review*, 66(6): 119–125.

Siu, W. (2000) 'Marketing philosophies and company performance of Chinese small firms in Hong Kong', *Journal of Marketing Theory and Practice*, 8(1): 25–37.

Slater, S. F. and Narver, J. C. (1994) 'Does competitive environment moderate the market orientation-performance relationship?', *Journal of Marketing*, 58(1): 46–55.

Slater, S. F. and Narver, J. C. (1998) 'Customer-led and market-oriented: let's not confuse the two', *Strategic Management Journal*, 19(10): 1001–6.

Slater, S. F., Narver, J. C. and Tietje, B. (1998) 'Creating a market orientation', *Journal of Market-Focused Management*, 2(3): 241–55.

Terpstra, V. and Sarathy, R. (1997) *International Marketing*, 7th edn, The Dryden Press, Harcourt Brace College Publishers, Fort Worth, TX.

Tjosvold, D., Hui, C. and Law, K. S. (2001) 'Constructive conflict in China: cooperative conflict as a bridge between East and West', *Journal of World Business*, 36(2): 166–83.

Tsang, E. W. K. (1998) 'Can guanxi be a source of sustained competitive advantage for doing business in China', *The Academy of Management Executive*, 12(2): 64–73.

Wong, Y. H. (1998) 'The Dynamics of Guanxi in China', *Singapore Management Review*, 20(2): 25–42.

Wong, Y. H. and Chan, R. Y. (1999) 'Relationship marketing in China: guanxi, favouritism and adaptation', *Journal of Business Ethics*, 22(2): 107–18.

Wright, R. W. and Etemad, H. (2001) 'SME and the global economy', *Journal of International Management*, 7: 151–4.

Yang, Mayfair (1994) *Gifts, Favours, and Banquets: The Art of Social Relationships in China*, Cornell University Press, Ithaca, NY.

Yeung, I. Y. M. and Tung, R. L. (1996) 'Achieving business success in Confucian societies: the importance of guanxi (connection)', *Organization Dynamics*, 24(3): 54–65.

Yin, R. K. (1993) *Applications of Case Study Research*, Sage, Beverley Hills, CA.

Yin, R. K. (1994) *Case Study Research: Design and Methods*, 2nd edn, Sage, Beverley Hills, CA.

Zhang, T. (2001) 'Achievement of development and trends of TVEs in China'. Available at http://www.agri.ac.cn/agri_net/02/2-11/bk13xz.htm

9 A management control assurance in the different cultures and institutions of China and the UK

Dermot Williamson

The cultural and institutional context, within which managers gain control assurance and manage operational risks, differs considerably between China and the UK. This is an example of how economic activities are embedded in society. Interrelations among culture, institutions and markets suggest that they can only develop in a hand-in-hand manner. The conclusion has implications for British companies wishing to do business in China, and for international regulation of companies' control.[1]

Introduction

Markets and business organizations operate within their social and institutional context. In the People's Republic of China (PRC)[2] and the UK these are very different. This chapter examines the interaction of managers as they seek to gain control assurance within their cultural and institutional contexts. Two field studies (Emmanuel *et al.*, 2001; Williamson, 2001) illustrate linkages between control assurance, its context, and the value placed on control assurance within the different cultures. Although these are cross-sectional studies, they provide a backcloth to the development of the PRC business environment. To achieve commercial success there, British businesses need to understand the influence of China's different culture and institutions.

International advances are being made in regulations calling for reporting by companies on their internal or management control[3] and on operational risk management, which is the modern risk-based approach to control. These advances in the UK (Turnbull Committee, 1999), the USA (Sarbanes–Oxley Act, 2002), and proposals by the Bank for International Settlement (Basel Committee, 2003) apply to banks and other companies throughout their worldwide operations. They are setting global standards for management control. No allowance is made in these regulations for the local context where these businesses operate, but differences in what control mechanisms are effective, and are seen to be effective, may shape how these standards are applied in different locations.

A premise of this chapter is that the effectiveness of control and how it is evaluated is subjective. Assurance provided by control mechanisms rests on subjective assessment of uncertainties of whether control objectives are likely to be achieved. It also rests on personal views of what is needed or contributes to control. These views may neither be shared between the managers who provide control assurance, nor by managers and stakeholders who receive that assurance. Effectiveness of control is therefore a matter of opinion, not capable of objective measurement, at least up to the point where control has clearly failed. Opinions may vary among cultures concerning the pertinence of uncertainties (Douglas and Wildavsky, 1983; Dake, 1992; Palm, 1998) and what control mechanisms are effective in the face of these uncertainties. This chapter shows how opinions on management control relate to cultural and institutional factors.

This chapter gives a brief background for the PRC and the UK, outlines the methods used in the two field studies, and then compares British and mainland Chinese managers' perceptions of six areas of control, which are related to cultural and institutional contexts. These contexts are analysed in the following section, in order to show how they may interact, affect and be affected by developments in markets and organizations. Examination of the field studies concludes with their limitations. The next section shows how control assurance, that is dependent on social and institutional context, can affect perceptions of commercial success or failure. It illustrates how the process of creating value is embedded in the culture and institutions of a society (Granovetter, 1985) and draws a parallel with a social capital (Putnam and Goss, 2002). The chapter concludes by drawing implications of 'socially embedded control assurance' for the development of the PRC's market economy and for international regulation.

Business context in the PRC and the UK

Political economies

The PRC is a Socialist country governed by the Chinese Communist Party. It has a socialist market economy, which is reforming its State-Owned Enterprises (SOEs), increasing market orientation, and increasing its openness to the outside world (Jiang Zemin, 1997). Since these studies were conducted in 1997–9, the PRC has joined the World Trade Organization (WTO). This has accelerated the reform of the PRC's markets and financial institutions. But, at the time of the fieldwork substantial obstacles to reform remained, and progress varied between regions. Besides established local interests and political pressures, 'regulatory fatigue' of new inexperienced and understaffed agencies battled with incomplete and inconsistent guidelines on deregulation. The UK, in contrast, has a long tradition of parliamentary democracy and a market economy. It is a member of the EU and the WTO.

Cultures

The Han people of China have had the longest span of homogeneous development in the World (Child, 1994), with relatively little foreign influence, from the Xia dynasty of 2000 BC. Even when invasions from Mongolia in AD 1271 and Manchuria in AD 1610 created the Yuan and Qing dynasties, the new foreign elites were absorbed into and adopted the local Han culture. In more recent times, despite debilitation from the decline and collapse of the Qing dynasty, China fought against foreign incursions by Western and Japanese colonial powers from the first Opium War in 1839 through to 1945 (Fairbank, 1987; Spence, 1990). Introduction of European institutions during this period was often resented, as were the 'unequal treaties' through which Western powers sought to protect their interests in China; these have recently been expunged with the handover of Hong Kong and Macao. Chinese traditions and culture, in the sense of shared beliefs, attitudes and values, are deep rooted.

Among Taoist, Buddhist, folklore and other sources, Confucian tradition and philosophy stand out as a defining foundation of Chinese culture. While it is impossible to summarize the richness of cultural beliefs, values and assumptions in a few paragraphs, four cultural values based on Confucian thoughts are often referred to. These are respect for age and hierarchy, group orientation, preservation of 'face' and the importance of interpersonal relationships (Child, 1994; Lu, 1996; Hoon-Halbauer, 1999).

Among attempts to measure and compare national cultures, Hofstede's (2001) survey is most widely followed.[4] Unfortunately he did not include the PRC. Some researchers extrapolate from his measures for Taiwan, Singapore and Hong Kong to a 'Chinese culture'. This is problematic (Bond, 1996), not least because national culture is learnt not inherited, and therefore reflects local history. However, Cragin (1986) has applied Hofstede's instrument to the PRC.[5] Scores for Hofstede's cultural dimensions that are referred to in this chapter, are compared in Table 9.1 for Great Britain, the PRC and the predominantly Chinese countries measured by Hofstede.

Individualism as a cultural dimension is defined as the extent that ties between individuals are loose, and that people are expected to look out for themselves. The opposite pole on this dimension, collectivism or group orientation, is the extent that people are integrated into strong cohesive in-groups, and are protected in exchange for unquestioning loyalty. Uncertainty avoidance is the extent that people feel threatened by uncertain or ambiguous situations. Power distance is the extent that less powerful people within society expect and accept that power is distributed unequally. Unlike Hofstede, Trompenaars and Hampden-Turner (1997) have surveyed mainland Chinese as well as British cultures. They confirm that mainland Chinese culture is collectivist (they use the term 'communitarian'), while British culture is individualist. They find that mainland Chinese culture tends to ascribe status according to kinship, gender, age, social connections or educational record. In contrast, British

Table 9.1 Hofstede's cultural dimensions

	Individualism index	Uncertainty avoidance index	Power distance index
The PRC	36c	117c	56c
Hong Kong	25	29	68
Taiwan	17	8	58
Singapore	20	69	74
Great Britain	89	35	35

Source: Hofstede, 2001; Cragin, 1996 for data with suffix 'c'.

culture tends towards achieved status based on a person's personal achievements. They find Chinese culture to be diffuse, so that how Chinese people relate to others tends to be carried across multiple roles, whereas British culture tends to be specific in people relating to others according to specific roles or areas of life. They also find Chinese culture generally to be particularist, giving greater weight to particular relationships with people and to particular situations, than the universalist assumptions of British culture that principles should apply in all situations.

The studies and methods

The case study

This study used Strauss and Corbin's (1990, 1998) version of grounded theory[6] and was informed by the work of Yin (1994) on case studies. The case study was done between August 1997 and January 1998 in the UK, Prague and Beijing with two Western-based multi-national companies (MNC) who have operations at all three of these locations. The Czech part is omitted as outside the scope of this chapter. The MNCs have asked to remain anonymous. Because they are major players in their fields, their industries and markets must also remain confidential. One of them supplies products to industrial customers. The other MNC provides corporate services. Data were gathered from interviews, documents, emails, systems and observation, while data from the business and national press added to the contextual data.

There were 65 British and 24 mainland Chinese interviewees. Those interviewed included 5 Britons in Beijing, 3 Chinese in the UK, 17 other nationalities in Beijing and 6 of other nationalities in the UK. Interviewees were initially chosen for the potential variation in views and insights that they might offer. Further interviewees were selected from those expected to challenge and extend the emerging theory.

Interviews were conducted in English, the working language for the MNCs in all six sites. Discussions focused initially on credit control, which was selected by the researcher and two MNCs as an area of management control that practical managers could explain. They then extended to management control in general, in terms of what provided assurance that a business is under control.

While the case study focused on perceptual differences between managers from different countries, differences were also checked between other groupings for the managers, such as which MNC they worked in, functions, levels of seniority and gender. This demonstrated that differences apparently detected between national cultures were not simply due to organizational or professional cultures. Prior assumptions and emerging ideas were repeatedly challenged through constant comparison with the field data, and from checking the emerging theories with interviewees.

National culture was identified as an interviewee's country of upbringing, because of the importance of childhood in acquiring national culture (Hofstede, 1991). Cultural data was collected by observation, from attitudes expressed in interviews, and in a cultural survey using a shortened version of Trompenaars and Hampden-Turner's instrument (1997). A total of 36 British and 36 Chinese respondents completed the cultural survey.

The trade credit control survey

This was conducted in 1999 among Chinese and British managers working respectively in the PRC and the UK for mainly locally owned companies. It was distributed to British managers by Experian in the UK and to Chinese managers by Sinotrust in the PRC, where they are well-established in providing credit-reference information. The surveys were given predominantly to clients of these companies. The UK questionnaire[7] was mailed to 250 managers, of whom 46 (18 per cent) gave usable replies.

The Chinese questionnaire was translated into Chinese and back-translated into English, in order to reduce differences in meaning. It was given to and completed by 60 Chinese managers, of whom 20 were in the vicinity of each of Beijing, Shanghai and Guangzhou.

Twenty-one interviews were conducted with managers who completed the survey. This helped bring out some of the thinking behind the survey responses.

Contracts and relationships

This is the first of six areas where differences between perceptions by mainland Chinese and British managers of gaining control assurance are compared. These perceptions are themselves manifestations of cultural differences. They illustrate how the different cultural contexts appear through responses to everyday challenges of maintaining control over a business.

Chinese relationships and contracts

While many Chinese interviewees[8] recognized the importance of contracts, most thought that relationships are in practice more important for resolving disputes with customers. The traditional Chinese preference for relationships over contracts was explained as follows: a social commitment based on attitudes and beliefs in a relationship is more trustworthy than the written word of a contract, because a contract is open to forgery or alteration. It was, however, recognized that China's managers are increasingly familiar with contracts. Chinese use of contracts, which may tend to focus on dealings with Westerners, appears to be an example of the Chinese preferring to follow Western examples when it is to their advantage.

Chinese managers were concerned about the likelihood that going to court would destroy relationships with a counterparty, and even sour their relationships with the counterparty's customers and suppliers. Besides the risks of damaging relationships, reasons for not going to court to settle contract disputes included strong preference for dealing with problems privately rather than in public (Child, 1994; Ch'ng, 1997).

British contracts and relationships

The weight of opinion[9] among British interviewees was evenly divided between favouring the use of contract or relationships for regulating affairs and resolving disputes. In this they were significantly different from Chinese managers who generally favoured relationships over contracts.

Some British interviewees described using relationships at the first stage problems are encountered, then negotiating how the contractual terms are to be applied, and only in the end taking customers to court. In progression from relationship to legal action, the latter was seen as being important to show that you are not a 'soft touch', and 'to tell the customer we expect them to abide by the contractual terms, to give a clear signal to the industry'. This concern, to show willingness to enforce contractual obligations, contrasts interestingly with a Chinese concern to avoid gaining a reputation in the market of one who overthrows relationships by taking legal action.

Guanxi *and* renqing

Although British as well as Chinese managers saw relationships as important, the nature of British and Chinese relationships tended to be different. Chinese interviewees recognized that they include an element of *guanxi* (Ch'ng, 1997) if not also of *renqing*. Yang (1994) describes *guanxi* as:

> dyadic relationships that are based implicitly (rather than explicitly) on mutual interests and benefit. Once *guanxi* is established between two people, each can ask a favour of the other with the expectation that the debt incurred will be repaid sometime in the future.
>
> (Yang, 1994: 1)

Guanxi has a wide meaning, well beyond business relationships. In this study, it was exemplified by treating a customer favourably when in difficulties. There was an expectation that the favour would be returned when fortunes are reversed. It could be called upon to regulate problems between suppliers and customers and to expedite recovery of debt without using legal remedies. Although *guanxi* relationships might be described as cronyism and can involve corruption, no one suggested that business relationships of these MNCs might be built on exchange of valuable gifts or benefits. This possibility was expressly excluded by interviewees, who nevertheless recognized the possibility existed in other organizations within China.

Interviewees described *guanxi* as being personal between individuals, rather than between organizations. They also referred to the long-term nature of *guanxi*. Interestingly, an interviewee pointed out that while the Communist Party of China has discouraged *guanxi*, books on 'relationship marketing' were appearing in the PRC at the time of the fieldwork. As a result, people were beginning to see *guanxi* in a different way, and trying to use it to improve their businesses.

Interviewees explained that *renqing* can arise as long term relationships between Chinese people who share common experiences such as between class mates from school. Yang (1994) describes *renqing* as ethical and emotional feelings between humans beings, and the proper conduct within a circle of people such as family, kin and close friends with whom one is bound by emotion and affection.[10] Interviewees gave examples where *renqing* affected business between enterprises. They also described how *renqing* can be part of strong interpersonal relationships within a company, such as between a boss and subordinate, and how Chinese people may invest in *renqing* as an alternative to reliance on corporate trust.

Yang (1994) claims that *renqing* is peculiarly Chinese. Nothing equivalent to *guanxi* or *renqing* was found in these studies among British interviewees or at the UK sites of the two MNCs. British relationships lacked the *guanxi* expectation that favours should be exchanged and be repaid, and lacked the emotional strength of long-term *renqing* relationships. Relationships were also generally described by British managers as between organizations rather than between individuals.

Other researchers show that access to PRC markets may depend upon *guanxi* connections (Bjorkman, 1996; Fukasaku and Lecomte, 1998). Boisot and Child (1988) pointed out that, if society progresses from status to contract, this had yet to occur for mainland Chinese society. Development of Chinese market transactions does not match Western-style markets. This is because of Chinese reliance on trust and social ties, including *guanxi* type relationships, more than on contracts (Boisot and Child, 1996). Reliance on legalistic behaviour is likely to be offensive as it indicates lack of trust (Child and Yan, 1999).

Yang (1994) recounts how the practice of *guanxi* has varied through China's history. It largely disappeared after 1949, when Communist ideals suppressed patronage. At the same time, party allocation of resources and jobs removed most of the transactions that *guanxi* supported. She places its major revival during the chaos and terror of the Cultural Revolution in 1966–76 (see also Cheng, 1986). Reasons for its revival included cultural, institutional and economic factors. Among cultural reasons were traditional Chinese attitudes to relationships and gift giving, which were never wholly eradicated by Communism. The lack of *renqing* and humaneness[11] between people during the chaos of the Cultural Revolution, as well as intrusion of state control into family affairs, led to demand for humaneness in relations. Institutional reasons included the explosion of mutual mistrust between people and collapse of moral norms as people retreated into ever smaller private circles. The collapse of production and distribution created the economic need to obtain food, clothing and shelter, when urban parents were trying to prevent separation and forced exile of their children to poor rural areas. In a time of extreme uncertainty and institutional chaos, Chinese society drew on its traditions to develop networks of interpersonal relationships. Therefore, the pace at which contracts and arms-length market transactions gain ground over *guanxi* arrangements within the PRC may depend upon security of both prosperity and the reliability of institutions.

Clarke (1996) puts forward interesting arguments about whether legal rights are a necessary precondition for economic development, or whether economic development stimulates development of enforceable legal rights. He argues that relationship transactions diminish the need in Chinese society for universally enforceable contractual and other legal rights. Thus relationship-based solutions, cultural particularism and local partiality may stand as impediments to development of Western-style market transactions. But, continuing economic reform and growth of market-based transactions create demand for universal legal rights and solutions. Indeed, since the fieldwork, the PRC has developed its legislation on contract law following international models.

Contextual factors

Guanxi and *renqing* relationships are examples of the Chinese variety of group orientation or cultural collectivism. They were also found to be manifestations of the relatively diffuse Chinese culture, which was associated with reliance on interpersonal relationships rather than contracts, and with interpersonal relationships being based more on mutual obligation than calculative self-interest.

The use of contracts and relationships were related by both Chinese and British interviewees to legal institutions and to possibilities of resolving disputes through legal action.

Law, regulation and rules

Interviewees commented on the relatively low regard for the rule of law held by Chinese compared to Westerners. Chinese say it is people who rule, *renzhi*, not the law, *fazhi* (Ch'ng, 1997; Kapp, 1997; Beamer, 1998). Just as Chinese interviewees expressed trust in relationships with people more than contracts, they tended to rely more on people within their network of relationships, than on legal institutions. Therefore, differences in views concerning whether relationships should be based on contracts or on social ties, extended to wider assumptions about the part that laws and rules play in society.

Interviewees attributed some of these attitudes to historical developments. One interviewee expected development of legal institutions and cultural attitudes in the PRC to take many years, perhaps even a century. On the other hand, changing attitudes, influenced by Western MNCs and even by television soap operas such as 'LA Law', were associated with increasing legal awareness.

The study pointed to problems with using the Chinese legal system. Some interviewees thought that Chinese courts could be biased against foreigners, show favouritism to local interests, be short of judicial experience in commercial matters and be reluctant to make or enforce judgements. Both of the MNCs in the case study seldom, if ever, sought redress through the courts or arbitration in the PRC.

These findings support Clarke (1996), who explains why the PRC legal system is not yet achieving the uniformity of legal process and consistent authority over government that is expected in Western countries. This is part of a larger problem of partiality. First, without sufficient economic reform in the PRC and a 'level playing field' in markets, applying general rules without recognition of particular circumstances would be unfair. Second, Chinese courts do not fit into Chinese thinking on power and authority. They lack sufficient vertical authority, or *tiao*, because without constitutional separation between executive, legislative and judicial arms of the state, they are just another bureaucracy. They also lack horizontal authority, or *kuai*, because of the pervasive influence of the Communist Party of China. Finally, he claims that the universal authority of a legal system, before which all people are equal, is alien to Chinese thinking. Development of the Chinese legal system therefore faces cultural problems from particularism and high power distance.

Using relationships and mediation rather than public dispute

Besides a general Chinese dislike for resolving disputes through the courts, the studies found a feeling that to admit to a dispute in public is to lose face. A Chinese manager explained: 'It is very shameful for both parties if they have to go to arbitration.... They don't like to expose the problem to the public.'

Several interviewees maintained that Chinese people prefer to follow instructions where there is the warmth of a personal relationship, rather than following cold regulations. For example: 'Managers have to rule from the heart; it's meaningless to just tell them. More important who gives the policy than whether the rule is good. Chinese respect the person, westerners respect the law.'

Plethora of regulations

There appears to be a paradox however between, on the one hand, Chinese preferences for using relationships and private negotiation and, on the other hand, a propensity to issue large volumes of regulations. This paradox was deepened by Chinese managers who thought that procedures usually involve too many people, take too long and are a waste of time.

Two explanations emerged. First, procedures may be looked to where there is lack of leadership and relationships are not working. Second, a manager may prefer the organization to issue a procedure, if there is any risk that his or her personal relationships may not work.

Mitigating the impact of regulation

Chinese legislation was criticized for ambiguity, having loopholes and terminology that is neither consistent nor defined (see also Clarke, 1996; Ch'ng, 1997). This may reflect an underlying Chinese assumption that it is dangerous to commit oneself to principles that may later conflict with dictates of particular situations or relationships. Interviewees explained how authorities do not like to give oral, let alone written, clarification of regulations. They recounted how a Western Finance Director refused to authorize an investment in a Special Economic Zone (SEZ) until the tax authorities had confirmed the tax-exempt status of the investment. The tax authorities refused, and the impasse continued until the project was cancelled. In the eyes of the Chinese narrators, what was remarkable was the Westerner's expectation that Chinese authorities would commit themselves to applying what was required by law.

Flexible interpretation also extended to those subject to rules. Examples appeared of people following laws and internal company procedures in ways that met their own agenda, while circumventing the purpose for the law or procedure.

British views

Among British interviewees, the predominant weight of opinion was that procedures and similar internal regulations contribute to control assurance. For example, procedures were thought to increase certainty for staff and enable staff to do their job in the face of frequent job transfers. As people move between jobs or employers, and as systems are 're-engineered', knowledge is lost of who is supposed to do what, when and why. Internal regulations are therefore an antidote to dissipation of corporate knowledge. Growing British support for written procedures was also identified with increasing litigiousness of British society.

Some British managers emphasized the contribution of policies to control assurance. Policies give direction for the business and set limits to the risks or the types of business that may be entered. This view was not apparent among Chinese managers and staff, but appeared to be vulnerable to the Chinese propensity for following the letter of regulations while avoiding the purpose of any broader policy.

Cultural factors

Several cultural factors help explain the patterns of perceptions found in the field concerning law, regulations and procedures. Concern for losing 'face' and use of interpersonal relationships have been identified as characteristics of Chinese culture (Child, 1994; Lu, 1996). British concerns for general principles and for the rules of law indicate the cultural dimension of universalism, whereas Chinese concern for people and relationships suggests particularism. Chinese reluctance to constrain future executive action, either with precise rules or commitments on how these would be interpreted, are a form of uncertainty avoidance.

Procedures are situation specific, and view that they are important to control assurance were associated with specific culture. This association is supported by a significant correlation found between opinions that procedures contribute to control assurance and specific culture measured in the cultural survey.

The institution of law

These findings are consistent with different legal traditions in Europe and the PRC. Carver (1996) contrasts private law as an institution for Western business, to the paucity of private law in the PRC. Central to the Western concept of civil society is the concept of individuals' privacy and how social bonds can tie the individual to society. She points to how Western legal systems arose from Roman justice and the bonding of Christian morality with law, which arose both from establishment of Christianity as the State religion and through ecclesiastical law.

In contrast, Confucian thinking was hostile to the concept of law, basing good government on the moral character of rulers and administrators rather than on systems of government (de Bary *et al.*, 1960). Chinese law still has a tradition of secrecy (Carver, 1996). This contrasts with the Western tradition, dating back to the Roman Twelve Tables of 450 BC, of making the law transparent and open to public scrutiny.

Empowerment and hierarchy

Empowerment, which featured in about two-thirds of British explanations of gaining control assurance, was not mentioned by Chinese managers. It seemed to be based upon reciprocal trust by British subordinates that superiors give them latitude in how they do their work, perhaps subject to some monitoring. British superiors expected subordinates to act sensibly in furthering wider objectives for the organization. Empowerment was a counterpart to accountability, another characteristically British expectation, and was linked to views that bosses should coach their staff and nurture staff development.

In contrast, Chinese interviewees expected bosses to instruct their staff, and subordinates were expected to be reliable. One quoted the saying: 'bu qiu you gong, dan qiu wu guo' (you don't need to earn merit, just don't make mistakes).

British staff were described as loyal generally to themselves and to a lesser extent their organization or team. In contrast, half of the weight of opinion among interviewees was that Chinese staff are loyal to their superior. This Chinese loyalty to bosses appeared in peculiarly Chinese terms, and was at times linked to *renqing*. The job market in Beijing was very attractive for English-speaking staff with experience of working in MNCs. However, Chinese interviewees made less mention of this market condition than of their boss when giving reasons for staying or moving job, for example resigning because their boss was transferred to another position.

The predominant Chinese view on organizational structure was in terms of hierarchy. For example, in the words of a Chinese junior manager:

> In China, like other communist countries, decisions are made at a very high level. . . . Our education is wide and superficial, so we are not experts in any field. The boss is worried he will lose face if you have a brilliant idea, which can be very embarrassing. You can have a brilliant idea, but it depends on the leader whether they listen.

Contextual factors

This Chinese preference for hierarchy reflected the cultural attributes of high power distance and ascribed status. Market forces were evident in British views on the effect of business process re-engineering and de-layering of organizations on staff attitudes. In contrast, the job markets were not identified as a factor with Chinese staff loyalty.

Education featured in several explanations for attitudes to hierarchy and knowledge. It was explained that Chinese school children learn to receive knowledge, whereas in Western education systems emphasis is given to competing arguments and reasoning. Even before school age, Chinese children tend to be told by their parents not to do this, and to be careful; in contrast Western parents are more likely to say 'go outside, try this, try that'. Education in the PRC may therefore foster more respect for authority of paternal hierarchy, than does British education. It may also discourage the empowerment and contribution expected by British bosses.

Information

Information is central to management control as well as to markets. Differences in attitudes to information affect the operation of both.

Availability of information

Both studies found differences in public availability of information, from relative secrecy in the PRC to relative openness in the UK. Availability of public information was reflected in attitudes to transparency.

The trade credit control survey found a statistically significant difference ($p < 0.0001$) in preferences for providing information to all who ask for it, or to only a few suppliers. Whereas, British managers tended to prefer widely held information, typically in order to demonstrate honesty, Chinese managers tended to prefer narrowly held information, and this was often in order to maintain relationships.

These survey findings supported the case study, in which British views were that monitoring within an organization should be done with free flow of information, transparent to all. One interviewee said that assumptions on which critical decisions were made should be transparent, so that others could monitor the decisions. Another stressed the importance of an audit trail so as to demonstrate that sufficient steps have been taken. Performance league tables were found to be pinned up in a UK office beside the coffee machine where all staff could not fail to see them, demonstrating greater symbolic transparency than was necessary for monitoring.

Interviewees explained how Chinese people are reluctant to appear conspicuous from volunteering information or ideas: to stand out is to risk losing face. Subordinates may be encouraged to make suggestions for improvement only where they can be sure that their suggestion will work (see also Beamer, 1998). Related to this was Chinese concern for the virtue of studied modesty, based on a desire not to stand out as better than others. A Chinese interviewee explained:

> We are influenced by Confucius who said you should be obedient and modest. Also proverbs we were told by our elders when we were young, and are still told by mothers today to their children, such as, *yu shi wu zheng*, hold oneself aloof from the world, stand aloof from success [and you will be safe]. *Ren pa chu ming, zhu pa zhuang*, man fears fame, like pigs fear getting fat.

Chinese employees appeared to foster less horizontal flow of information across departments than their British counterparts. Chinese information flows seemed to be mostly vertical (see also Child and Lu, 1996).

There were, however, a number of examples where Chinese managers communicated more than might be expected by British managers. These were communications within strong interpersonal relationships, whether between subordinate and superior, between members of a management team, or within *guanxi* networks spanning across organizations. It appears that Chinese reluctance to be open with information may be reversed where it is a matter of maintaining valuable relationships.

Other researchers have found that obtaining information in the PRC can be difficult (Bjorkman, 1996) and that Chinese accounting has a tendency towards relative secrecy compared to transparency in the UK (Roberts *et al.*, 2002).

Absolute or relative truth

The case study found a general opinion among interviewees that, whereas Westerners may look for absolute truth, Chinese people tend to look for relative truth dependent upon the particular situation and upon relationships with people. When a Western person might expect absolute truth in a business partner, a Chinese person might expect his or her business partner to give support rather than to stand on principle. Information may therefore be withheld or modified in order to maintain the relationship or to protect the provider of information. Examples included information provided by customers to their supplier's auditors, and low credence given by investors and banks to audited accounts of unlisted Chinese companies.

There were British expectations that information should always be accurate. Although accurate, it might be influenced by the interests of the person providing the information. Safeguards to prevent misleading information included concern that there should be no conflicts of interest, and the importance of transparency about the information provider, including transparency about his or her interests.

Contextual factors

These findings on transparency are consistent with the cultural theory that contrasts high context communication, typical of oriental cultures, to low context communication usually found in Anglo-Saxon business cultures (Hall, 1977; Trompenaars and Hampden-Turner, 1997). Whereas low context communication requires a relatively large volume of data about specific content of a topic, high context communication conveys more information about the context. Market information subject to standard contracts and accounting information that follows accounting standards are examples of very low context communication. High context information is more usual, where both parties already have some mutual understanding, such as where there is an interpersonal relationship. The contrast found here between relatively high context communication within a Chinese culture to relatively low context communication in the UK has also been found by Boisot and Child (1988, 1996). Trompenaars and Hampden-Turner (1997) attribute low context communication to specific culture and high context communication to diffuse culture.

Difference in attitudes to whether information should be volunteered and transparent appeared to reflect uncertainty avoidance, which was high for Chinese and low for British interviewees. It also reflected Chinese concern for losing face, which has been linked to cultural dimensions of diffuse culture (Trompenaars and Hampden-Turner, 1997) and collectivist culture (Hofstede, 2001). Smith and Berg (1997) point out that concern for saving face is an opposing cultural attribute to concern for honesty.

Process – opportunities

Discussion of planning and control over implementation of plans brought out contrasting paradigms of control processes: one seeks to ensure achievement of objectives, the other, resilience through flexible positioning so that opportunities can be seized as they arise. The former was the view of all the British managers, as well as about half of the Chinese managers in the case study. It saw the need to reduce uncertainty through identifying objectives and steps to achieve those objectives. The latter paradigm of resilience and opportunities was peculiar to the Chinese interviewees. It used uncertainty by taking advantage from the unexpected. In the strongest versions of this view, detailed planning constrained action, was time consuming, focused inwards within the organization away from markets and diverted attention away from opportunities.

Further analysis showed that these paradigms related to contexts of relatively turbulent market conditions and uncertain legal institutions within the PRC compared to the UK. It also showed that the contrasting paradigms rested on cultural attitudes. British views of time were seen as sequential. Chinese interviewees complained that British managers planned their action linearly as a series of steps towards a goal. Chinese synchronous[12] view of time saw successful management as following more from ability to co-ordinate concurrent activities, and being in a strategic position from where opportunities can be selected. The cultural dimension of universalism – particularism was also evident. Particularism appeared in Chinese concern for opportunities and solutions in a particular context, in contrast to universalism of Western concern for general principles that may determine what processes are likely to work.

Interviewees related these contrasting paradigms to educational systems and to philosophical traditions of European and Chinese learning. Chinese managers were described as being able to plan faster than British managers, as the latter attempt to identify all alternatives and weigh up consequences; Chinese more than British educated minds have a tendency to jump straight to what is seen as the correct solution. The faster Chinese approach was attributed to Chinese education, where more is learnt and less debated than in the British education system. This direct thinking, as well as synchronous time, was related by an interviewee to relatively greater emphasis on imagination by Chinese Taoist philosophers such as Lau Tzu (1994) and Chuang Tzu (1964). It was contrasted with deductive logic of ancient Greek philosophers. Another Chinese manager illustrated the paradigm of flexibility and opportunities by quoting:

Yu qiong qian li mu,
Geng shang yi ceng lou

from the Tang poem *Deng Guan Que Lou* by Wang Zhihuan. He explained it as meaning that success comes only from looking at the broad vista from an upper floor, not by looking at details in the basement, that a broad or long-term view is important in order to identify context and opportunities, and that time can be viewed as an eternal cycle.

Attitudes to risk and uncertainty

The trade credit control survey indicated that British managers responsible for credit were concerned about the effectiveness of their credit control systems, whereas Chinese managers tended to be more concerned about maintaining relationships with particular customers. British managers tended to be concerned about the availability of information and expertise. Chinese managers were more concerned about competitors and the state of the business environment.

The British systems' view of trade credit risk management may reflect cultural factors, such as low uncertainty avoidance, low concern for losing face, preference for transparent information and achieved status shown in credit performance reports. It may also be consistent with the relatively stable UK market environment. System-based exception reporting is much easier to design and maintain, when there is a stable history of transactions to form the basis for setting norms and intervention levels.

In contrast, the Chinese tendency to focus on customers rather than control systems may reflect concern for the particular customer within the market context, interpersonal relationships between managers and their customers, and higher concern for losing face from the ignominy of one's customer failing to honour commitments. The practice of linking salesmen's annual bonuses to absence of bad debts, which was more prevalent in the PRC than the UK, increased the impact of uncertainty avoidance on trade credit transactions.

Interaction between control assurance and contextual factors

The context for control assurance in the case study is illustrated in Figure 9.1. The central envelope represents cultural, institutional and market factors for the patterns in which the managers in the study perceived gaining control assurance for their business. Constituent elements of the cultural and institutional context are broken out into separate ovals and oblongs. These include cultural dimensions such as specific–diffuse culture. Examples of institutions identified in the study included educational and legal systems.

The effect of historical, philosophical and other social traditions on the cultural context are represented in Figure 9.1 with arrows indicating direction of influence. They included historical development of the PRC, Confucian and Taoist philosophy and European hypotheco-deductive logic. Social traditions included *guanxi* and *renqing*.

Markets both influenced this institutional context and were influenced by it. For example, the presence of Western MNCs within Chinese markets was seen to create demand for effective legal remedies, by both these MNCs and indigenous Chinese enterprises. At the same time, the effectiveness of legal action for recovery of debt was seen as affecting how companies do business in markets.

Change and uncertainty were identified by interviewees as affecting what gave them control assurance, and as endemic in the context of gaining control assurance. The extent of this change and uncertainty was seen to be generally greater in Chinese than in British markets and institutions.

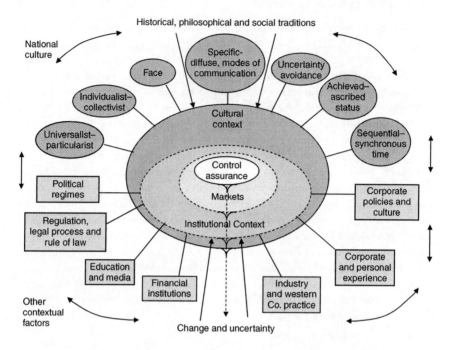

Figure 9.1 Context of gaining control assurance.

Although particular cultural dimensions, such as ascribed status, could be identified, as were particular institutions such as effects of education systems, the boundaries were indistinct between the overall cultural, institutional and market contexts. For example, an explanation for changing loyalties of British staff referred to personal aspirations, market conditions and norms expected of organizations and peers. Explanations for complex Chinese supply arrangements through multiple importers referred to markets, trust in relationships and preference for obfuscation, whether from cultural roots or to confuse Chinese Customs authorities.

Interactions among cultural, institutional and market factors were detected. For example, managers' views on the state of control of their business, within its particular markets and regulatory context, were integrated into organizational cultures at each site and reflected in emerging organizational routines, local information systems and other control mechanisms. These were in turn reflected in economic activities, such as granting credit to customers and investing in joint ventures. Cultural, institutional and economic factors, together with managers' control perceptions, therefore influenced each other in complex social ecologies, which were distinctly different for the British and the Chinese managers.

There were also longer term factors. Historical and philosophical traditions have been handed down by one generation to the next, and by education systems, to shape cultural values, which in turn shape education systems and create further historical and philosophical traditions. Change was therefore endemic over longer term cycles than those of the market transactions and the organizational operations.

The complex of interacting social and market forces shown in Figure 9.1 illustrates control assurance as a social construction (Berger and Luckmann, 1967; Ahrens, 1996). Views on whether a particular business is under control may be socially constructed within a management team, within an audit team, between such teams and within the community of capital markets. How managers perceive gaining control assurance may inject further dynamism into the interdependencies between markets, institutions and their cultural context. For example, the perceived importance and effectiveness of accountability is likely to affect corporate cultures and how organizations operate in the market. Factors described by new institutional sociologists (DiMaggio and Powell, 1991; Meyer and Rowan, 1977) encourage similar practices between firms (Firth, 1996). This might be through copying prevalent management responses to uncertainty and competition, normative power of professional best practice and sometimes coercive regulation. The risk-based approach to external and now internal auditing (McNamee and Selim, 1998) is an example of good practice, spread by professional standards of required best practice (APB, 1995) and now appearing in market regulation (Turnbull Committee, 1999; FSA, 2000).

Limitations of the empirical studies

The limitations of these studies should be recognized. The case study was confined primarily to managers of two Western-based MNCs and did not study indigenous organizations. There were the biases inherent in the researcher's academic training and prior experience as an accountant and internal auditor.[13] Both studies were cross-sectional research and did not study the extent of change in perspectives.

Inferences that can be made from these studies are necessarily limited. They should not predict what might be found in other populations. The samples were small and not representative. The case study used theoretical sampling to select interviewees who might test and extend the emerging grounded theory (Strauss and Corbin, 1998). Samples for the trade credit control survey were selected according to availability among the two credit reference agencies' clients. Care should be taken not to fall into the ecological fallacy of assuming that individuals conform to stereotypes for their culture (Lloyd and Trompenaars, 1993; Hofstede, 2001). These findings are therefore offered not as a predictive, but a skeletal theory (Laughlin, 1995). They may help explanation, understanding and learning, but they should not be used for prediction.

Discussion

This chapter gives examples of how the cultural and institutional context for business organizations in the PRC and the UK interact with perceptions by managers of management control. Going beyond the scope of the two empirical studies, I suggest that the assurance gained by stakeholders outside a company also varies with their cultural and institutional context. That is to say, the value that shareholders, lenders, customers, suppliers and other stakeholders place on their expectations for the company, varies with the context from which they evaluate a company's strategy, its managers and control over implementation of that strategy.

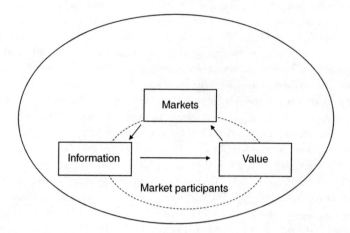

Figure 9.2 Social context of cultural, institutional and economic factors.

Figure 9.2 illustrates how value placed on market transactions by market participants is embedded in their social context. Markets comprise individuals and organizations interacting within an economic community that has its explicit and tacit rules, norms and expectations. Markets sometimes display imitative tendencies of following fashions and shared interpretations, such as expected standards of corporate governance. Participants interpret market data within a background of economic and social information. Their understanding of what data are relevant and reliable is based on assumptions, beliefs and ways of interpreting the world built from learnt knowledge, norms of their communities and personal experience. For example, their interpretation of data may be shaped by capital asset pricing theories, policies of organizations where they work, and personal belief in the veracity of sources. The value that market participants place on interpreted data is shaped by their aspirations and standards of the societies to which they belong. A fund manager may be concerned to meet the investment aims of his or her clients for performance, security or ethical investment, while at the same time valuing his or her status among the community of fund managers and related job markets. The values are in turn reflected in market transactions, for example, selling shares of a company if the company's strategy and implementation are not improved.

This argument has a parallel with the concept of social capital (Bowles and Gintis, 2002; Putnam and Goss, 2002), which is used to redress the under-socialized conception of man within economics (Granovetter, 1985; Durlauf, 2002). Individuals may make rational decisions within markets and, to a greater or lesser extent, within the constraints of the law and regulation. But, individuals are also members of a society. They value social relations with implicit levels of trust; they form social networks based on perceptions of trustworthiness and norms of reciprocity; they are members of their society through acceptance of the norms expected of its members. Extending from social capital, it can be said that individuals, as social beings, are to a greater or lesser extent influenced by the coercive, normative and imitative forces of society's institutions (DiMaggio and Powell, 1991). These institutional factors, acting generally at a subconscious level, subject individuals to shared assumptions, meanings and cognitive patterns (Scott, 1995). Cultural theorists similarly argue that culture shapes shared values and perceptions (Adler, 1991; Schein, 1992). Institutional and cultural theories indicate that society constructs the scope of what is acceptable, feasible and recognizable (Berger and Luckmann, 1967; Douglas, 1986). It was argued at the beginning of this chapter that the effectiveness of management control is subjective, at least until the point when it fails. Similarly, the value placed upon management control is subjective. It is susceptible not only to the aspirations and needs of the people who expect to benefit from a company's productive efforts, but also to the shared norms, values and perceptions of the society to which they belong.

The findings of these two studies illustrate how the nature of social relations and bases for trust, which comprise social capital, can differ between the British and the Chinese managers. For example, differences in their tacit knowledge of effective ways of working and in the nature of their networks of relationships represent different contours of social capital within organizations (Stiglitz, 2000). The studies provide evidence of variation in types of social capital between countries (Fukuyama, 1995; Putnam, 2002). This chapter indicates how the social contexts for the British and the Chinese stakeholders may influence their perceptions of value, which are in turn reflected in their market transactions.

Potential future developments

The studies and prior research illustrate tensions and synergies between contextual factors that may give some clues about the potential future development of China's markets and institutions. Chinese interpersonal relations, such as *guanxi*, appear to reduce Chinese reliance on contracts, and at the same time dampen the expanding role for contracts. Cultural particularism impedes the development of the Chinese legal system towards Western models (Clarke, 1996). Low predilection for transparency may also hinder Chinese progressing towards Anglo-Saxon or European styles of legal system, which are premised on private rights protected by processes open to public view.

But, cultural collectivism or group orientation, perceived unreliability of the Chinese legal system, together with uncertainty from economic transition and reform of China's SOEs, provide reasons why *guanxi* may remain important to transactions in the PRC. *Guanxi* and *renqing* provide normative and emotional bases for interpersonal trust within Chinese society. These studies found that concern for transparency and conflict of interests were more important to British than to Chinese interviewees. It shows how bases for the social capital of trust can differ between China and the UK, and how this difference is rooted in culture and long standing social traditions.

The transition from status to contract, which is claimed to have still been in progress during the late twentieth century, reflects high context communication (Boisot and Child, 1988). It may also reflect ascribed status as well as Chinese preferences, seen here, for warmth of personal feelings over the cold objectivity of contracts. Furthermore, the connectivity of interpersonal relationships offers greater flexibility for responding to uncertainty, than avoiding uncertainty through the relative certainty of contractual commitments. An array of cultural factors, as well as *guanxi* traditions, work against China rapidly grasping Anglo-Saxon use of contracts. This is not to say that China cannot greatly increase its use of contracts. The evidence offered here cannot support prediction.

It is tempting to postulate how China's markets may develop, although again no prediction is made. Markets may thrive where they offer flexibility for Chinese participants to respond to opportunities. But, preferences for interpersonal relationships over contracts, secrecy over transparency and reluctance by some Chinese managers to invest in control systems, may limit the potential of markets that impose overheads of onerous contracts, requirements for formal information systems or heavy regulatory bureaucracy. There are other possibilities. One is that use of contracts may increase, perhaps with the Chinese characteristics, which may support great expansion of open market transactions. In the absence of social uncertainty, expansion of markets may reduce the demand for *guanxi* transactions.

Conclusions

Subject to the limitations outlined here, this chapter illustrates how the PRC's social traditions, institutions and culture are reflected in economic activity. It explains how the hand-in-hand development of markets and institutions can support value creation, if they remain true to cultural values. It shows how China's markets and institutions may continue to have strongly Chinese characteristics. At the same time, cultural values are themselves developing, influenced by markets, and changing institutions and society, but developing slowly. The implications for enterprises from the UK, seeking to operate within China, are that managing risks and making profits will continue to require deep appreciation of these Chinese characteristics.

By illustrating the cultural and the institutional differences between the UK and the PRC, this chapter adds to the extant literature on how social factors, such as social capital (Bowles and Gintis, 2002; Durlauf, 2002) and social embeddedness (Granovetter, 1985) intervene between market transactions and state regulation. It suggests that the operation of transaction cost economics (Williamson, 1975), in shaping the boundaries between firms and markets, may differ between countries such as UK and China. It contributes evidence to show how cultural and institutional factors shape the control mechanisms and predominant types of organizations that populate different national economies (Whitley, 1991, 1999).

International and extra-territorial regulation, such as the Basel capital accord (2003), Sarbanes–Oxley Act (2002) and Turnbull Committee (1999) requirements, set requirements for risk management and reporting on control by companies operating throughout the world. They harmonize requirements and are a step towards levelling standards between countries, both through regulating worldwide operations of international companies falling within their jurisdiction, and through setting international standards for regulators in other countries. These regulations, however, fail to recognize the dependence of management control and risk management on cultural, institutional and market contexts. They may create surprises for international managers and stakeholders, if they expect uniform implementation of these standards. Assurance based on ethnocentric regulation and systems is unlikely to be sensitive to what is pertinent in different markets, and to what gives local investors and managers assurance that their businesses are under control. Differences in local contexts for management control, operational risk management and value creation are likely to shape how these international standards are applied in the PRC, and how Chinese markets respond to these standards.

Notes

1 Support is gratefully acknowledged from the Research Foundation of the Chartered Institute of Management Accountants for the trade credit control survey, and from the Lancaster Centre for Management in China for continuing research into management control and risk management in China.

2 The cultures and institutions of the PRC, discussed in this chapter, exclude those of Hong Kong and Macao, which are very different from those of mainland China and which were excluded from the field studies discussed here. Unless stated otherwise, 'Chinese' refers to mainland China, its people and culture.

3 'Internal control' and 'management control' are used here synonymously to mean the provision of some level of assurance of achieving one or more objectives (standard, goal, objective or purpose) for an organization, including avoiding undesirable outcomes. The term management control is preferred because the focus is on control provided by managers, rather than on what is internal to a company. Its scope is wider than internal control supporting financial accounting, although regulations over control in the Sarbanes–Oxley Act 2002 do not extend beyond control over financial reporting.

4 Hofstede (1980, 2001) surveyed work related values of IBM staff in 50 countries. He identified four and later a fifth cultural dimensions from factor analysis of his survey data. Hofstede measured culture with an index for each dimension ranging between 0 and 100. Of his dimensions, 'masculinity' and 'long-term orientation' were found not to be relevant to these field studies.

5 Cragin (1986) used Hofstede's instrument to measure cultural values of Chinese managers. He found their uncertainty avoidance to be stronger than reported by Hofstede for any country.

6 Grounded theory was developed by Glaser and Strauss (1967) as a predominantly qualitative approach to theory generation. Their research approach induces theory from data, rather than fitting data to existing theory. Data gathering and emerging theory therefore mutually interact during fieldwork.

7 The cultural questionnaire and trade credit survey instrument are available from the author on request.

8 National patterns in perceptions included the views of expatriates, such as Chinese managers working in the UK and British managers working in the PRC.

9 A simple ordinal scale was constructed to represent the strength of opinion for each view, which combined across interviewees to give a weight of opinion. This represents a position on a range for a category in Strauss and Corbin's (1998) grounded theory research method. Significance of differences in weights of opinion between interviewees from different countries and other groupings were checked with the Mann–Whitney or Kruskal–Wallis test.

10 Other authors give different definitions of *renqing* (Chen, 1995; Dana, 2000). Explanations by interviewees in the case study were generally consistent with those of Yang (1994).

11 Humanity or humaneness, *ren*, was for Confucius (1993) the supreme or perfect virtue (de Bary *et al.*, 1960).

12 Sequential and synchronous time is the terminology of Trompenaars and Hampden-Turner (1997). They are largely equivalent to Hall's (1977) monochronic and polychronic time.

13 This academic training and prior experience contributed to the researcher's awareness of the meaning of data, which is termed 'theoretical sensitivity' within the grounded theory method (Strauss and Corbin, 1990, 1998). While interpretation depends on theoretical sensitivity, the inseparable biases are monitored and constrained through constant comparison of the emerging theory against new data. These data are selected to test and extend the theory. The grounded theory method also constrains theoretical sensitivity by requiring depth of support for the theory from multiple data sources in different situations. In this study, triangulation included checking findings through discussion and confirmation by research subjects.

References

Adler, N. (1991) *International Dimensions of Organizational Behavior*, PWS-Kent, Boston, MA.

Ahrens, T. (1996) 'Styles of accountability', *Accounting, Organizations and Society*, 21: 139–73.

APB – Audit Practices Board (1995) *SAS 300 Accounting and Internal Control and Audit Risk Assessments*, APB, London.

Basel Committee (2003) *Overview of the New Basel Capital Accord*, Bank for International Settlements, Basel, Switzerland. Online. Available at http://www.bis.org/bcbs/cp3ov.pdf (accessed 18 May 2004).

Beamer, L. (1998) 'Bridging business cultures', *China Business Review*, 25(3): 54–8.

Berger, P. and Luckmann, T. (1967) *The Social Construction of Reality: A Treatise on the Sociology of Knowledge*, Penguin, London.

Bjorkman, I. (1996) 'Market entry and development in China', in J. Child and Y. Lu (eds), *Management Issues in China*, Vol. 2, International Enterprises, Routledge, London.

Boisot, M. and Child, J. (1988) 'The iron law of fiefs: bureaucratic failure and the problem of government in the Chinese economic reforms', *Administrative Science Quarterly*, 33: 507–27.

Boisot, M. and Child, J. (1996) 'The institutional nature of China's emerging economic order', in J. Child and Y. Lu (eds), *Management Issues in China*, Vol. 1, Domestic issues, Routledge, London.

Bond, M. (1996) 'Chinese values', in M. Bond (ed.), *The Handbook of Chinese Psychology*, Oxford University Press, Hong Kong.

Bowles, S. and Gintis, H. (2002) 'Social capital and community governance', *The Economic Journal*, 112: 419–36.

Carver, A. (1996) 'Open and secret regulations and their implication for foreign investment', in J. Child and Y. Lu (eds), *Management Issues in China*, Vol. 2, International Enterprises, Routledge, London.

Chen, M. (1995) *Asian Management Systems*, International Thomson Business Press, London.

Cheng, N. (1986) *Life and Death in Shanghai*, Collins, London.

Child, J. (1994) *Management in China During the Age of Reform*, Cambridge University Press, Cambridge.

Child, J. and Lu, Y. (1996) 'Introduction', in J. Child and Y. Lu (eds), *Management Issues in China*, Vol. 2, International Issues, Routledge, London.

Child, J. and Yan, Y. (1999) 'Investment and control in international joint ventures: the case of China', *Journal of World Business*, 34: 3–15.

Ch'ng, D. (1997) 'Managing the relationship factor in East Asia', *Monash Mt. Eliza Business Review*, 1: 62–73.

Chuang Tzu (1964) *Basic Writings*, trans. B. Watson, Columbia University Press, New York.

Clarke, D. (1996) 'Power and politics in the Chinese court system: the enforcement of civil judgements', *Columbia Journal of Asian Law*, 10: 1–92.

Confucius (1993) *The Analects*, trans. R. Dawson, Oxford University Press, Oxford.

Cragin, J. (1986) 'Management technology absorption in China', in S. Clegg, D. Dunphy and S. G. Redding (eds), *The Enterprise and Management in East Asia*, University of Hong Kong, Hong Kong, Centre of Asian Studies.

Dake, K. (1992) 'Myths of nature: culture and the social construction of risk', *Journal of Social Issues*, 48: 21–37.

Dana, L. (2000) 'Culture is of the essence in Asia', in *Financial Times*, 12 September, pp. 12–13.

de Bary, W. T., Chan, W.-T. and Watson, B. (1960) *Sources of Chinese Tradition*, Columbia University Press, New York.

DiMaggio, P. J. and Powell, W. W. (1991) 'The iron cage revisited: institutional isomorphism and collective rationality in organizational fields', in W. W. Powell and P. J. DiMaggio (eds), *The New Institionalism in Organizational Analysis*, University of Chicago Press, Chicago, IL.

Douglas, M. (1986) *How Institutions Think*, Syracuse University Press, Syracuse, New York.

Douglas, M. and Wildavsky, A. (1983) *Risk and Culture*, University of California Press, Berkeley, CA.

Durlauf, S. (2002) 'On the empirics of social capital', *The Economic Journal*, 112: 459–79.

Emmanuel, C., Williamson, D. and Zhao, M. (2001) *Perceptions of Trade Credit Control in Mainland China and the UK*, Chartered Institute of Management Accountants, London.

Fairbank, J. K. (1987) *The Great Chinese Revolution 1800–1985*, Chatto & Windus, London.

Firth, M. (1996) 'The diffusion of managerial accounting procedures in the People's Republic of China and the influence of foreign partnered joint ventures', *Accounting, Organizations and Society*, 21: 629–54.

FSA – Financial Services Authority (2000) *A New Regulator for the New Millennium*, Financial Services Authority, London.

Fukasaku, K. and Lecomte, H.-B. (1998) 'Economic transition and trade policy reform: lessons from China', in O. Bouin, F. Coreicelly and R. Lemoine (eds), *Different Paths to a Market Economy: China and European Economies in Transition*, Centre for Economic Policy Research Development Centre of OECD, Paris.

Fukuyama, F. (1995) *Trust: The Social Virtues and the Creation of Prosperity*, Hamish Hamilton, London.

Glaser, B. and Strauss, A. (1967) *The Discovery of Grounded Theory: Strategies for Qualitative Research*, Weidenfeld and Nicholson, London.

Granovetter, M. (1985) 'Economic action and social structure: the problem of embeddedness', *American Journal of Sociology*, 91: 481–510.

Hall, E. (1977) *Beyond Culture*, Anchor Books, New York.

Hofstede, G. (1980) *Culture's Consequences: International Differences in Work-related Values*, Sage Publications, Beverly Hills, CA.

Hofstede, G. (1991) *Cultures and Organizations: Software of the Mind*, McGraw-Hill, Maidenhead.

Hofstede, G. (2001) *Culture's Consequences: Comparing Values, Behaviors, Institutions and Organizations across Nations*, Sage Publications, Thousand Oaks, CA.

Hoon-Halbauer, S. K. (1999) 'Managing relationships within Sino-foreign joint ventures', *Journal of World Business*, 34: 344–71.

Jiang Zemin (1997) 'Report by Jiang Zemin, General Secretary, at the 15th National Congress of the Communist Party of China, on 12 September', in *China Daily*, pp. 1–5.

Kapp, R. (1997) 'China, the United States and the rule of law', *China Business Review*, 6–7.

Lao Tzu (1994) *Tao Te Ching*, trans. Legge, J., Little, Brown & Company, Boston, MA.

Laughlin, R. (1995) 'Empirical research in accounting: alternative approaches and a case for "middle-range" thinking', *Accounting, Auditing and Accountability Journal*, 8: 63–88.

Lloyd, B. and Trompenaars, F. (1993) 'Culture and change: conflict or consensus?' *Leadership and Organization Development Journal*, 14: 17–23.

Lu, Y. (1996) *Management Decision-Making in Chinese Enterprises*, Macmillan Press, London.

McNamee, D. and Selim, G. (1998) *Risk Management: Changing the Internal Auditor's Paradigm*, The Institute of Internal Auditors Research Foundation, Altamonte Springs, FL.

Meyer, J. W. and Rowan, B. (1977) 'Institutionalized organizations: formal structure as myth and ceremony', *American Journal of Sociology*, 83: 340–63.

Palm, R. (1998) 'Urban earthquake hazards: the impacts of culture on perceived risk and response in the USA and Japan', *Applied Geography*, 18: 35–46.

Putnam, R. D. (2002) *Democracies in Flux: The Evolution of Social Capital in Contemporary Societies*, Oxford University Press, New York.

Putnam, R. D. and Goss, K. A. (2002) 'Introduction', in R. D. Putnam (ed.), *Democracies in Flux: The Evolution of Social Capital in Contemporary Societies*, Oxford University Press, New York.

Roberts, C., Weetman, P. and Gordon, P. (2002) *International Financial Accounting: A Comparative Approach*, Pearson Education, Harlow.

Sarbanes–Oxley Act (2002) US Congress 107, Vol. H.R.3763.

Schein, E. (1992) *Organizational Culture and Leadership*, Jossey-Bass, San Francisco, CA.

Scott, W. R. (1995) *Institutions and Organizations*, Sage, Beverley Hills, CA.

Smith, K. and Berg, D. (1997) 'Cross-cultural groups at work', *European Management Journal*, 15: 8–15.

Smith, P. B. and Wang Zhong-Ming (1996) 'Chinese leadership and organizational structures', in M. H. Bond (ed.), *The Handbook of Chinese Psychology*, Oxford University Press (China) Ltd, Hong Kong.

Spence, J. D. (1990) *The Search for Modern China*, Century Hutchinson, London.

Stiglitz, J. E. (2000) 'Formal and informal institutions', in P. Dasgupta and I. Serageldin (eds), *Social Capital: A Multifaceted Perspective*, The World Bank, Washington, DC.

Strauss, A. and Corbin, J. (1990) *Basics of Qualitative Research: Grounded Theory Procedures and Techniques*, Sage Publications, London.

Strauss, A. and Corbin, J. (1998) *Basics of Qualitative Research: Techniques and Procedures For Developing Theory*, Sage Publications, Beverley Hills, CA.

Trompenaars, F. and Hampden-Turner, C. (1997) *Riding the Waves of Culture: Understanding Cultural Diversity in Business*, Nicholas Brealey, London.

Turnbull Committee (1999) *Internal Control: Guidance for Directors of Listed Companies Incorporated in the United Kingdom*, The Turnbull Report, ICAEW Institute of Chartered Accountants of England and Wales, London.

Whitley, R. (1991) 'The social construction of business systems in East Asia', *Organization Studies*, 12: 1–28.

Whitley, R. (1999) 'Firms, institutions and management control: the comparative analysis of coordination and control systems', *Accounting, Organizations and Society*, 24: 507–24.

Williamson, D. (1975) *Markets and Hierarchies: Analysis and Antitrust Implications*, The Free Press, New York.

Williamson, D. (2001) 'Perceptions of management control by mainland Chinese, Czech and British Managers', PhD thesis, University of Glasgow, Scotland.

Yang, Mayfair (1994) *Gifts, Favours and Banquets: The Art of Social Relationships in China*, Cornell University Press, Ithaca, NY.

Yin, R. K. (1994) *Case Study Research: Design and Methods*, Sage Publications, Beverley Hills, CA.

10 China's insurance industry in the twenty-first century

Challenges facing Chinese insurers

Xiaoling Hu

This chapter is based on the author's field research undertaken between June and October 2003. The project was sponsored by the British Academy and British Economics and Social Research Council (ESRC). This is the first part of the project, which provides a holistic view of China's insurance industry in a rapidly changing business environment. It examines how the marketplace has changed since China adopted the 'open-door' policy in 1978. It also tries to identify the key drivers of changes and to predict the future trend of the market, taking into consideration the impact of globalisation and China's accession to the World Trade Organisation (WTO).

Brief history of the Chinese insurance industry

The earliest Chinese insurance company, Canton Insurance Company was established in August 1805 with help from British and Indian businessmen (Jardine Matheson Archive, 1805). The first Chinese insurance company set up by the Chinese themselves, Yi He Insurance Company, was established in Shanghai on 25 May 1865 (Ma, 1994). Due to the lack of management experience, however, indigenous insurers proved less competitive than their foreign counterparts. For a long time, Chinese insurance was effectively controlled by foreign insurers even though there were only 63 foreign compared with 178 indigenous insurers in China in 1949. Nevertheless, the former controlled 80 per cent of insurance business (D'Arcy, 2003). As soon as the Chinese Communist Party (CPC) took power, it immediately founded the state-owned insurance company, the People's Insurance Company of China (PICC), on the 20 October 1949. Under the regulation of the People's Bank of China (PBOC), the then regulatory body of the bank and insurance industry, the PICC became the sole provider of insurance services in China. In parallel, all the foreign insurers were forced to move out, because the market for insurance and re-insurance in China was cut off by the Chinese government. As a result, the PICC expanded rapidly. By the end of 1952, it had become a monopoly insurer with 1,300 branches, 34,000 employees and more than 3,000 agents (Ma, 1994). The business lines of the PICC ranged from fire insurance, transportation insurance and property liability insurance to personal insurance. During the period of social and economic disruption between 1958 and 1979, the domestic insurance market was virtually suspended. It was not until 1979 that the PICC (which became directly responsible to the State Council in 1983)

Table 10.1 Chinese insurance premium income 1980–2002

Year	Total premium income (RMB 100 million)	Growth rate (%)	Life insurance premium income (RMB 100 million)	Growth rate (%) (RMB 100 million)	Property insurance premium income	Growth rate (%)
1980	4.6	—	0	0	4.6	—
1981	7.8	69.5	0	0	7.8	69.5
1985	33.1	65.5	4041	508.3	28.69	49.9
1990	135.17	34.4	28.41	45.1	106.76	36.8
1995	594.9	18.9	204.2	24.93	390.7	16.0
2000	1595.9	14.5	997.5	14.4	598.4	14.8
2001	2109.4	32.2	1424.0	42.8	685.4	14.6
2002	3023.1	43.4	2274.8	59.8	748.3	9.2

Source: The CIRC (2003), *China's Insurance Statistic Yearbook.*

began the process of reviving the sector. By the late 1980s, it was operating 5,700 branches, in both urban and rural areas, with a staff of 120,000, as well as maintaining a network of 110,000 agencies and 200,000 sales agents (Ma, 1994).[1]

China's insurance market (writing all types of insurance) has undergone a rapid expansion since the country adopted the 'open-door policy' in 1979. Over the last 20 years, the value of premium payments collected by insurance companies operating in China has increased at a remarkable rate of 47 per cent per annum between 1982 and 2002, as compared with the country's growth rate of about 9 per cent per annum over the same period.

The data in Table 10.1 shows that the Chinese insurance market grew at an incredible speed. The growth rate of the premium income of life insurance was 81 per cent between 1982 and 2002 and the premium income of property insurance was 24 per cent for the same period. In 1997, the premium income of life insurance surpassed the premium income of property insurance for the first time. In 2002, the premium income of life insurance accounted for 75 per cent of China's total premium incomes, reaching RMB 227,480 million China Insurance Regulatory Commission (CIRC, 2003).

Understanding the growth and current underdevelopment of insurance

Several factors contributed to the rapid expansion of China's insurance market, especially that of life insurance market. First, growth started from a low base. Over much of the last 50 years, the rigid political and ideological constraints made commercial insurance virtually unavailable. At the same time the traditional welfare system that looked after people from cradle to grave, made people think individual insurance to be unnecessary. Hence, when China opened its doors to the outside world, the country represented the world's largest untapped insurance market. Second, rising living standards, brought about by economic reforms, has turned many of the 1.3 billion Chinese population of potential buyers of insurance products into genuine consumers. Third, the unique 'one child policy' had not only increased the demand for health insurance for the young generation, but had also increased the demand for the elderly pension insurance since the tradition of offspring caring for their parents post-retirement had been eroded by this policy (Asia Insurance Review, 2003). However, during the period between November 1997 and early 2000, the PBOC, the Chinese central bank, had reduced the deposit interest rate eight times (Wang, 2002). The continuing decline of interest rates made savings unprofitable, so that people started to look for other investment opportunities. In 2002, private savings in mainland banks totalled more than 8 trillion RMB compared with just 40 billion RMB in 1980 (Hong Kong iMail, 2002). However, Fifth, the immature and volatile stock exchange market has made many investors, especially the small ones, feel unsafe. Finally, the entry of foreign insurers into China's insurance market has intensified the competition and forced indigenous insurers to improve their market strategies and service provision. It, thus, increased consumers' awareness and their demand for insurance products (Cheng, 2000).

In spite of this remarkable expansion of China's insurance market, the market is still underdeveloped and under-served, as measured by its low insurance depth[2] and insurance density.[3] In China per capita spending on insurance was only US$15.2 in 2000, as against an average of US$2,384 for developed countries and an average of US$42 for emerging markets including India and China (Jeffrey, 2002). China's insurance industry only accounts for a very small proportion of the market share in Asia with 6 per cent by value in 2002 (Datamonitor, 2003).

The underdevelopment of China's insurance market may be attributed to several factors including the low base of China's insurance and the lack of suppliers in the last 30–40 years. In concert with other 'gradual' economic reform measures, it opened its insurance market only slowly to foreign insurers. Foreign insurers and brokers have to go through a strict licensing-approval procedure before they can sell insurance products in China. For example, according to China's Insurance Law, a foreign insurance company applying for a licence needs (i) to have engaged in insurance business for a minimum of 30 years; (ii) to have established a representative office in China for at least two years at the time of applying. (The representative offices are not allowed to conduct any direct business and can engage in non-business activities only such as market research and product promotion, technical exchange or liaison work for business purposes); (iii) prior to application, the company needs to have total assets of more than US$5 billion at the end of the previous year. Parallel to the inadequate supply of insurance, there is also a lack of demand for insurance in China. Compared to consumers in Western countries, Chinese consumers have some salient characteristics bearing on their readiness to purchase insurance products. First, many Chinese consumers still have little knowledge of insurance. A survey conducted by the Future R&D Company in 1997 showed that, when asked about their knowledge of insurance, only 1.7 per cent of the respondents said they 'understood insurance well'; 18.6 per cent of them said they 'partly understand' compared to 44.6 per cent who 'did not understand well' and 36.1 per cent who 'did not understand at all' (Sun, 2002: 32). The survey conducted by the Development Research Centre of the State Council produced a similar result also showing that a lack of insurance awareness among Chinese consumers. In a survey of 22,182 families across 50 cities, only 6 per cent surveyed said confidently that they had enough insurance knowledge compared to 36 per cent who answered that they knew little of insurance (Xin Hua News Agency, 2002). Second, the lack of insurance knowledge is compounded by the superstition held by a large number of Chinese that purchasing insurance products is a curse on the insured and that buying insurance will bring bad luck. Third, the traditional values that are deep-rooted in a farmer-dominant society. One of the traditional values has been the idea of 'raising the children to support the elderly'. This traditional value, although being gradually eroded in urban areas has hampered the development of insurance, especially life insurance in rural China. And finally, insurance demand is unevenly spread in China. According to the most recently available statistics, the major buyers of insurance products in China are concentrated in the developed, coastal areas. Shanghai and Shen Zhen alone accounted for 45 per cent of the country's insurance demand in 2002 (the CIRC, 2002).

Market structure and key market players

The Chinese insurance market has, with liberalisation and opening-up to foreign competition, undergone a remarkable transformation in recent years. The situation has evolved from the provision of insurance services by a state monopoly to intense competition in an increasingly open market, with state and private sector, joint-venture, domestic and foreign-owned companies, vying with each other to attract business through the innovation of insurance products and new marketing strategies.

In 1992, the first foreign licence was granted to the American International Group (AIG), 12 years after it had opened a representative office in Shanghai. AIG's resumption of Chinese operations was a milestone on the road to an open insurance market in China. Following AIG, a series of companies received permission to operate in China. For example, in 1994 the Tokyo Marine and Fire Insurance Company obtained a permit to sell non-life insurance in Shanghai and in 1996 Manulife of Canada was permitted to establish a joint-venture life insurance company in Shanghai. Since then, more and more insurance companies have been granted licences to do business in China. But in the 1990s the industry was still tightly regulated: the companies' areas of operation, the range of policies which could be written and the ownership of the insurers were all closely controlled by the sole regulator – which, up to November 1998, was the PBOC and subsequently has been the CIRC. Shanghai was the only open window for foreign insurance companies until 1995, when Guangzhou was also opened. (At one time, in the Shanghai market, the number of foreign insurers exceeded that of domestic insurers.)

It was not until 1996 that the regulatory body started to make an effort to ensure that the insurance needs of other regions were met. As a result, several companies, including the Hutai General Insurance Company, the Xinhua and the Tai Kang Life Insurance companies, the Yong An General Insurance Company in Xian and the Sinosafe General Insurance Company, were established. It must be noted, however, that, during this period, both the foreign and the domestic insurers were still concentrating on serving a few large cities.

However, with the growth of both foreign and domestic joint-stock insurance companies the pre-1992 role of the state-owned insurance companies had been reversed by the end of the decade (Table 10.2).

In terms of the business volumes, however, the state-owned companies still dominate the life insurance market.

Table 10.3 shows that China's life insurance market is still highly monopolistic or oligopolistic. The effort made in the last decade to break the monopoly status of China Life Insurance Co. only resulted in the emergence of an oligopoly insurance market. A term 'tripartite confrontation' has been used to refer to this kind of market structure in China's insurance industry (Cheng, 2000). China Life Co., Ping An Insurance Co. and Pacific Insurance Co. accounted for over 80 per cent of the market by value in 2002 (China Statistics Bureau, 2003). The major reason contributing to the evolution of this highly concentrated market before 1988, has been the strict entry requirement set by the regulatory body, the Bank of China and later by the CIRC.

The participation of foreign companies not only contributed to the expansion of China's insurance market, but also brought into the country valuable expertise in marketing, distributing, underwriting, rating and other operations (Lai, 2002). One example of this was the distribution technology the indigenous firms learned from their foreign counterparts. When AIG resumed operation in Shanghai in 1992, it

Table 10.2 Number of insurance companies in China by ownership

Year	Total	State-owned	Joint-stock (Chinese)	Joint-venture	Individual (Foreign)
1999	29	4	10	5	10
2000	32	4	9	7	12
2001	52	5	15	19	13

Source: CIRC, www.financialnews.com.cn (5 February 2002).

Table 10.3 Chinese life insurance market share, 2002

Company	Premium income 100 million RMB	Market share (%)
China Life Insurance Co.	1287.00	56.58
Ping An Insurance Co.	534.80	23.51
Pacific Insurance Co.	148.90	6.55
Xinhua Insurance Co.	79.83	3.51
Tai Kang Insurance Co.	65.63	2.89
Others	158.64	6.97
Total	2274.80	100.01

Source: Calculated from the China's Insurance Association Report, August 2003.

Table 10.4 Individual agents and their contribution to life insurance

	1996	1997	1998	1999	2000	2001	2002
Number of individual agents (×10,000)	12	20	30	40	60	100	130
Premiums collected (×0.1 billion RMB)	40	200	300	500	700	900	1200

Source: China Insurance Association, Annual Report, 2002.

adopted the exclusive agent system in selling its life insurance policies. An exclusive agent, although not technically the insurance company's employee, is perceived as being so, because he/she is trained and paid on commission by the company and can represent only that one company. The introduction of this type of distribution channel was so successful because it completely changed the traditional way of selling insurance products to consumers, by switching from a counter-based and product-centred approach to a personalised, protection-focused, needs-based approach. AIG quickly gained a 90 per cent share of all life premiums paid in the Shanghai market in 1992 (Gauthier and Peng, 1999). However, domestic competitors and other foreign insurance companies in China immediately followed AIG's lead and all adopted this effective new channel of distribution, so that since 1992 exclusive agents selling on commission have formed the principal method of sale of personal life insurance in China. In 2001, over 1 million individual agents collected 114.52 billion RMB, amounting to 80.4 per cent of the total life assurance premium income (www.zgbxb.com.cn, 9 October 2002).

The development of the individual agents and their contribution towards the Chinese insurance industry is listed in Table 10.4.

As other companies followed AIG's strategy of heavy reliance on individual agents to sell their products, especially life insurance, the initial competitive advantage gained by AIG began to diminish. By 2001, AIG's market share for life insurance in Shanghai had dropped to 14 per cent from 90 per cent in 1992 (www.china-insurance.com).

Regulation

Another important market player in China's insurance market is the CIRC. In the early years of the development of China' insurance industry, following resumption of trading activities in 1979, the business regulations were inadequate. The rapid development of the insurance market pushed the Chinese government to strengthen its regulation and supervision over the industry and a series of laws and rules relating to insurance were promulgated from the mid-1980s. Among these, China's Insurance Law, which was issued and which took effect in 1995, is the most important. It lays out the rules concerning the establishment of insurance organisations, their business operation, market behaviour and intermediaries' management. On 18 November 1998, the CIRC was established. It replaced the PBOC to become the sole regulator of China's insurance industry. Jeffery (2002) has detailed the role and powers of the CIRC. These regulations and rules can be categorised into four areas:

Market access regulation

An indigenous insurer can be a solely state-owned company or a joint stock company, but it can not operate both life insurance and property insurance businesses. To encourage the growth of life insurance, the minimum paid in capital for establishing a life insurance company has been reduced from 500 million RMB to 200 million RMB in contrast with the 300 million RMB requirement for a non-life insurance company. It also requires that an insurer obtain approval from the CIRC for any shareholder to hold more than 10 per cent of the company's shares.

Market conduct regulation

China is adopting the prior-approval system to prevent insurers using price-cutting strategies to gain market share. Because of the high risk of immature domestic stock markets along with the insurers' lack of risk management capabilities, investments of Chinese insurance firms were limited before 1999 to bank deposits, government bonds and corporate bonds. After the 'Securities Law' was issued in 1999, insurance companies began to be allowed to invest 5–15 per cent of their previous year's total assets or 5 per cent of total assets in newly issued stock options in mutual funds in the primary market which was an indicator of the maturity of China's stock market. This was later increased to 10 per cent in 2002 and 20–25 per cent under the revised China Insurance Law, which took effect in January 2003.

Financial and accounting regulation

All the insurers were to send their balance sheets and profit-loss account to the CIRC every year using accepted accounting principles. Those who falsified books and records, or hindered examination by the CIRC, were to be penalised. Punishments would include business restrictions or cessation, a fine up to RMB 50,000–300,000 and/or prosecution.

Solvency regulation

The minimum solvency ability of an insurer should be commensurate with the size of its business which is 'the difference between the actual assets and the actual liabilities' (China's Insurance Law, 1995). On 24 March 2003 the CIRC issued 'Administrative Rules on solvency Capacity and Supervision Indices for Insurance Companies', which took effect on the same day. These rules stipulated different minimum solvency standards and supervision indices for property insurance companies, life insurance companies and reinsurance companies. If an insurance company fails to meet the relevant minimum solvency standard, the CIRC may require the company to rectify the situation within a certain period. For those who are not compliant, the same corrective measures mentioned earlier may be taken against them.

Overall, the Chinese insurance regulatory regime is moving from rigid governmental intervention to an insurance industry concentrating on the market conduct of insurers to a more market-oriented style concentrating on monitoring solvency and unfair trade practices (LeBoeuf *et al.*, 2003).

The challenge of liberalisation

Since its accession to the World Trade Organisation (WTO) on the 11 December 2001, China has committed to comply with the General Agreement on Trade in Services (GATS) (WTO, 2001). Specific commitments on opening its insurance sector included the following.

Lifting/relaxing regional restrictions   Before 1996, foreign insurers were allowed to operate only in Shanghai. In 1996, this was extended to Guanzhou, Dalian, Shengzhen and Foshan. Under WTO all the geographical restrictions will be eliminated by 2004.

Expanding business scope   Before China's accession to the WTO, foreign property and casualty companies were allowed to provide property-liability insurance only for foreign companies operating in China. Similarly, the foreign life insurance companies' business scope was limited to individual (non-group) life insurance to both Chinese and foreign citizens. By the end of 2003, foreign property and casualty insurers were allowed to underwrite any large-scale risk for either indigenous or foreign firms without any geographical jurisdiction. Foreign life insurers are allowed to extend their business scope from individual (non-group) to group insurance. The business lines that they are allowed to write also include health and pension insurance, which represent about 85 per cent of the total life insurance premiums collected from the whole country.

Increasing equity ownership   China has allowed 51 per cent foreign ownership for non-life and reinsurance since its accession to the WTO, and it will permit wholly foreign-owned subsidiaries after five years of its accession.

Lifting restrictions on insurance brokerage operations   The minimum-total-assets requirement for an insurance broker will be reduced from US$500 million to US$400 million one year after accession, to US$300 million two years after accession and to US$200 million four years after accession. Foreign insurance brokers could enter the China market as joint-venture partners with a ceiling of 50 per cent equity share upon WTO accession or up to 51 per cent after three years of accession. After five years, wholly foreign-owned subsidiaries will be allowed.

Adopting prudential criteria   China will issue licences solely on the basis of prudential criteria, which means that the regulatory body, the CIRC, will adopt transparent process and objective criteria for all applicants when issuing licenses. At the same time, economic-needs tests, or quantitative limits on the number of licenses, are abolished (Sun, 2003).

Challenges for China's enterprises

China's accession to the WTO will have a far-reaching impact on its insurance industry. 'Floodgates of competition' opened up by China's accession to the WTO's rules are throwing a challenge to both indigenous insurance companies and the regulator. At the time of writing, there are 40 foreign insurance companies from 13 countries and regions operating in China. They have set up 62 insurance branches and received insurance premiums of 4.65 billion RMB (US$561.5 million) during 2003 (BCG, 2004). To compete with their foreign counterparts, Chinese insurance companies face three main challenges as described in the following sections.

Management and efficiencies

> The overall level of professionalism [of Chinese insurers] is far lower than that of successful international players who operate in mature markets.
>
> (BCG, 2004)

Compared to their foreign counterparts, Chinese insurance companies have some advantages. For instance, they started Chinese business earlier, thus have acquired and accumulated local knowledge through their local operating experience. This local knowledge may include information and know-how about local politics, economy, culture; or information on local demands and tastes, on how to access the local labor force, distribution channels and infrastructure (Makino and Delios, 1996). Some knowledge that is tacit and firm-specific is difficult to be learnt and acquired explicitly. As a result of these advantages Chinese insurance companies have built a vast consumer database and distribution networks. They also established certain brands and captured a large proportion of the market share. However, in opposition to these advantages, foreign insurers are more experienced in strategy and business planning, sales and underwriting, products and marketing, financial management and human resource management. Most important, they all have large asset bases directed by their headquarters. Typically, the minimum operation fund of a branch of a foreign insurance company is ten times that of their Chinese counterparts.

These large assets of foreign insurers will allow them not only to acquire information at low costs, but also generate economies of scale and economies of scope. Along with accumulated experience in actuarial work, underwriting, marketing, distribution and other managerial skills, foreign insurers find it relatively easy to instill confidence in potential customers in China (Leung and Young, 2002). Furthermore, although the investment channels for Chinese insurance companies have been increased, they may still not be able to compete effectively with foreign companies that invest their profits internationally.

Technological and product innovation

With the insurance industry facing ongoing liberalisation, combined with increasing commoditisation of core products, new products are emerging to meet the diverse and evolving needs of customers. This helps to diversify the sector's product range, in turn enabling insurers to reduce their reliance on less profitable products (Asia Insurance Review, 2003). Since life insurance products are less differentiated than those of property-liability insurance, a higher innovation rate would be expected in life insurance market as a result of intensified competition. In general, foreign insurers may gain competitive advantages in developing new products because of the technical support they obtain from their headquarters. It is reported that 90 per cent of insurance products provided by Chinese insurance companies are the same or similar (Xu, 2001). Most insurance products have some characteristics of savings. In contrast, foreign insurers are experienced in providing products spanning securities, insurance and banking businesses. To enhance the R and D capability and launch innovative products in order to meet consumers demand and to provide responsive and high quality products is a huge challenge facing the Chinese indigenous insurers.

Service qualities

Skipper (1997) summarised the effects of foreign competition in a local insurance market. One of these effects is the improvement in customer service and value. Fierce competition has led to intensive advertising campaigns and product promotion. Consequently, Chinese consumers' buying behaviour in relation to insurance products has gradually changed. In the past, Chinese consumers were 'sold' insurance products, since very few people would have any knowledge of insurance.[4] But Chinese consumers' awareness of insurance products has been stimulated by fierce competition. The marketing effort and rapid communication have made information more accessible and have made switching between insurers easier. As a result, improving service quality, which may include reducing the complaint ratio and handling consumers queries in the way they feel comfortable with has become a crucial element of business strategy for Chinese insurers.

Future trends

In the near future (between 3 and 5 years), the market structure of China's insurance will change significantly. Despite the fact that China's insurance market is still tightly regulated, there has been a move towards deregulation and divestment of state ownership. For example, the once wholly state-owned insurance company, the People's Insurance Company (PICC) group, was divided into three separate companies: China Life, PICC Property (both of which have become holding companies since late 2003) and PICC Reinsurance. All three separate state-owned insurance companies are now being transformed into joint-stock companies in order to increase their competitive strength. Along with Ping An Insurance, all of these insurance companies have started to sell shares overseas since the end of 2003. China Life itself has sold about 6.47 billion shares, valuing the company at about US$12.1 billion. (Reuters, 2 December 2003). It is expected that more state-owned insurance companies in China will become joint-stock companies, because this will allow them to sell their shares to the public or take on strategic partners (Asia Insurance Review, 2003). The other existing Chinese joint-stock insurance companies are likewise expected to increase their capital and improve administration in order to enhance their ability to compete against insurance companies from abroad.

Liberalisation of the insurance sector promises new opportunities for further deregulation on insurance contract and rates of premium. Before 2003, the CIRC set contract wording and prices for all kind of insurance. Since January 2003, however, the CIRC no longer stipulates the specific insurance terms to be employed by all insurance companies in China. In addition, alongside the prior-approval rate regulation system (which is applicable only to those products 'concerning public interests', compulsory insurance and newly developed life products, a file-and-use rating systems has been introduced. Thus, each company will have the right to design its own policies and charge the premium rate, especial those providing motor insurance. This two-tier rating system is considered to be appropriate for the current Chinese insurance market (Lai, 2002). On the one hand, it maintains healthy development of the insurance market, by preventing insurers adopting a price-cutting strategy to gain market share. On the other hand, the file-and-use system will give insurers a greater autonomy and allow them to respond to constantly changing market conditions. The liberalisation of insurance contract and rates of premium will enable insurers to introduce more sophisticated contract language and actuarial techniques into their practice more quickly and efficiently (LeBoeuf *et al.*, 2003). With the lowering of barriers of entry and stiff competition, it could therefore be expected that the market share of the state-owned insurance companies will be reduced in a few years time, whereas the market share of the joint-stocking companies, joint-ventures and wholly owned foreign subsidiaries of foreign insurers will increase. Meanwhile, foreign insurance companies could well outnumber Chinese companies, although the latter may still have a stranglehold on the insurance market.

Finally, it may be predicted that accompanying deregulation, China's insurance market will go through consolidation that may even take the form of mergers and acquisition (M&A). So far the regulator, CIRC, has made efforts to remove the ownership restriction on insurance companies, relax the geographical restriction of branching and even lift the control of the rate of premiums for auto insurance. All these can be viewed as incentives to increase competition and market efficiency. Inevitably, the market concentration will increase through consolidation. M&A is very likely to take place during this process.

Conclusion

China's insurance industry has undergone dramatic changes during the last decade. As China's insurance market moves from a literally closed and highly regulated marketplace to one that is gradually opening and becoming more competitive, more and more foreign competitors are moving into this important market with its huge potential. In the meantime, more and more domestic insurers are becoming the joint-stock companies, or forming joint-ventures with foreign partners. The market structure is changing rapidly. Although foreign insurance companies will outnumber Chinese insurers, the major business volumes, especially in life insurance, is likely to remain with the domestic insurers. The challenges for the latter, however, will be significant and of special importance will be their ability to adopt new technologies, innovate new products and routes to market and develop their financial management capabilities.

Notes

1 These sales agents were salaried employees of the insurance firms whilst the agencies were mainly branches of the insurers selling insurance products.
2 Also called insurance penetration, referring to the percentage of insurance premium income in GDP.
3 Per capita premium income.
4 In fact, the words 'safe' and 'insurance' have the same pronunciation in Chinese. There were cases in which people came to an insurance company to buy a safe (D'Arcy and Xia, 2003).

References

Allen, A. (1999) *The Insurance Industry in China, A Market Analysis*, Hong Kong, Asia Information Associates Ltd.

Asia Insurance Review (2003) 'China: the drivers of the market boom'. Available at http://www.asiainsurancereview.com/Stroy2.asp

Beijing Insurance Association (2001–2003) *Monthly Report*, Beijing.

Boston Consulting Group (BCG) (2004) 'Improve business practices now or risk being marginalized by multinational players in the future', *Business Report*, 10 March.

Cheng, D. W. (2000) 'A strategy for opening up the Chinese insurance industry', MACD Project MA in Commercial Diplomacy, Monterey Institute of International Studies. Available at http://www.commercialdiplomacy.org/ma_projects/ma_dawei1.htm

China Statistics Bureau (2003) *China's Economics Statistics Yearbook*, Beijing.

China's Insurance Association (2001 and 2002) *Annual Report*, Beijing.

China's Insurance Association (January–August 2003) *Monthly Report*, Beijing.

China's Insurance Law, *China Law Publications*, 1995.

China's Insurance Regulatory Commission (the CIRC) (2000–2003) *China's Insurance Yearbook*.

Chu, J. (2000) 'All eyes on China', *Best's Review*, 101(4): 67–9.

CNNIC (2003) *Semi-annual Survey Report on the Development of China's Internet*. Available at http://www.cnnic.net.cn

D'Arcy, Stephen, P. and Xia, H. (2003), 'Insurance and China's entry into the WTO', *Risk Management and Insurance Review*, 6(1): 7–25.

Datamonitor (2003) China Insurance, *Datamonitor* Plc, London, 25 October.

Gauthier, J. P. and Peng, E. (1999) *Insurance in China: a Holistic Approach to Understanding the Chinese Insurance Market*, London: FT Financial Publishers.

Goldman, Sachs (1998) *China Insurance Market*, Unpublished report. Available at http://www.towersperrin.com/tillinghast/publications/emphasis/Emphasis_2004_2/SaundersLu.pdf

Hong Kong iMail (2002) 'Past and future equity market activity', *Hong Kong iMail*, 27 March.

Hu, W. H. and Schanz, A. (1999) 'Asia's insurance markets after the storm', Swiss Re-working paper, No. 5, in *China Finance*, The People's Bank of China.

Jardine Matheson Archive (1805) *Correspondences in 1805*, Cambridge.

Jeffrey, E. T. (2002) 'The role and power of the Chinese insurance regulatory commission in the administration of insurance law in China', *The Geneva Papers on Risk and Insurance*, 27(3): 413–34.

Lai, Gene C. (2002) 'The future direction of the Chinese insurance industry after China enters the WTO', *China and World Economy*, 4: 50–8.

LeBoeuf, Lamb, Greene and MacRae (2003) 'China amends its insurance law', LLP, International Law Firm. Available at http://www.llgm.com

Leung, M. K. and Young, T. (2002) 'China's entry to the WTO: prospects and managerial implications for foreign life insurance companies', *Asia Pacific Business Review*, 9(4): 184–205.

Ma, M. Z. (1994) *China's Insurance Market*, Beijing: Chinese Commerce Publisher.

Makino, S. and Delios, A. (1996) 'Local knowledge transfer and performance: implications for alliance formation in Asia', *Journal of International Business Studies*, Special Issue, 27(5): 905–27.

Reuters (2003) 'China life to raise US$3 bn from IOP', *The star online*, 2 December. Available at http://biz.thestar.com.my/news/story.asp?file=/2003/12/2/

Shen, Y. (2000) 'China's insurance market: opportunity, competition and market trends', *The Geneva Papers on Risk and Insurance*, 25(3): 335–55.

Skipper, Harold D. Jr (1997) 'Foreign insurers in emerging markets: issues and concerns', *International Insurance Foundation Occasional Paper*, 16–24.

Sun, Q. X. (2003) 'The impact of WTO accession on China's insurance industry', *Risk Management and Insurance Review*, 6(1): 27–35.

Wang, X. J. (2002) 'An analysis on Chinese insurance market', in *Proceedings at the Overseas Chinese Forum*, Beijing: PR China.

WTO (2001) *The Report of the Working Party on the Accession of China*, WT/ACC/CHN/48/Add2, 1 October.

Xin Hua News Agency (2002) 'Chinese insurance awareness needs improving', Xin Hua News Agency, 30 July.

Xu, W. H. (2001) 'Changing mentality of insurance', *China Finance*, 11: 13–14.

http://www.china-insurance.com

http://www.circ.com

http://www.financialnews.com.cn www.sinopolis.com/archivesindex/topstory/ts_000121_full.ht

http://www.zgbxb.com.cn

11 Chinese business style in three regions

An exploratory study of Beijing, Shanghai and Guangzhou

Tony Fang

The existing knowledge of Chinese business style is based largely on the perception of China as one single homogeneous land and the Chinese as doing business in 'the Chinese style'. This 'one China, one style' approach had its advantages and was acceptable at a time when Western companies started embarking on their China mission. But, after many years of extensive operations on Chinese soil, Western managers have come to realize that there exist 'many Kingdoms' within the Middle Kingdom and there is a variety of 'Chineseness' among the Chinese. How to understand and cope with the diverse patterns of Chinese business behaviour within China poses an increasing challenge to management. The purpose of this chapter is to conduct an exploratory study of the diversity of Chinese business styles from a regional subcultural perspective. A survey was conducted among Swedish companies to identify the differences in Chinese business negotiating style between Beijing, Shanghai and Guangzhou. The profiles of businesspeople from the three regions are discussed and compared with each other. The chapter concludes with a number of theoretical and managerial implications.

Introduction

The People's Republic of China (PRC) has become 'the workshop of the world' (Chandler, 2003; Roberts and Kynge, 2003). In 2002, China overtook the United States as the world's largest FDI recipient (US$52.7 billion). The FDI in China further increased by US$53.5 billion in 2003 by which a total of 465,277 foreign-funded enterprises, including more than 400 of the Fortune Global 500, were operating on the Chinese soil. China's accession to the World Trade Organization (WTO) in 2001 and forthcoming hosting of the 2008 Beijing Summer Olympics and the 2010 Shanghai World Expo have lifted the PRC to the very frontier of international business. When this chapter was being written, the 2004 World Economic Forum was taking place in Davos, Switzerland. 'China' was the simple, one-word answer for many of the key questions facing the world:

> The world's fastest-growing economy? China. The market you can't afford not to be in? China. The source of the funds needed to keep the US economy from going bust? China. The engine behind global trade growth? China. The unfair trader manipulating the value of its currency at the expense of Europe and the United States? China. The giant gorilla siphoning off jobs from the West?

China. The indifferent employer pushing labour standards lower throughout the developing world? China.

(Pfanner, 2004: 15)

Never before have we been so closely linked to China and never before have we had such imperative demand to understand how to do business with the Chinese. In the mid-1990s Peter Drucker predicted an upsurge in interest in the 'secrets of Chinese management' in the years to come to be comparable to our earlier interest in the 'secrets of Japanese management' (Drucker and Nakauchi, 1997). Peter Drucker seems to be right again.

The 'one China, one style' paradigm

What is Chinese business style? Or put in other words: What are the basic characteristics of the Chinese way of doing business? This fascinating question has been touched on explicitly or implicitly from a number of perspectives in the existing literature since the 1980s, such as Chinese culture and Chinese business negotiation process (Tung, 1982, 1989; Pye, 1982, 1992; Chu, 1991; Chen, 1995; Goh, 1996; Blackman, 1997; Faure, 1998, 2000; Fang, 1999; Woo and Prud'homme, 1999; Chen, 2001; Ghauri and Fang, 2001; Shi and Wright, 2001; Woo *et al.*, 2001), Sino-Western business-to-business interactions (Fang, 2001), Chinese management structure (Lockett, 1988; Tan, 1990; Child and Markoczy, 1993; Child, 1994), mainland Chinese private businesses (Schlevogt, 2002) and some focused studies on Chinese concepts such as *guanxi* (Ambler, 1994; Xin and Pearce, 1996; Yeung and Tung, 1996; Luo, 2000; Fan, 2002). The Chinese approach business in a way which is generally sketched as relationship-focused, hardworking, face-conscious, bureaucratic, bargaining-oriented and harmonious.

Despite significant advances, the existing knowledge of Chinese business style is based largely on the perception of China as one homogeneous culture and the Chinese as negotiating business in 'the Chinese style' with a focus on differences between Chinese and Western managers (e.g. Buttery and Leung, 1998; Zhao, 2000).[1] This 'one China, one style' paradigm, though useful and important (e.g. for beginners or newcomers to Chinese business in the early stage of their China operations), does not seem to cope well with the richness of the Chinese business landscape.

China is a huge continent and may be better called the 'United States of China' given its vast land of 9.6 million square kilometre, a huge population of 1.3 billion inhabitants, and enormous ethnic, linguistic and subculture variations. Pye (1984) observed that the physical characteristics of China defy generalization of China as homogenous. China is about three times the size of the European Union, in territory and population, and more than one oral language is spoken. In many ways 'exporting' into other provinces has similar characteristics to exporting from the UK to other countries in Europe (Ambler *et al.*, 1999).

After many years of operations on the Chinese soil, many Western managers are realizing that there seems to exist 'many kingdoms' within the Middle Kingdom and there is a variety of 'Chineseness' among the Chinese people. How to understand and cope with the diverse patterns of Chinese business behaviour within China poses an increasing challenge to management. 'Anyone who has seen more of the country lately than the Great Wall and the terra-cotta warriors would laugh at the idea that there is but one China' (Pei, 2002: 8). A former vice president of a large Swedish multinational corporation in China told the author:

> One thing that struck me every time I was traveling in China, from province to province, was that the Chinese themselves are not the same. They seem to do business in different ways. Some are quite like our ways, straightforward, down-to-the-earth type; but some are extremely traditional. They seem to have different customs and etiquettes from region to region.... Coming back to Sweden I got the question from my headquarters colleagues: 'What's the temperature in China?' I replied, 'From −35C to +35C'. I'm not joking. The regional differences within China are enormous.

The regional differences within China are keenly sensed by many Western business-people especially those from Europe. Mr Kurt Hellström, Ericsson's President and CEO pointed out the potential challenges of doing business in China in an interview with the author in March 2003: 'China...has many cultures...the difference between south China and north China is as much as the difference between Italy and Sweden.'[2] Segmenting the China market and integrating China operations in terms of regions is a strategy increasingly adopted by foreign firms in China. Since the middle of the 1990s, Ericsson China's business operations have been organized in terms of Region North, Region South, and Region East and Central.

There are many markets within the Chinese market (Swanson, 1989; Polsa *et al.*, 2004). Chinese regions also vary in terms of economic development and foreign direct investment (Chen, 1996; Wu, 2002). The lack of sensitivity to the regional variations in the Chinese market is an important reason why many Western companies have failed in China (Cui and Liu, 2000). To gain a better understanding of Chinese business style and to be able to succeed in dealing with the Chinese, it seems crucial to shift our attention from the national level to regional or subcultural level; we need to focus more on regions and subcultures in China.

Stereotypes about Chinese regions

Stereotypes about Chinese regions do exist in a few texts. For example, Fang (1999: 92) quotes:

> Beijing people are straightforward; Shanghai people are clever and farsighted; Tianjin people are capable and seasoned; The people of Guangzhou, Zhejiang, and Anhui are decisive and full of stratagem; Fujian people are honest and sedate; Shandong people are forthright and generous; The people of Liaoning, Jilin, and Heilongjiang are reasonable and loyal; The people of Henan, Hebei, Hunan, and Hubei are open and direct; The people of Sichuan, Shannxi, Jiangxi, and Shanxi are upright; Those in Yunan, Haianan, Guangxi, Guizhou, and

Table 11.1 Western negotiators' perception of the Chinese regional differences

Beijing	Shanghai	Guangdong
Less knowledgeable	More sophisticated than Beijing	Friendly, more open
Friendly	Not flexible	Lead with their personal requirements, self-serving
Naïve claims	Rude, insulting	Practical, down to earth
More reserved, conservative	Sly, cunning	More quality and environmentally conscious
More politically correct	Show off, superior attitude	Least bureaucratic
Not fond of HK Chinese, prefer Taiwanese	Anti-foreign	Promise more than they can deliver
Very deferential to authority	Suave appearance	Wild west environment of anything goes
Most bureaucratic	Not fond of HK Chinese, unless Shanghai speaking	Like dealing with Hong Kong Chinese
Becoming more corrupt	Very corrupt	Corrupt

Source: Wong and Stone (1998: 211).

Qinhai always behave in an unhurried manner; The people of Inner Mongolia, Xinjiang, and Tibet are warm-hearted but dubious.

Wong and Stone (1998) also provides 'Chinese regional stereotypes' showing differences between Beijing, Shanghai and Guangzhou (see Table 11.1). But all these anecdotal accounts, though useful and important, do not seem to be well grounded in the existing culture studies. This is the gap that this chapter intends to start filling.

About this study

The purpose of this chapter is to conduct an exploratory study of the diversity of Chinese business style from a regional subcultural perspective. It attempts to answer a fundamental question: What are the differences in Chinese business style between Chinese regions as perceived by Western businesspeople with experience from working with these regions?

The scope of this chapter is narrowed to three major Chinese cities,[3] that is, Beijing, Shanghai and Guangzhou. These three cities are China's major growth engines and principal recipients of FDI where most multinational corporations are active. Beijing, as the Capital of China assumes the utmost importance in China's political and economic life. Shanghai and Guangzhou are important not only as developed and advanced municipalities in China but as leading dragons in the Yangtze River Delta and the Pearl River Delta, respectively.

Inspiration for conducting this research is also drawn from the growing interest in China's regions in macroeconomics and social development (Wei, 2000; OECD, 2002; Renard, 2002), work values (Ralston *et al.*, 1996), consumer behaviour (Cui, 1997, 1998; Cui and Liu, 2000), Chinese lifestyle (Vittachi, 2000a,b,c) and from the renaissance of Chinese literature on 'regional Chinese traits' (e.g. Yu, 2001;

Chen, 2002). But the focus of this chapter is not on macroeconomics or consumer behaviour but rather on regional business culture and behaviour.

Theory

We approach our subject from a culture point of view. There are two basic approaches to the study of culture: etic and emic (Brislin, 1993; Triandis, 1994). The former uses culture-general variables (i.e. cultural dimensions) to compare cultures, while the latter uses culture-specific variables (i.e. the idiosyncratic components of the culture) to understand one specific culture and behaviour. As such, this study is based on two clusters of literature: the dimensional theory of culture (etic) and Chinese business culture and behaviour (emic).

The 'etic' perspective

The conventional wisdom of cross-cultural business behaviour builds on analyses at the national cultural level. In the etic (culture-general) studies, national cultural dimensions are used to compare national cultures with each other (e.g. Hall, 1976; Hofstede, 1980, 1991, 2001), while regions and subcultures are not sufficiently tackled. Given the size and variation of the Chinese mainland (as noted earlier, businesses between Chinese provinces are comparable to those between EU nations), it is considered to be appropriate to employ dimensional analysis at the regional level (see also Ralston *et al.*, 1996).

We use a more manager-friendly version of etic cultural dimensions. Gesteland's (2002) four dimensional framework of cross-cultural business behaviour of international business negotiators suits our purpose: Deal-focused vs Relationship-focused; Formal vs Informal; Rigid-Time vs Fluid-Time; Reserved vs Expressive. We briefly discuss these four dimensions:

Deal-focused vs relationship-focused

Deal-focused (DF) people are task-oriented and transaction-minded, while relationship-focused (RF) people are more relationship-minded. 'RF people prefer to deal with family, friends and persons or groups well known to them – people who can be trusted' (Gesteland, 2002: 19). They are uncomfortable doing business with strangers. For RF people, trust building is important before a formal business process can be opened. In contrast, DF people do business even with those who they do not know. DF people rely on written agreements to prevent misunderstandings and solving problems. Some in particular tend to take a rather impersonal, legalistic, contract-based approach when disagreements and disputes arise. RF people, however, depend primarily on relationships to prevent difficulties and to solve problems. The DF–RF distinction is related to that of individualism vs collectivism often discussed in the cross-cultural literature and reflects the general trust in the society (Fukuyama, 1995). From the business process point of view, the RF people need a long pre-negotiation period to engage in what Graham and Sano (1996) call the 'non-task sounding' activities.

Formal vs informal

Formal cultures tend to be 'organized in steep hierarchies that reflect major differences in status and power', while informal cultures 'value more egalitarian organizations with smaller differences in status and power' (Gesteland, 2002: 45). In formal cultures, surname, title, formality are emphasized to show respect. Formal cultures tend to ascribe status according to one's age, gender, organizational rank and whether one is the buyer or the seller. Therefore, a young female export sales manager from a small private firm potentially suffers from a quadruple handicap when operating in formal hierarchical cultures. This dimension is associated with Hofstede's (1980, 1991, 2001) dimension of power distance. The Chinese value of respect for age and hierarchy (e.g. Lockett, 1988; Child and Markoczy, 1993; Fang, 1999) suggests that Chinese business behaviour is formal.

Rigid-time vs fluid-time

People perceive time and scheduling differently in different cultures. In rigid-time (RT) societies 'punctuality is critical, schedules are set in concrete, agendas are fixed and business meetings are rarely interrupted'; in contrast, the fluid-time (FT) cultures, people 'place less emphasis on strict punctuality and are not obsessed with deadlines' (Gesteland, 2002: 57). This RT–FT dimension is directly anchored in Hall's (1976) dimension of Monochronic-time vs Polychronic-time (or M-time vs P-time). Apart from the issue of punctuality emphasized by Gesteland (2002), Hall (1976) also suggests that P-time people have the tendency of doing a number of things at a time, while M-time people prefer to undertake only one task at a time. Given this difference, China is regarded as a RT culture in Gesteland (2002) but P-time (suggesting an FT orientation) in Hall (1976).

Reserved vs expressive

In communication, two cultures are distinguished from each other: Reserved vs Expressive. This divide creates a major communication problem. Reserved people are comfortable communicating nonverbally, while expressive people tend to communicate verbally. Expressive people tend to be uncomfortable with more than a second or two of silence during conversation. They tend to interrupt and overlap each other. In contrast, reserved people feel at ease with longer silence. This dimension has its roots in Hall's (1976) famous High-context (HC) vs Low-context (LC) distinction of communication style. Chinese culture is a typical HC (Hall, 1976) and reserved culture (Chen, 2001; Gao *et al.*, 1996).

The 'emic' perspective

Fang (1999) synthesized the Chinese business culture and negotiating style literature by identifying three fundamental dimensions in Chinese business culture. First, business in China is influenced by the so-called 'PRC condition' (politics, economic planning, legal framework, technology, great size, uneven development within China and rapid change). Second, the Chinese business mindset is driven by Confucian traditions (moral cultivation, importance of interpersonal trust and *guanxi*, family-orientation, respect for age and hierarchy, avoidance of conflict and need for harmony and the concept of face). Finally, Chinese business behaviours are fundamentally shaped by the strategic Chinese thinking called the 'Chinese stratagems' which is grounded in the Taoist Wu Wei philosophy. Existing studies are classified along these three different but interrelated dimensions.

The Chinese way of life is characterized intrinsically by paradox (Chen, 2001; Fan, 2002). Given the paradoxical influences of Chinese sociocultural forces, a Chinese businessperson plays different roles in different situations. More specifically, the Chinese business personality integrates three roles into one: 'Maoist bureaucrat in learning', 'Confucian gentleman' and 'Sun Tzu-like strategist' (Fang, 1999). In this chapter, this '3-in-1' metaphor is modified to highlight the three different business profiles of Chinese businesspeople: 'Bureaucrat', 'Gentleman' and 'Strategist'.

Bureaucrat

As a 'bureaucrat', the Chinese businessperson follows the government's plans for doing business. He gives first priority to China's political interest and never separates business from politics. He avoids taking initiatives, shuns responsibility, fears criticism and has no final say. He is a shrewd and tough negotiator because he is trained daily in a Chinese bureaucratic system in which subtle bargaining is an integrated element. His negotiation strategy comes naturally from his culture, which can be called a mix of 'Confucian-type cooperation' and 'Sun Tzu-type competition'. At present, his international business experience improves and he learns fast.

Gentleman

Being a 'Gentleman', the Chinese businessperson acts on the basis of mutual trust and benefit, seeking cooperation or 'win–win' solutions for both parties to succeed. He places high value on trust and sincerity on his own part and that of the other party. For him, cultivation of righteousness is more important than the pursuit of profit. He shows a profound capacity to conclude business *without* negotiating. He does not like lawyers to be involved in face-to-face negotiations. He may not like the word 'negotiation' since the term suggests somewhat disagreeable connotations of conflict, which must be avoided at all costs. He is well-mannered and generous; a mere handshake or exchange of business cards implies a lifelong commitment. He views contracting essentially as an ongoing relationship or problem-solving process rather than a once-off legal package. He associates business with *guanxi* and friendship. He is group-oriented, self-restrained, superstitious, face-conscious, suspicious of outsiders, and sensitive to age, hierarchy and etiquette.

Strategist

As a 'Strategist', the Chinese businessperson believes everything is a 'win–lose game' and 'The marketplace is like a battlefield'. He sets out to 'win–lose' you in the interests of his group. He never stops bargaining. He is a skilful negotiator, endowed with a formidable variety of Chinese stratagems from his ancestors. At the heart of his bargaining technique lies Sun Tzu's admonition: 'To subdue the enemy without fighting is the acme of skill'. He seldom wages a physical war; rather, he is skilled in the psychological wrestling of wit to manipulate you into doing business his way. His actions tend to be deceitful and indirect. He often creates favourable situations to attain his objectives by utilizing external forces. He is always ready to withdraw from the bargaining table when all else fails, but that is only a Chinese stratagem for fighting back.

Which role the Chinese negotiator would play depends on trust between business partners. Given the fundamental influence of the PRC condition, foreign companies, especially when negotiating large projects, will always encounter Chinese bureaucrats. When trust is high, the Chinese will do business as a gentleman. When trust is not in place, the same Chinese would play the role of strategists and could use whatever strategies and tactics are necessary to knock the opponents off balance. Therefore, the Chinese way of behaving is dynamic, paradoxical and changing. Trust is the ultimate indicator of Chinese business style.

Chinese business negotiating tactics are discussed in many studies (e.g. Pye, 1982, 1992; Blackman, 1997; Fang, 1999). Fang (1999), in particular, lists 36 Chinese stratagems and negotiating tactics. A number of mostly discussed Chinese negotiating tactics are singled out in this research to see if they are employed differently in different regions: stalling, playing competitors off against each other, camouflaging, surprising and other tricks.

Guanxi (connections or personal contacts, e.g. Chen, 1995; Davies *et al.*, 1995; Xin and Pearce, 1996; Luo, 2000; Chen, 2001), *face* (*mianzi*, see, e.g. Hu, 1944; Redding and Ng, 1982; Redding and Wong, 1986; Redding, 1990; Bond, 1991; Child and Markoczy, 1993) and *superstition* (Eitel, 1984; McDonald and Roberts, 1990; Seligman, 1990; Baker, 1993; Lip, 1995; Schmitt, 1995; Feng, 1996; Pan and Schmitt, 1996) are among the most frequently discussed Chinese concepts in the literature. In this research, *guanxi* is viewed as a relationship building process which is involved in the RF dimension discussed earlier. We, therefore, only use 'face' and 'superstition' as two extra variables in our analysis.

Summing up the theoretical discussions stated earlier, the core variables to be used to study the regional Chinese business style in this research are: (1) DF vs RF, (2) Formal vs Informal, (3) RT vs FT, (4) Reserved vs Expressive, (5) 'Bureaucrat', (6) 'Gentleman', (7) 'Strategist', (8) Superstitious and (9) Face. In addition, items concerning Chinese business negotiation and Chinese negotiating tactics will be measured across the three regions.

Methodology

Given the purpose and research question of this study a quantitative survey is desired (Yin, 1994). In the spring of 2001, a questionnaire was sent by a team of MSc candidates under the supervision of the author of this chapter to 247 Swedish companies actively doing business in China. The companies were approached via email through the network of the Swedish Trade Council that has its regional offices in Beijing, Shanghai and Guangzhou. A total of 39 companies responded in the questionnaire survey among which 22 are complete valid answers on which the analysis was based. This is a relatively small sample; one reason is that the persons we tried to reach were division chiefs or responsible executives who happened to be very busy and could not answer the questionnaire within the designated time frame (one month). But the 22 companies come from various industries in which Sweden has a strong profile (telecommunications, machine processing, banking, energy, service, etc.) both internationally and in China. The sample companies were well represented in Beijing, Shanghai and Guangzhou through its own compa-nies, representative offices, productions or agents. Apart from the questions involv-ing the above nine variables, a few background questions were also asked. The empirical data were processed using 1–6 scale (1 strongly disagree...6 strongly agree) structure.

Survey findings

The average years of conducting business negotiations in China for these Swedish businesspeople are 9.16 (with a Standard Deviation 6.54). There appear to exist two clusters of respondents; those who have business experience in China for more than ten years and those for less than five years (see Figure 11.1).

- As Table 11.2 shows, when asked if they have perceived substantial regional differences in Chinese business style, 20 out of 22 answered 'Yes' (about 91 per cent) and two answered 'No' (9 per cent).
- Beijing businesspeople are found to be the most RF (4.50). Guangzhou is the least RF (3.10), suggesting that they are most DF. Shanghai is in the middle but towards being significantly DF (3.20).

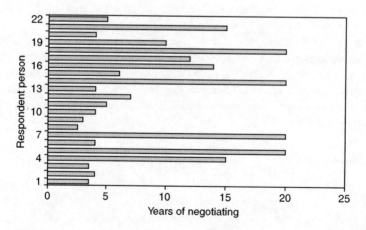

Figure 11.1 Number of years of experience by respondent.

Table 11.2 Chinese business style: summarizes the findings of the core
measured items across Beijing, Guangzhou and Shanghai

Item	Region	Mean	SD
1 Relationship-focused	Beijing	4.50	1.06
	Guangzhou	3.10	1.23
	Shanghai	3.20	1.02
2 Informal	Beijing	2.68	1.17
	Guangzhou	3.73	2.24
	Shanghai	3.27	0.94
3 Fluid-time	Beijing	3.86	0.83
	Guangzhou	3.73	1.12
	Shanghai	3.36	0.85
4 Expressive	Beijing	3.32	1.17
	Guangzhou	4.41	0.80
	Shanghai	3.77	0.92
5 'Bureaucrat'	Beijing	4.73	0.77
	Guangzhou	3.24	0.94
	Shanghai	3.62	0.67
6 'Gentleman'	Beijing	3.15	1.09
	Guangzhou	2.85	1.04
	Shanghai	3.25	0.91
7 'Strategist'	Beijing	4.27	0.98
	Guangzhou	4.18	1.14
	Shanghai	4.32	0.84
8 Importance of face	Beijing	5.19	1.05
	Guangzhou	4.48	1.03
	Shanghai	4.71	0.85
9 Superstitious	Beijing	3.84	0.86
	Guangzhou	4.72	0.84
	Shanghai	3.72	0.77

- Guangzhou seems to have the most informal business culture (3.73) whereas Beijing, the least informal (2.68) and Shanghai being in the middle (3.27). Notice that the standard deviation for Guangzhou is pretty high (2.24).
- In Beijing, time seems to move in the most fluid fashion (3.86), while in Shanghai, time seems to be the most structured (3.36). Guangzhou is in the middle (3.73).
- Beijing businesspeople seem to be the most reserved (3.32). Guangzhou businesspeople are the most expressive (4.41), Shanghai in the middle (3.77).
- Who is a 'Bureaucrat'? Beijing businesspeople seem to have the greatest tendency to play the role of 'bureaucrat' (4.73) with Guangzhou being the least bureaucratic culture (3.24) and Shanghai in the middle (3.62).
- Who is a 'gentleman'? The difference between the three regions is not significant. Shanghai businesspeople are perceived to be the most 'gentleman'-oriented (3.25), followed by Beijing businesspeople (3.15) and Guangzhou businesspeople (2.85). The mean value seems to suggest the respondents' low interest in this item.

- Who is a 'strategist'? Shanghai seems to possess the most strategic-oriented business culture (4.32), followed by Beijing (4.27) and Guangzhou (4.18). The mean value seems to suggest the respondents' high interest in this item.
- Is face important? Face is regarded as important in China (suggested by the high mean value). Face seems to be most important in Beijing (5.19), then Shanghai (4.71) and then Guangzhou (4.48).
- Are businesspeople in Beijing, Shanghai and Guangzhou superstitious? How superstitious are they? It shows that 77 per cent believe Guangzhou and Shanghai businesspeople are superstitious, 73 per cent believe Beijing business-people are superstitious. Guangzhou businesspeople seem to be the most super-stitious (4.72), those in Shanghai the least superstitious (3.72), whereas those in Beijing fall in the middle (3.84).

Four other questions were asked (not included in Table 11.2):

- Who are the easiest to negotiate business with? The survey shows that most respon-dents point to Shanghai as the easiest people to negotiate business with (Shanghai 50 per cent, Beijing 27 per cent, Guangzhou 18 per cent, No opinion 5 per cent).
- Who are the toughest to negotiate business with? The answer points, paradoxi-cally, to Shanghai as well (Shanghai 45 per cent, Guangzhou 32 per cent, Beijing 18 per cent, No opinion 5 per cent).
- Who takes the longest time to negotiate with? The survey shows that negotia-tion in Beijing seem to be the most time-consuming (45 per cent) followed by Shanghai (27 per cent) and Guangzhou (23 per cent), No opinion 5 per cent.
- Negotiating tactics? The Chinese tactic of playing competitors off against each other seems to be the most frequently used negotiating trick by the Chinese negotiators. The exception is Beijing where stalling just prevails. Stalling is also the second most used tactic by the Chinese negotiators: 'stalling' (Beijing 13 : Guangzhou 11 : Shanghai 12), 'playing competitors off against each other' (12 : 15 : 13), 'camouflaging' (9 : 8 : 7), 'surprising' (8 : 8 : 9), other tactics (9 : 8 : 9). Figure 11.2 provides a spider's-net view of differences between the three cities (based on the mean value).

This study suggests that significant regional differences in Chinese business style exist between Chinese businesspeople in Beijing, Shanghai and Guangzhou (20 out of 22 answered 'Yes'). But the measured items are not equally significant; some differences are marginal such as 'FT', 'Gentleman' and 'Strategist'. More significant variations are found on the items such as 'RF', 'Informal', 'Expressive', 'Bureaucrat', 'Importance of face' and 'Superstitious'. The survey seems to suggest that Chinese businesspeople in the three regions are all strategic-minded. The Beijing's business style is *relational* while Guangzhou's is *entrepreneurial* in nature. Beijing's political status and the importance of the central government networks may have contributed to making the Beijing business culture more RF than others. This study seems to support the existing stereotype about Guangzhou as being a more open and action-oriented business culture (Wong and Stone, 1998). Both Beijing and Guangzhou are more fluid in the use of time than Shanghai. Sudden changes of networks balancing and political interference may be possible reasons behind a fluid business culture in

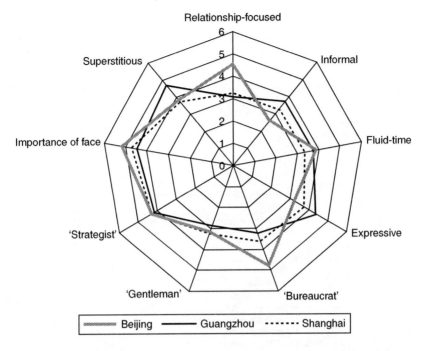

Figure 11.2 Differences in business styles between Beijing, Guangzhou and Shanghai.

Beijing; while the FT mentality in Guangzhou may be better explained from the region's long-standing tradition of entrepreneurship and risk taking. We, therefore, call the Guangzhou business style an entrepreneurial business style and the Beijing business style a relationship-oriented one.

Shanghai seems to be a more complex case. On many significant items, Beijing and Guangzhou serve as the two ends of the spectrum while Shanghai is located somewhere in the middle (see 'RF', 'Informal', 'Expressive', 'Bureaucrat' and 'Importance of face'). But, simply claiming that the Shanghai business style is between those of Beijing and Guangzhou can be gravely misleading. In this study, Shanghai businesspeople are found to be the least superstitious with the most structured use of time, negotiating as both the most gentle and the most strategic negotiators. The Shanghai businesspeople are also found to be, paradoxically, both the easiest and the toughest negotiators. One explanation is the history of Shanghai as the trader between China and Western businesses. Shanghai's culture does not seem to be grounded in the old Chinese traditions but rather developed from a mixture of Western style and local Chinese traders' culture. Some call Shanghai businesspeople the least loyal businesspeople (Yu, 2001; Chen, 2002). The more structured or rigid perception of time may also reflect the lack of boldness in the character of Shanghai in defiance of the central power in Beijing (Yatsko, 2000). This study sees Shanghai as being characterized by a *professional* business style. Figure 11.3 offers general profiles of business styles in Beijing, Guangzhou and Shanghai based on the investigation from this study.

```
┌─────────────────────────────────────────┐
│ Beijing                                  │
│ (A relationship-focused business style)  │
│                                          │
│ Relationship-focused                     │
│ Formal                                   │
│ Fluid-time                               │
│ Reserved                                 │
│ Most bureaucratic negotiators            │
│ Least strategic                          │
│ Most face-conscious                      │
│ Least tough negotiators                  │
│ Longest time to negotiate with           │
│ Favourite negotiating tactic: stalling   │
└─────────────────────────────────────────┘
        ┌─────────────────────────────────────────┐
        │ Guangzhou                                │
        │ (An entrepreneurial business style)      │
        │                                          │
        │ Deal-focused                             │
        │ Informal                                 │
        │ Fluid-time                               │
        │ Expressive                               │
        │ Least bureaucratic                       │
        │ Least 'Gentleman'                        │
        │ Most strategic negotiators               │
        │ Least face conscious                     │
        │ Most superstitious                       │
        │ Quickest to negotiate with               │
        │ Favourite negotiating tactic: playing    │
        │    competitors off against each other    │
        └─────────────────────────────────────────┘
                ┌─────────────────────────────────────────┐
                │ Shanghai                                 │
                │ (A professional business style)          │
                │                                          │
                │ Deal-focused                             │
                │ Formal                                   │
                │ Structured time                          │
                │ Expressive                               │
                │ Most 'Gentleman'                         │
                │ Least superstitious                      │
                │ Easiest to negotiate with                │
                │ Toughest negotiators                     │
                │ Favourite negotiating tactic: playing    │
                │    competitors off against each other    │
                └─────────────────────────────────────────┘
```

Figure 11.3 General profile of business styles in Beijing, Guangzhou and Shanghai.

We are aware of the strengths and weaknesses of this study. The study has advanced the existing knowledge of Chinese business style mainly through efforts, however preliminary it may be, to fine-tune Chinese business style from a regional perspective based on the empirical investigation. This regional approach to the study of culture is not only rare in Chinese business studies (one exception is Ralston *et al.*, 1996) but also uncommon in cross-cultural management behaviour literature in general. For decades, the field of cross-cultural management research has been dominated by a 'nation-state' paradigm of analysing national culture at the national culture level (e.g. Hofstede, 1980, 1991, 2001). But the paradigm does not cope well with the intricacies, diversities and dynamisms within a culture. This study supports the speculation that there may exist different cultures within a national culture (Punnett, 1998). Deeper studies on 'region-states' need to be encouraged. Implications for practitioners are many. One is that managers who are to work in Shanghai may need to think nationally (China) and act regionally (Shanghai). For example, *guanxi* is certainly a national trait in China but professional skills and expertise may be equally important in Shanghai business communities.

The main weakness of this study is the lack of real-life contexts (industry or business-related processes, situations, and people) in which to examine the suggested variations between the three cities. Another weakness is the small amount of empirical samples (22 Swedish companies) being presented in the study, which could have weakened the generality of the conclusions and possibly introduced some biases. Although these companies are well represented in various industries in China and with extensive business networks in Beijing, Shanghai and Guangzhou, efforts to involve more Western firms in the research would be appreciated. Given the Yin Yang principle (Chen, 2001; Fang, 2003) that everything embraces Yin and Yang, there must be variations even within each of the studied regions. Floating population and work forces active in all the Chinese large cities (Fang, 1999) may have contributed to making the regional culture more dynamic than before. In addition, gender issues in Chinese business style should be explored (Woo *et al.*, 2001). In short, in-depth case studies and more extended surveys to include even Chinese managers' own perceptions and to include more Chinese regions, especially, China's inland regions need to be undertaken if a fuller understanding of the subject is to be reached.

Acknowledgement

The preparation of this work was partially financed by a research grant from the *Jan Wallanders och Tom Hedelius Stiftelse och Tore Browaldhs Stiftelse*.

Notes

1 Exceptions are anecdotal accounts of regional differences in China in Chu, 1991; Ralston *et al.*, 1996; Wong and Stone, 1998; Fang, 1999; Schlevogt, 2002.
2 Tony Fang's personal interview with Mr. Kurt Hellström, Ericsson's then President and CEO, LM Ericsson Headquarters, Telefonplan, Stockholm, 19 March 2003.
3 China is administratively divided into 22 provinces, 5 autonomous regions and 4 provincial-level municipalities.

References

Ambler, T. (1994) 'Marketing's third paradigm: *guanxi*', *Business Strategy Review*, 5(4): 69–80.
Ambler, T., Styles, C. and Wang, X. (1999) 'The effect of channel relationships and *guanxi* on the performance of inter-province export ventures in the People's Republic of China', *International Journal of Research in Marketing*, 16: 75–87.

Baker, H. (1993) 'Symbolism in cross-cultural trade: making Chinese symbols work for you', in T. D. Weinshall (ed.), *Societal Culture and Management*, de Gruyter, Berlin, pp. 271–8.

Blackman, C. (1997) *Negotiating China: Case Studies and Strategies*, Allen & Unwin, St Leonards, NSW.

Bond, M. H. (1991) *Beyond the Chinese Face: Insights from Psychology*, Oxford University Press, Hong Kong.

Brislin, R. W. (1993) *Understanding Culture's Influence on Behavior*, Harcourt Brace College Publishers, Fort Worth, TX.

Buttery, E. A. and Leung, T. K. P. (1998) 'The difference between Chinese and Western negotiations', *European Journal of Marketing*, 32(3–4): 374–89.

Chandler, C. (2003) *Coping with China*, Fortune, pp. 66–70.

Chen, C.-H. (1996) 'Regional determinants of foreign direct investment in mainland China', *Journal of Economic Studies*, 23(2): 18–30.

Chen, G. R. (2002) *Zhongguo gedi shangren* [*The Businessmen from All Over China*], Dandai Zhongguo Press (in Chinese), Beijing.

Chen, M. (1995) *Asian Management Systems: Chinese, Japanese and Korean Styles of Business*, Routledge, London.

Chen, M. J. (2001) *Inside Chinese Business: A Guide for Managers Worldwide*, Harvard Business School Press, Boston, MA.

Child, J. (1994) *Management in China during the Age of Reform*, Cambridge University Press, Cambridge.

Child, J. and Markoczy, L. (1993) 'Host-country management behavior and learning in Chinese and Hungarian joint ventures', *Journal of Management Studies*, 30(4): 611–31.

Chu, C. N. (1991) *The Asian Mind Game*, Rawson Associates, New York.

Cui, G. (1997) 'The different faces of the Chinese consumer', *China Business Review*, 24(4): 34–8.

Cui, G. (1998) 'The emergence of the Chinese economic area (CEA): a regiocentric approach to the markets', *Multinational Business Review*, 6(1): 63–72.

Cui, G. and Liu, Q. (2000) 'Regional market segments of China: opportunities and barriers in a big emerging market', *Journal of Consumer Marketing*, 17(1): 55–72.

Davies, H., Leung, K. P., Luk, T. K. and Wong, Y. H. (1995) 'The benefits of "*guanxi*": the value of relationships in developing the Chinese market', *Industrial Marketing Management*, 24: 207–14.

Drucker, P. F. and Nakauchi, I. (1997) *Drucker on Asia: A Dialogue Between Peter Drucker and Isao Nakauchi*, Butterworth-Heinemann, Oxford.

Eitel, E. J. (1984) *Feng-shui: The Science of Sacred Landscape in Old China* (First published in 1873), Synergetic Press, London.

Fan, Y. (2002) 'Questioning *guanxi*: definition, classification and implications', *International Business Review*, 11(5): 543–61.

Fang, T. (1999) *Chinese Business Negotiating Style*, Sage, Beverly Hills, CA.

Fang, T. (2001) 'Culture as a driving force for interfirm adaptation: a Chinese case', *Industrial Marketing Management*, 30(1): 51–63.

Fang, T. (2003) 'A critique of Hofstede's fifth national culture dimension', *International Journal of Cross Cultural Management*, 3(3): 347–68.

Faure, G. O. (1998) 'Negotiation: the Chinese concept', *Negotiation Journal*, 14(2): 137–48.

Faure, G. O. (2000) 'Negotiations to set up joint ventures in China', *International Negotiation*, 5: 157–89.

Feng, J. C. (1996) 'Festival highlights life culture', *China Daily*, 12 March, Beijing.

Fukuyama, F. (1995) *Trust: The Social Virtues and the Creation of Prosperity*, Penguin Books, Harmondsworth, Baltimore, MD.

Gao, G., Ting-Toomey, S. and Gudykunst, W. B. (1996) 'Chinese communication processes', in M. H. Bond (ed.), *The Handbook of Chinese Psychology*, Oxford University Press, Hong Kong, pp. 280–93.

Gesteland, R. R. (2002) *Cross-cultural Business Behavior: Marketing, Negotiating, Sourcing and Managing Across Cultures* (3rd edn), Copenhagen Business School Press, Copenhagen.

Ghauri, P. N. and Fang, T. (2001) 'Negotiating with the Chinese: a socio-cultural analysis', *Journal of World Business*, 36(3): 303–25.

Goh, B. C. (1996) *Negotiating With the Chinese*, Dartmouth, Brookfield, VT.

Graham, J. L. and Sano, Y. (1996) 'Business negotiations between Japanese and Americans', in P. N. Ghauri and J. C. Usunier (eds), *International Business Negotiations*, Pergamon Press, Oxford, pp. 353–67.

Hall, E. T. (1976) *Beyond Culture*, Doubleday, Garden city, NY,

Hofstede, G. (1980) *Culture's Consequences: International Differences in Work-related Values*, Sage, Beverly Hills, CA.

Hofstede, G. (1991) *Cultures and Organizations: Software of the Mind*, McGraw-Hill, Maidenhead.

Hofstede, G. (2001) *Culture's Consequences: Comparing Values. Behaviors, Institutions, and Organizations Across Nations*, Sage, Beverley Hills, CA.

Hu, H. C. (1944) 'The Chinese concepts of "face" ', *American Anthropologist*, 46(1): 45–64.

Lip, E. (1995) *Feng Shui for Business*, Times Books International, Singapore.

Lockett, M. (1988) 'Culture and the problems of Chinese management', *Organization Studies*, 9(4): 475–96.

Luo, Y. (2000) *Guanxi and Business*, World Scientific, Singapore.

McDonald, G. M. and Roberts, C. J. (1990) 'The brand-naming enigma in the Asia Pacific context', *European Journal of Marketing*, 24(8): 6–19.

OECD (2002) *Foreign Direct Investment in China: Challenges and Prospects for Regional Development*, Organisation for Economic Co-operation and Development (OECD), Paris.

Pan, Y. and Schmitt, B. H. (1996) 'Language and brand attitudes: impact of script and sound matching in Chinese and English', *Journal of Consumer Psychology*, 5(3): 263–77.

Pei, X. M. (2002) 'China's split personality', *Newsweek* (Special Issue), Fall/Winter: 6–13.

Pfanner, E. (2004) 'The talk of the town at Davos: China', *International Herald Tribune*, 25 January, p. 15.

Polsa, P., So, S. L. M. and Speece, M. W. (2004) 'The People's Republic of China: markets within the markets', in C. Shultz and A. Pecotich (eds), *Handbook on the Markets and Economies of East Asia, Southeast Asia, Australia and New Zealand*, M.E. Sharpe (Forthcoming).

Punnett, B. J. (1998) 'Culture, cross-national', in R. L. Tung (ed.), *The International Encyclopedia of Business Management (IEBM) Handbook of International Business*, International Thomson Business Press, London, pp. 51–67.

Pye, L. W. (1982) *Chinese Commercial Negotiating Style*, Oelgeschlager, Gunn & Hain, Cambridge, MA.

Pye, L. W. (1984) *China: An Introduction* (3rd edn), Little, Brown & Company, Boston, MA.

Pye, L. W. (1992) *Chinese Negotiating Style: Commercial Approaches and Cultural Principles*, Quorum Books, New York.

Ralston, D. A., Yu, K. C., Wang, X., Terpstra, R. H. and He, W. (1996) 'The cosmopolitan Chinese manager: findings of a study on managerial values across the six regions of China', *Journal of International Management*, 2: 79–109.

Redding, S. G. (1990) *The Spirit of Chinese Capitalism*, de Gruyter, Berlin.

Redding, S. G. and Ng, M. (1982) 'The role of "face" in the organizational perceptions of Chinese managers', *Organization Studies*, 3(3): 201–19.

Redding, S. G. and Wong, Y. Y. (eds) (1986) *The Psychology of Chinese Organizational Behavior*, Oxford University Press, Hong Kong.

Renard, M. F. (ed.) (2002) *China and Its Regions: Economic Growth and Reform in Chinese Provinces*, Edward Elgar, Cheltenham.

Roberts, D. and Kynge, J. (2003) 'How cheap labour, foreign investment and rapid industrialization are creating a new workshop of the world', *Financial Times*, 4 February, p. 13.

Schlevogt, K. A. (2002) *The Art of Chinese Management: Theory, Evidence, and Applications*, Oxford University Press, Oxford.

Schmitt, B. H. (1995) 'Language and visual imagery: issues of corporate identity in East Asia', *Columbia Journal of World Business*, 30(4): 28–36.

Seligman, S. D. (1990) *Dealing with the Chinese: A Practical Guide to Business Etiquette*, Mercury, London.

Shi, X. and Wright, P. C. (2001) 'Developing and validating an international business negotiator's profile: the China context', *Journal of Managerial Psychology*, 16(5): 364–89.

Swanson, L. A. (1989) 'The twelve "nations" of China', *Journal of International Consumer Marketing*, 2(1): 83–105.

Tan, C. H. (1990) 'Management concepts and Chinese culture', in J. Child and M. Lockett (eds), *Advances in Chinese Industrial Studies*, Part A, JAI Press, Greenwich, CT, 1: 277–88.

Triandis, H. C. (1994) *Culture and Social Behavior*, McGraw-Hill, New York.

Tung, R. L. (1982) *U.S.–China Negotiations*, Pergamon Press, New York.

Tung, R. L. (1989) 'A longitudinal study of United States–China business negotiations', *China Economic Review*, 1(1): 57–71.

Vittachi, N. (2000a) 'China's elite: global generation' (First of a three-part series), *Far Eastern Economic Review*, 5: 63–72.

Vittachi, N. (2000b) 'China's elite: the good life' (Second of a three-part series), *Far Eastern Economic Review*, 12: 53–62.

Vittachi, N. (2000c) 'China's elite: connected to the world' (Third of a three-part series), *Far Eastern Economic Review*, 19: 65–74.

Wei, Y. D. (2000) *Regional Development in China: States, Globalization and Inequality*, Routledge, London.

Wong, G. Y. Y. and Stone, R. J. (1998) 'Chinese and western negotiator stereotypes', in J. Selmer (ed.), *International Management in China: Cross-Cultural Issues*, Routledge, London, pp. 207–22.

Woo, H. S. and Prud'homme, C. (1999) 'Cultural characteristics prevalent in the Chinese negotiation process', *European Business Review*, 99(5): 313–22.

Woo, H. S., Wilson, D. and Liu, J. (2001) 'Gender impact on Chinese negotiation: some key issues for western negotiators', *Women in Management Review*, 16(7): 349–56.

Wu, Y. (2002) 'Regional disparities in China: an alternative view', *International Journal of Social Economics*, 29(7): 575–89.

Xin, K. R. and Pearce, J. L. (1996) '*Guanxi*: connections as substitutes for formal institutional support', *Academy of Management Journal*, 39(6): 1641–58.

Yatsko, P. (2000) *New Shanghai: The Rocky Rebirth of China's Legendary City*, John Wiley, New York.

Yeung, I. Y. M. and Tung, R. L. (1996) 'Achieving business success in Confucian societies: the importance of *guanxi* (connections)', *Organizational Dynamics*, 25(2): 54–65.

Yin, R. K. (1994) *Case Study Research: Design and Methods* (2nd edn), Sage, Beverly Hills, CA.

Yu, Q. Y. (2001) *Dong xi nan bei ren: Zhongguo ren de xinge yu wenhua* [*East West South North: Personality and Culture of the Chinese People*], Dangdai Shijie Press (in Chinese), Beijing.

Zhao, J. J. (2000) 'The Chinese approach to international business negotiation', *The Journal of Business Communication*, 37(3): 209–30.

Index

Note: Page numbers in italics indicate illustrations.